Books by Everett S. Allen

ARCTIC ODYSSEY
The Biography of Rear Admiral Donald B. MacMillan

FAMOUS AMERICAN HUMOROUS POETS
(*For young people*)

THIS QUIET PLACE
A Cape Cod Chronicle

CHILDREN OF THE LIGHT
The Rise and Fall of New Bedford Whaling and the Death of the
Arctic Fleet

A WIND TO SHAKE THE WORLD
The Story of the 1938 Hurricane

THE BLACK SHIPS
Rumrunners of Prohibition

The Black Ships

The

BY EVERETT S. ALLEN

Black
Ships

Rumrunners of Prohibition

LITTLE, BROWN AND COMPANY   BOSTON   TORONTO

FIRST EDITION

The author is grateful to Frederic F. Van de Water, Jr., for permission to
reprint material from *The Real McCoy* by Frederic F. Van de Water; and
to the I.H.T. Corporation for permission to reprint an excerpt from the
August 15, 1924, edition of the *New York Herald Tribune*.
A portion of this book appeared in *Yankee*.

Library of Congress Cataloging in Publication Data

Allen, Everett S
  The black ships.
  Bibliography: p.
  Includes index.
  1. Smuggling — Atlantic States. 2. Prohibition
— Atlantic States. I. Title.
HV5089.A56   382'.45'663500974   79–15100
ISBN 0–316–03258–1

BC

Designed by D. Christine Benders

Published simultaneously in Canada
by Little, Brown & Company (Canada) Limited

PRINTED IN THE UNITED STATES OF AMERICA

To
Jo and Bill Wood
with love

PREFACE

M Y YOUTHFUL RECOLLECTIONS of rum-running are personal, not only because some people very close to my family were elaborately involved, but especially because I knew, as did all the young in coastal towns of the Northeast, both the rumrunners and the Coast Guardsmen who pursued them by night.

What I remember concerns that area in and about New Bedford and Martha's Vineyard, Massachusetts, and what comes to mind first is how illogical the whole business seemed, as it was carried on in the mid- to late '20s and early '30s. By day, the draggers that never went fishing lay at the dock; mostly, they carried no nets and never a working line had furrowed their quarter bitts, which were as bright as the day they came from the yard. Sometimes, on a warm, still day, these vessels smelled of liquor.

Outboard of them, as often as not, lay a gray Coast Guard 75-foot patrol boat, dubbed a "six-bitter," because of her length. Late in the afternoon, the patrol boat would cast off to allow the draggers to depart for wherever and would trail them slowly, out of the harbor and finally, out of sight. This happened almost every day and it seemed to me an odd kind of ceremonial.

At that age, I had clear-cut ideas about sin and sinners, notions born of regular Sunday School attendance. I had never heard of "The Portrait of Dorian Gray," but I assumed that what you were on the inside eventually would show on the outside. It seemed reasonable that criminals ought to look like criminals and that if those charged with law enforcement knew any criminals, they would lock them up. I felt that *I* certainly didn't know any criminals.

But there was this fellow named Charlie and he had a brand-new boat; everybody knew nobody could afford a brand-new boat in those days unless he was a rumrunner. I stood on the dock one day and a Coast Guardsman on the patrol boat hollered, "Hey, Charlie, got a cigarette?" Charlie was just coming up from below on his dragger and he said, "Sure," and reached into the pocket of his woolen shirt, fished out the pack, and passed it over the rail to the Coast Guardsman.

"Thanks, Charlie," the Coast Guardsman said, handing the pack back. Then he said, "See you tonight, Charlie," and Charlie said, "Not if I can help it," and they both laughed.

This did not square with any of the Saturday afternoon movies I had ever seen, in which enemies remained enemies from the first reel on, both waking and sleeping, so that when one eventually nailed the other, it was not only predictable, but right.

What is more, two of the 75-footers came into Vineyard Haven one afternoon and men came ashore from both of them, drunk enough so they tried to sell liquor in bottles right on the street. They kept it up until Captain Ralph

Packer, who ran a bottling plant on the wharf, phoned their base at Woods Hole to complain, and Captain Henry Stevenson of the freight boat *Eben A. Thacher* confronted the Coast Guardsmen and, in my father's words, "bawled them out until the flies wouldn't land on them."

The daylight visibility of the rum-running fleet and the occasional candor of some of its members compounded my confusion. "On most days," Selectman Walter Silveira of Fairhaven, Massachusetts, recalled, "there would be twelve to fifteen rum boats testing their engines and roaring around New Bedford harbor, while a patrol boat kept an eye on them. Then as it got later in the day, one by one, they would disappear, speeding out across Buzzards Bay until they were all gone to sea."

Frank Butler never made any bones about telling the world what he was up to. He had been a fisherman all of his life and one day he was fitting out a new boat in New Bedford. Some men came down on the dock and one of them asked, "How much do you figure she will ice up?" which is to say, "How many pounds of fish do you think she will carry?" Frank didn't even look up at them, but he shifted his cigar and said, "About seventy-five cases."

At school, Frank Butler was elevated to legendary status, principally, because my friend, Leslie "Kaiser Bill" Tilton always seemed to know how Frank had outwitted his government pursuers the night before. At eight in the morning, on the school ground, I did not see how this could be unless Mr. Butler had had breakfast with the Tiltons, yet each chapter was so exciting that I preferred to accept it rather than question it. I think one of the best concerned the time when Frank was being chased by patrol boats and had engine trouble.

Kaiser Bill said, "He knew he couldn't get away, so he ran his boat ashore, jumped out, ran up the beach to a marsh, squatted down in the water with his head under and breathed for two hours through the hollow stalk of a plant that he broke off. They looked all over hell for him and never came close." I was aware that a movie about a fugitive from a Georgia chain gang was playing at the Capawock Theater in town at about that time and it contained a similar episode of underwater breathing. Nevertheless, Mr. Butler *may* have done just that, for he did possess certain derring-do and besides, the whole rum-running business lent itself to extraordinary feats of seamanship, to intrigue, mystery, and cunning.

Thus, the common place and the common man sometimes assumed an unexpected fascination because of the aura of lawlessness that surrounded them. I stood at a wholly uninspiring intersection of North Street in the West End of New Bedford late one afternoon, staring at an empty carriage factory and wondering why there wasn't somebody of my own age about with whom I could play ball. A black touring car, traveling west toward Providence, came whizzing along North Street at what seemed to me to be a high rate of speed. There were three or four men in the car, and when it was nearly opposite me, one of them leaned out and hurled a bundle, which landed on the sidewalk about a hundred feet from me.

I waited until the car was gone and walked toward the bundle, swallowing a little nervously and feeling my heart pound. The thing was about a foot and a half long, wrapped carefully in newspaper and tied with heavy twine; it was roughly cylindrical, and approximately six inches in diameter. Very briefly, I thought that it might explode if I unwrapped it, but then it occurred to me it was much more likely to be a clandestine payoff. My hands shook as I tore at the wrappings; if this was a package of money, it was a lot of money.

It was not money, and it did not blow up. It was a log of firewood, split and with the bark on one side, unmarked and without message. Disgusted, I threw wood, paper, and string into the tall grass near the factory wall and scuffed glumly to my uncle's house, where I was staying.

I told him what had happened and he listened very carefully. Then he put on his hat and coat and said, "Come with me." We went to where I had thrown the stuff and he rewrapped the package very carefully and asked me to show him exactly where I had first found it on the sidewalk. It was almost dark when he put the package down and he said to me quietly — almost as if he expected somebody to be listening — "This means something to somebody." Then he looked around, and I half-expected, and feared, that the touring car would come speeding past again. My uncle said, "We aren't looking for trouble," and we went home in silence. The next morning I approached the site with caution, drawn by irresistible curiosity. The package was gone. To this day, I do not like that intersection at nightfall because when young and innocent, I was made afraid there, having had thrust upon me a confrontation with something the more frightening because it concerned ordinary ingredients employed in an extraordinary manner for dark purpose.

Manuel was extraordinary, too. He was a lean man who had been to sea and his clothes hung on him like a shirt on a handspike; he loped when he walked, wore a floppy straw hat, and sailed an old knockabout that needed paint. In one of the first conversations we ever had (he initiated it by yelling, "Hey, boy!" at me as I rowed past his moored sloop), he related how a fellow with whom he had shipped on a vessel contracted venereal disease and chose not to tell anyone about it or have it treated.

"What happened was," said Manuel, "he wound up having the top of his skull sawed off and they put in a silver plate. You get anything wrong with you like that from some woman, you go to the doctor, you understand?" That was nearly fifty years ago; I have never forgotten the message.

Manuel's house was on the edge of town. He lived alone and was quite a good cook, ship fashion; once in a while, I would walk past his place and he would yell, "Hey, boy!" and give me a couple of warm sugar cookies. The area where he lived was wooded and once or twice I wondered why the path through the pine needles to his door seemed so well worn, for he had few friends and I do not know to this day why I was one of them.

One morning, I was walking by his house and the chief of police and a patrolman were just leaving. Manuel called to me and I walked up the path, wondering what kind of trouble he was in.

"They gone?" he said.

"They've gone. Sure have."

"Come in, boy. Gonna tell you somethin'. Gonna show you somethin'."

The house had no more than a kitchen and a bedroom; we stood next to the sink. Manuel put his big hands on his hips; he had a strange look, half-irritated, half-wry. "Boy," he said, "that's the fourth time them po-licemen come to my little house. They think I sell likka because a lot of people come to my house after dark and I got a new jib for my boat. They look all over my house, even down on they hands and knees, and they don't find nothin'. They go away mad. Four times."

I sensed that he had been drinking and I was slightly uneasy, although the door was open and I thought I probably could run faster than he. Then he said, in a baritone whisper, "I *do* sell likka. And I'm smarter'n them. And I'm gonna tell you where my likka is, because I know who I kin trust in this here town."

I didn't really want to know where it was, but before I could say anything, he turned to the single cold-water faucet at the kitchen sink, opened it a hair, swiped his forefinger across it, and brushed my lips with the moisture. "Lap it," he commanded. I did, and it was like fire. "That's likka," he said, grinning. "They never thought to look there. They ain't got brains enough to know that if you want a drink, you go to the tap. Got it hooked to a tank in the loft, behind some junk. And you ain't goin' to tell the po-licemen, are you? Or your old man? Or anybody? Are you?"

"No," I said. And I never have, until this day, even though it was a terrible burden for a boy who went to Sunday School regularly. For a while, whenever I saw the chief of police — usually standing in front of the post office — I would cross to the other side of the street for fear that the awful urge to bare my soul would prove too much to withstand.

One was aware, of course, that all elements of the rum-running situation were not benign or of the Main Street temperament. A fellow with a boatload of booze developed limping engines off Menemsha Creek, docked at the Vineyard, and arranged with an islander to unload the liquor after dark, store it in a shed, and keep it until the boat owner could get his engines fixed and return. The Vineyarder, short of money, as most people were in those days, looked at the liquor in his shed and calculated the market value until he could stand the temptation no longer. He moved it to another building, passed the word that he had a lot of liquor for sale, and awaited a buyer.

Two off-islanders showed up and invited him to discuss the matter with them in their room at the Mansion House in Vineyard Haven. He accepted the invitation, at which time his hosts urged him to return the liquor to its owner because, as they pointed out, they did not wish anything to happen to him. He returned the liquor.

Sometimes on Sunday evenings, our family would drive to Gay Head, and if it was before dark, often as not, we would see the rumrunners bound offshore, out past the Head and Nomansland. Nothing else looked like them; nothing else sounded like them, and I can hear the unmistakable distant hum of those finely tuned engines now. One night, we were later than usual, and the rum boats were coming back in the dark, engines running faster and higher pitched. Suddenly, more than halfway across Vineyard Sound, there were brief orange flashes. I looked at my father and he said, "Gunfire." I thought it quite possible that I might know the man who was firing the gun and the man at whom he was shooting and that they might very likely know each other. I thought about Charlie and the Coast Guardsman, and the cigarettes.

That is the curious mixture that it all was.

There are two additional footnotes before we get on to the major business at hand. The first is that George Sweet and my father were offered one hundred dollars apiece to take a boat out of Westport, Massachusetts, load her from an offshore vessel, and bring the liquor back to the beach. The man who made the offer had one boat running very successfully; he came into New Bedford regularly with a fish cart and peddled hot-water bottles full of whisky, which were pinned to the lining of his overcoat. He wanted to operate a second boat; he wanted my father to run her. We did not have much money and a hundred dollars was a great deal in those days; my father and George Sweet agonized over the offer and finally turned it down because they both had small children. Another skipper and his mate took out the boat; the Coast Guard caught her that night.

Lastly, there is the matter of identifying people mentioned in this book. In general, I have identified vessels and individuals on which there is public record already. In the cases of people whom I have interviewed, I have concealed identities because otherwise there would have been no interview and since this is, in essence, a history, it seemed to me that what they had to offer was worth more than giving the public a name that would mean nothing to most. A large majority of the people who were engaged in rumrunning at the level with which this book is concerned were ordinary folks. In many instances, this was the only manner in which they ever broke the law and a surprisingly fierce code of silence persists among them because, as one former rumrunner said to me, "They would rather forget than remember, they will protect the others, because they expect the others to protect them, and they don't want their second wives and their grandchildren to know where the family money came from."

In suggesting that these rumrunners were "ordinary," I mean only that they never would have been likely to make headlines had it not been for Prohibition.

With further regard to names, it was commonplace — and federal officials were forced to take this into account — for the rumrunner to give an alias when he was arrested. On occasion, these aliases were not discovered and remain part of the official record. Sometimes, the rumrunner gave the name of an innocent contemporary as his own. On one occasion, to which I have alluded in this book, a couple of dozen men, apprehended by law-enforcement officers, all gave the same name — that of a common acquaintance who was not present. In several instances, a rumrunner had several aliases. Obviously then, the matter of names is complicated, often of questionable value, and made further so by the use of false addresses and straw men. However, I have made a point of using the names or numbers of boats in almost all instances since these are matters of record and a desirable constant.

One final matter. There are three pieces of verse in this book, written by my father, Joseph Chase Allen of Vineyard Haven and published in the early 1920s in the New Bedford (Massachusetts) *Evening Standard*. I have included them because they express sentiments that were shared by many in the coastal communities of the Northeastern United States, a fact that did not escape the astute newspaper editor who chose to publish them, George A. Hough.

Cast off, and all ahead full.

E. S. A.

Poverty Point
Fairhaven, Massachusetts

THE SMUGGLERS' CHANTY

"Oh, we don't give a damn for our old Uncle Sam
Way-o, whisky and gin!
Lend us a hand when we stand in to land
Just give us time to run the rum in."

From sunny southern island ports
That dot the Spanish Main,
A brand new gang of pirate sports
Have put to sea again.

But differing from men of old
Who counted all fair prey
These modern pirates gain their gold
In quite a different way.

Unto our unprotected shores
Forbidden rum they bring
Patrol boats chase them by the scores
But still the pirates sing:

"Oh, schooners and steamers and cruisers and all
Way-o, whisky and gin!
Chase us with cutters and battleships tall
Still we have time to bring the rum in."

And so it goes, our agents grow
More haggard every day
They form new plans each week or so
But nothing works their way.

They spread wild rumors round about
That all the booze is dope
But even this doesn't help them out
And they are losing hope.

Each day they claim "The peak is passed,
The job is well in hand,"
Each day we read "Rum fleet is massed
A few miles off the land."

Our laws are dry as dry can be
Although the land is moist
And jolly pirates out at sea
Chant loudly as they hoist:

" 'Tis easy and free for us boys out at sea
Way-o, whisky and gin!
Pigs will all fly when the country goes dry
Give us the word, we'll run the rum in."
— Joseph Chase Allen
1921

The
Black
Ships

CHAPTER I

POLARIZATION WAS the hallmark of the Prohibition era. There was among some a sense that America was going to hell in a handbasket. One of them was the Rev. John Roach Stratton of Calvary Baptist Church in New York City, who preached a sermon entitled "Does the Recent Dempsey-Carpentier Fight Prove that We Have Relapsed into Paganism?"

Dr. Stratton said that he had attended the bout to study the psychology of the crowd before, during, and after the fight, and he concluded the event was "more than a mere boil on the body social. A boil has but one head and one channel for the discharge of corruption, but a carbuncle has several. It is complex, it gathers corruption from all over the human body, finds the weakest spot in the system, breaks down the remaining tissue there and generates its corruption until it heads up in a half-dozen spots and unless it is lanced, drained, and thoroughly disinfected, it will poison the entire body and finally produce death.

"This prize fight was just that sort of thing. It meant not simply the presence of one class of our defectives and moral degenerates, but it gathered all the poison elements of our modern society. The gamblers and the horse racers and the touts, the home neglecters, the baby-killers and the pug-dog nurses, the burglars and the pickpockets and the strongarm men, the promoters, the plutocrats and the profiteers, the liquorites and the painted Amazons, the double livers, the society divorcees, and the polygamous movie stars whose coming was heralded across the continent, the vaudeville performers and the proprietors of the degraded theaters, and all the other women exploiters, the Sabbath-breakers, the church-scorners, and the God-defiers, yes, all of those elements whose influences are making for the overthrow of our American ideals and customs, were on hand in force.

"The poison from all over the land drained to that huge amphitheater and this moral carbuncle naturally came to a head at the weakest spot in our body politic, the State of New Jersey, with its pro-liquor, anti-Constitution, anti-Sabbath governor. . . ."

When he criticized the women who attended the boxing match, Dr. Stratton specifically mentioned the women of the Roosevelt family. In response, Mrs. Kermit Roosevelt replied that she saw nothing debasing in the affair. She said, "I enjoyed the fight thoroughly. I think boxing is a wonderful sport and I am going to have it taught to my children." Informed that Dr. Stratton had declared he felt sure that if Colonel Theodore Roosevelt were still living, he would not have gone to "this disgraceful affair," Mrs. Roosevelt commented, "What a perfectly dreadful thing to say."

Still, they were upsetting times for many. In Chicago,

Bill Burns, the state's star witness, testified that indicted White Sox players, after agreeing with a clique of gamblers to throw the 1919 World Series to Cincinnati for $100,000, became sick of the deal when they were not paid the bribes promised and, at a meeting before the third game, decided to play their best and win the series.

And in New Bedford, more than 1,800 residents applied to Chief of Police Doherty for permission to carry revolvers in the two-month period ending January 25, 1921. Only 100 permits had been granted in the entire twelve months preceding and Chief Doherty said, "Requests to carry arms began to pour into my office a short time ago when the so-called 'crime wave' first gained its start in New York City."

Some looked upon Prohibition as a means of national salvation. "Nation Would Fall Like Rome Without Dry Law — Hobson" declared the headline in the New London (Connecticut) *Day*. The reference was to an address by Richmond Pearson Hobson, who, as a member of Congress from Alabama, had introduced the first proposed amendment to the Constitution that would have banned the sale of alcoholic beverages. Hobson became a popular naval hero during the Spanish-American War after he tied up a Spanish fleet at Santiago, Cuba, by sinking a collier at the mouth of the harbor. It is recorded that when he returned to the United States, he "was the subject of a series of wild demonstrations in a number of cities during which he was kissed by thousands of hysterical women."

Speaking in behalf of the Volstead Act, Mr. Hobson said, "All the nations of the earth are watching America and they will follow after they are convinced of the results, but in the meantime, the liquor traffic is waging a war against this nation with a program of great wealth and cunning strategy that is sound to the core.

"This traffic has invested today throughout the world exactly 20,000 millions of dollars. Is it not reasonable to believe that they would spend ten percent of this amount to save 90 percent?" He noted that 5 percent of the liquor traffic's total investment would give them a campaign fund of a billion dollars with which to fight for repeal of the Eighteenth Amendment. He scoffed at the "propaganda" that the amendment had been "put over" on the people, observing that over the years, 3,500 amendments had been proposed and only nine had prevailed.

There were those not necessarily in favor of the Eighteenth Amendment who nevertheless thought that a law on the books ought to be enforced, lest the total fabric of orderly society and due process come unraveled. The following is a letter written by a resident of Philadelphia that was received by the commandant of the Coast Guard in Washington on May 14, 1931:

Sir, here is a proposition to save a lot of money for the government, stop graft, stop lawbreaking, and be honest. Lend me a good subchaser with a gun, a load of torpedoes, a few machine guns and shot; I will supply a crew. No one will know. I will go to sea and sink without trace every rum boat I can find and croak all on it. They will disappear and that will stop the game.

I, with a few million more, am sick and tired of reading the fool things this yellow government is doing, and doing nothing useful, making a bluff and spending millions of the people's blood money and letting the graft flow. I am sick of seeing foreigners [Author's note: Here, he drew a sketch of a person thumbing his nose] at Americans.

I will do this silently, secretly, and no one will blame our "statesmen." If caught, I will guarantee to shoot it out with any ship, and be sunk, and that includes any U.S. ship. It might mean war. All right. You would call it a war to make Morgan's money safe, as Wilson did. The country needs a war and a white man for president.

I am putting this proposition up honestly, and know a crew I could take. They are not stuffed shirts like you Washington politicians, but men. Am I for Prohibition? Hell, no. Just tired of fiddling, fooling, and graft. I'll clean the seas of the graft as Forrest cleaned the woods of niggers, part of. [Author's note: Presumably, the reference is to Major-General Nathan Bedford Forrest of the

6

Confederate Army and his capture of Fort Pillow. The supposed massacre of the Negro troops who composed its garrison was bitterly discussed, following the incident in 1864, but Forrest denied there had been any wanton slaughter.]

If you won't do this, give me a job on the Prohibition force. I need the money. Thanking you. L.----- G.-----

Of course, not everyone thought the nation was going to hell. Those who wondered whether the much-discussed flapper was sounding the death knell of the so-called old-fashioned woman were much interested in the comments of writer Fannie Hurst, who observed, "The girl of tomorrow will regard the flapper as we regard the mid-Victorian era of silk mitts and swoons."

Miss Hurst was being interviewed, the conversation had turned to Lily Becker, heroine of her first novel, *Stardust*, and, noted the interviewer, "as if by force of gravity, to the flapper."

In the eyes of the flapper, Lily Becker is a high conservative, said Miss Hurst. Just as the flapper of today who stands on the brink, as it were, of a new ethical pool for women, will be the old-fashioned girl of tomorrow. The unrest of the flapper is the result of her being the grist between the millstones. There is just enough of the old generation and enough of the stirring consciousness of the new to create an enormous unrest. It is not entirely a case of off with the old and on with the new, but a sort of compromise of both. We'll outgrow all institutions and all moralities and all ethics, although women have been slow to cast off moss-grown tradition. The only institution which withstood change and weathering and which has not kept up with the new demands is marriage.

Q. Would you like to see marriage cast off as an institution?

A. No, I would not, but the truths of yesterday are not necessarily the truths of today. What we consider the scientific facts of yesterday are in some cases ludicrous today. In other words, the one institution which has not adapted itself to the social, moral, economic, political and industrial changes is marriage.

Q. What is wrong with the average marriage of today?

A. It does not fit the status of women. The shoe no longer fits. The last should be changed. But not discarded. Due to the various emancipations such as suffrage, industrial opportunities, and education, woman has been elevated from chattel to individual. Marriage is no longer a woman's whole existence. It is a fundamental part of her existence, if you will, but one which she approaches in an utterly different manner from her sisters of a less emancipated and less enlightened generation.

Lily Becker antedated the age of the flapper, Miss Hurst said. She was the standard-bearer for the first generation that was actually to emerge from the chrysalis of women's serfdom. So the flapper condition of today is not a malignant one, it is the inevitable result of the lid-off of years of suppression and repression. The flapper is merely nouvelle riche. She suddenly finds herself in possession of liberties that she sometimes turns into license, merely because the various emancipations have rushed to her head, turning it. The flapper will soon get her bearings and, instead of "going giddy on new conditions once she accepts them, her new status will become a matter of course and not of newspaper headlines."

Others were confident of the country's ability to endure for different reasons. In the wheelhouse of a broad-beamed workboat, I interviewed a fellow whom I had known since childhood in an effort to recreate the spirit and feelings of this particular period in history. I knew that he had been a successful rumrunner. He knew that I knew. As a matter of fact, he had bought the workboat with some of the money he made running liquor.

He leaned against the chart table, patting a tiger cat with a battered ear. "Well," he said, "I don't know what they might of thought down in Washington, but anybody I knew didn't expect Prohibition to produce any miracles except maybe in reverse. People who drank we figured would keep on drinking. They did, and they had to pay more for the habit. Poor people who drank and couldn't afford to pay more either made moonshine back in the woods or drank Jakey."

"Jakey?"

"Jamaica ginger. You could buy it in two-ounce bottles. Then there were some people never had drunk booze at all and they drank it because it was illegal. Like goin' swimming with no clothes on.

"Personally, I figured the whole thing was a fluke. Seemed to me that when the country got tired enough of going to all that work to get a drink, and maybe watered-down at that, they'd make liquor legal again. Which they did. They took longer'n I thought to get to it. Some fellows in the rum business got burned; when repeal come, they got stuck with expensive boats and engines — I guess they thought it would go on forever. It was a case of getting in, making a good dollar, and getting out. . . ."

"Did you think that stopping drinking in the United States would save the country?"

"If I thought the country hung on such a skinny thread as that, I'd probably jump down a well. In the first place, I know any number of people in reasonably high places that couldn't do a day's work if they didn't have a drink to steady them up, and besides, I didn't think the country needed savin'."

Even within the ranks of those who had taken a clear stand on the matter of legalized liquor, there apparently were differences of opinion as to how this related to the direction and destiny of American society as a whole.

On January 31, 1927, a Connecticut daily newspaper

9

published a two-column picture with the caption, " 'We won't drink, smoke or pet,' that's the pledge taken by the Misses Harriett Whitford and Helen P. Gatley, Washington, D.C. society debs who are seen as pages at the WCTU meeting at the capital. Are they setting the pace for the rest of society? WCTU speakers flayed flagrant drinking by members of the society."

Four pages later, same newspaper, same date, there was published a one-column picture distributed by Pacific and Atlantic, the same syndicate that took the first picture, bearing this caption: "Four out of seven Washington debutantes, including Miss Helen P. Gatley, above, serving as pages at the WCTU convention, have resigned because they were heralded over the nation as non-smokers, non-drinkers, and non-petters."

The fellow in the wheelhouse of the workboat lit a cigarette and watched the smoke sift across his fingers and out the open door to starboard. "I think in the beginning, most people were willing to go by the law, but breakin' it kinda caught on. The word got around that some of the people supposed to be enforcing it were winking an eye. You knew they had to be.

"So you said, 'What the hell, I might's well get mine.' Maybe you didn't like some of the people you had to associate with; they weren't exactly church-goin'. . . "

So Main Street found itself in a loose and unlikely marriage with another kind of world, of which the following excerpt offers a glimpse:

U.S. Attorney Thomas E. Dewey and his staff ("in tones matching the defendant's for softness, yet dripping with scorn and disbelief," according to an observer) were interrogating "Waxey" Gordon, described in nothing less than the *Encyclopaedia Britannica* as one of three "underworld characters" who "dominated the New York area bootleg market." The matter at hand concerned Max Greenberg and Max Hassell, who were shot dead in an Elizabeth, New Jersey, hotel.

Q. You were in the hotel at the time — is that right?
A. I was.
   Gordon cleared his throat.
Q. You had been in the room up to about a minute before these men were killed by somebody?
A. Well, no, I wasn't . . . well, I'll tell you. I left
   Max Hassell sitting in a room. Mr. Greenberg
   hadn't been there. I think I went to see some people
   in a different room.
Q. Yes?
A. And I heard sort of like the rattle of dishes out in
   the hall and I opened the door of the room and I
   saw some of the men that worked for Mr. Hassell
   and Mr. Greenberg running along the hall and I
   says, "What's the excitement?" They says, "Well,
   they just shot Max" or what we call him . . . we
   always called him Jimmy.
Q. That is, Hassell was called Jimmy.
A. That is right.
Q. How long had you known Greenberg?
A. Since 1916.
Q. How long had you known Hassell?
A. Since about 1927.
Q. You three men were friends, weren't you?
A. Very dear friends.

There were many dear friends bereft before the era of
rum-running was over.

CHAPTER II

A GOOD WAY to obtain a perspective on rum-running is to follow the course of a bottle of booze from Europe to the high-water mark on the North Atlantic coast, where it was finally landed, and that is what I intend.

Bundles of consular cables, now gathering dust in the National Archives, reveal the intense degree to which the American government kept tabs on the foreign connection, without which there would have been no rum traffic. These messages, principally on the movements of vessels loaded with liquor that were bound for "off New York trading" and similar destinations, reveal how varied and wide-ranging the ocean operation was. They covered such matters as departure of the German steamer *Apis,* with 437,000 liters of liquors and wines, from Copenhagen, reportedly for

Africa. American officials in Denmark added, "[It is believed] the intent is to smuggle the cargo into the United States."

And when the French steamer *Celte* sailed from Marseilles for St. Pierre and Miquelon off southern Newfoundland "with a cargo of spirits for the same shippers as that of the steamer *Mulhouse*," the State Department was notified, the dispatch adding that "she is described as having a yellow funnel and two masts."

How were such transactions handled? Consider the activities of Thomas Godman and Schooners Associated Limited of London, described in documents in possession of the U.S. government in the 1920s as "engaged in running liquor into the United States."

In a letter datelined Gruppenbahren, dated September 3, 1927, and marked "private and confidential," Godman described his role in rum-running:

My Dear Warrle:
Please understand clearly that my job is to arrange sales that show a profit, either in the Atlantic or elsewhere. I cannot handle 8,000 in six weeks and no one can, not on the coast. There is a rush of orders from my friends for cheap whisky to meet the Christmas trade, goods for St. Pierre showing a profit of about 40 percent, in two months, without risk. Where goods are sold from the ship, payment is made to the supercargo on board.

The boats come off with the money; it is all very simple. Any bootlegger in the States who really means business will send his boat off with actual cash to pay for what he takes, and any other kind of proposition is a fraud, without any exception. What I do in the matter is to arrange for a ship to be in certain positions at stated times and then let my customers know where to find her. There is no possibility of fraud, as the goods are never in any danger. It requires on my part absolute knowledge of the U.S. system of patrols, but that is my mystery.

It was common practice for the offshore rum vessels to carry supercargoes who were responsible for the commercial concerns of the voyage; they usually represented the owners of the cargo — if sales were over the rail at random, they were charged with keeping track of the number of bottles and the number of dollars; if sales were in large lots and prearranged before the vessel sailed from her port of loading, it was they who verified the signals, documents, or identities of the shoreside people who came out to pick up the cargo, because very possibly money would not change hands at sea in this kind of transaction.

On occasion, supercargoes were asked to perform security functions. In a letter from Bremen dated March 18, 1924, and titled "Secret Circular, No. 15 to Our Captains," Godman wrote:

Captains will understand that the only danger that need be feared on the Atlantic Coast is the danger from rum pirates. These pirates are usually Nova Scotia schooners who will attempt by some trick to get on board your vessels, when they will hold you up, generally with guns, and endeavor to steal whatever cargo you have on board, or they may attempt to take any money which may be on board resulting from the sale of your liquor.

We do not think that such people would open fire, but the human element under certain circumstances is always doubtful, and we expect our captains to defend their vessels should such an occasion arise. The best method of defense, of course, is to prevent these people coming on board, and the most effect plan is to limit the number of people on board to buy liquor to two. While these two are boarding the vessel, the supercargo should be stationed, say on the poop with a rifle, and he will keep them covered, taking such action to disable them as he may think necessary in the event of their making any action toward drawing a weapon.

If an open attack is made, the most effective means of dispersing such is by hand grenades hurled into the attacking vessel. . . . We will endeavor to supply our gunner and also machine guns, grenades and other suitable weapons, but it must be understood that these things should be used only in self-defense, where the question is one of life and death. Rum pirates are sea robbers only and to draw a short line through the whole of the above, a captain will defend his ship the same as a man would defend his house from robbers ashore.

Godman concluded that there "is no risk from rum pirates provided a proper watch is kept and reasonable precautions taken," but I am aware of one instance in which the pattern of attack was unorthodox. Ordinarily, one would expect the pirates to board a vessel that was not under way, which had the hold open, and was selling liquor. However, I know a fellow who was master of a steamer that transported liquor from German ports to Rum Row. Off the Nova Scotia coast, while bound for the New York area with a load, his vessel was struck by gunfire from a craft in pursuit. Greater speed enabled him to outrun the pirate eventually, but the attack was sobering because he had always declined to carry weapons on the steamer as a matter of principle. Rather than sail armed, he decided to make that the last trip to Europe, although he remained active in coastal rum-running for years.

The schooner *Tom August,* one of the vessels owned by Godman's company, offers an illustration of how the Rum Row operation worked. This particular trip by the *August* is selected because it also reveals a number of problems with which international liquor traffickers had to contend.

Sometime in the spring of 1924, the master of the *Tom August,* Captain William R. Whitburn, received orders from Schooners Associated Ltd. to fit out and proceed to Bremen "to take a full cargo of liquor from J. D. Bode and proceed direct to a point 25 miles south true from Montauk Point." Montauk Point is at the eastern extremity of Long Island. At Bremen, the schooner took abroad 14,935 cases of whisky and 1,355 cases of champagne; at $30 a case, the cargo was worth $488,700. The supercargoes who came aboard were named Bottcher and Prohl; they both came from Bremerhaven and had orders from the owners, European investors, to "sell the cargo out of the zone of the United States."

By the middle of June of that year, the schooner was lying off Jones Inlet, at the western end of Long Island, and complications of several kinds had developed. Bottcher became ill, was taken ashore and hospitalized, leaving Prohl in charge of selling the cargo. What appears to have happened was that the Godman organization had no established shoreside apparatus, so putting together a deal between buyers and sellers was a cumbersome and even risky kind of business.

Prohl made contact with a couple of middlemen named Charbonneau and Schrivaneck; the latter was described in government documents as "a Slavonian, a tall, lanky fellow with a straggly mustache, weighing about 175–180 pounds, about 50 years of age, sloppy dresser, with a very strong foreign accent." Schrivaneck, who had figured in rum-running escapades that brought him before the courts of Halifax, Nova Scotia, eventually was arrested on similar charges in New York, failed to show up to stand trial, and finally was deported to Czechoslovakia by Canada. At this time, however, he was still in business off the Northeast coast and did, in fact, sell 2,000 cases of the *August*'s cargo, although not without friction. Trouble arose, both among the supercargoes — who evidently had differing ideas about disposal of the liquor — and among members of the ship's company as well.

Captain Whitburn was somewhat bothered by June 18 and wrote to Godman:

The two supercargoes [Prohl and Schrivaneck] called the Prohibition cutter alongside as she passed today and asked the captain to order me to proceed to Halifax or that he would take the ship into New York as a capture.

At this, the [Coast Guard] captain only laughed at them and told them they had better order me to Halifax themselves. Last night, the supercargoes talked of protecting the cargo with their lives and threatened that if Mr. Charbonneau or anyone else, without their permission, attempted to board the vessel, they would be shot.

This afternoon, when Mr. Charbonneau came on board, bringing some fresh provisions, Mr. Schrivaneck met and spoke to him as if bloodshed had never entered his mind.

The first mate is simply useless in every way and hand in glove with the supercargoes. The first machinist is also on their side. I am having a lively time on board this vessel, as there are too many foreigners here and only two Britishers, myself and the bosun.

A week later, the *August* had moved to a point 18 miles southeast of Block Island. Charbonneau had promised to come back to that location with orders for more liquor but had not shown up. The price offered for "a case of good whisky," Whitburn said, "is at present $20." But he added, "A vessel arriving here without having her cargo consigned to an agent ashore stands a very poor chance of selling. The bootleggers are few and only take 10 to 50 cases at a time. There is a good trade to be done here yet, but it is absolutely necessary there should be a well-connected agent ashore. Otherwise, a vessel arriving without a representative ashore is liable to wait around for months before she will be clear of her cargo."

Some mail found its way to the schooner; as a result, every member of the crew complained to the master that their families had received no money since the vessel had sailed from England. They refused to work, except to keep anchor watch, wash down, and heave up the anchor. Captain Whitburn, frustrated, complained, "I have to be careful not to exceed the law, as I wish to punish them when we get home. Nevertheless, it is very annoying not to be able to get the ship cleaned and painted, as I should like to do."

Nor did he come to think any better of the first mate, ". . . a Dane [who] is absolutely useless to me, being neither a navigator nor a sailor and frightened to dirty his hands. Also, he appears to be hand in glove with the men. I would not carry him again in any ship I was master of, even for ballast. . . ."

By early July, the *August* was still off Block Island. Sales had been sluggish, and the average price was $15 to $20 a case. Whitburn reported to Godman,

Last night, Schrivaneck went on shore to bank the money and today, I believe they are coming for another 800 cases. After they get the money for these, I should not be surprised to hear that Schrivaneck had cleared out with all the cash, for he is a crook and old Captain Prohl is soft and does what Schrivaneck tells him.

I may have to go elsewhere to sell, perhaps to Halifax or St. Pierre, where I can dispose of it. I have certainly got to watch my step, for I am up against people who would doublecross me if they can. . . . I have to smuggle my letters on shore the best way I can. I don't trust any one of the crowd I am up against. After my letters being opened in Bermuda [Author's note: The *August,* and other rumrunners, often put in at Bermuda because the ship's papers listed it as the vessel's destination, even though most of them actually were bound for waters off Block Island, Long Island, or Atlantic City.] they would certainly open any letters I am sending and find out what I am telling you. Schrivaneck has acknowledged that they confiscated a letter from you to me dated June 5 and forwarded to Bremen. I don't know what the contents of the letter was [sic] but they seem to think they have done a very smart trick.

At about this time, a Mr. Weitzman was sent from Germany to New York "on behalf of the concern" to see what he could do about speeding up the sales. In a letter dated July 11 to Captain Whitburn, Godman fumed,

This business has been dirty from the beginning. The shippers of the cargo in the first place tricked me and now they are fighting among themselves. Furthermore, the agents they sent over are totally unreliable and when all is said and done, I shall be very glad to wash my hands of that cargo. . . . I do not know whether Mr. Weitzman or Mr. Bottcher or Mr. Schrivaneck is chief over there; as a matter of fact, it is all so mixed up that no one seems to know, and the point we must bear in mind is to look to ourselves.

Godman said the European shippers of the cargo owed him $20,000 balance on the freight charges and ordered Whitburn to retain aboard the schooner enough liquor to cover this amount. That was one of several things that did not quite work out.

Weitzman replaced the supercargoes with a Mr. Pell and Mr. Baker, who agreed to take over the balance of the cargo. At the outset, the Pell-Baker team discovered that nobody really knew how much liquor had been sold. Captain Whitburn said, "According to a rough tally that I have been keeping, 2,195 cases of whisky and eight cases of champagne have gone overside and been sold. . . ." Schrivaneck and Prohl, offering a final accounting before they went ashore, put the figure at 1,200 cases. Pell-Baker, after a quick count, decided on 1,700; at $17 or $18 a case, which is about what the liquor was going for, these variations left some bottles and dollars unaccounted for. In any event, the *Tom August* began to get rid of her cargo, but not her problems.

At some point, Whitburn's son, who was boatswain aboard the vessel, went ashore with 210 cases of liquor, for which he was apparently to be paid by somebody. He failed to return to the *Tom August*.

The first mate, the machinist, and a seaman also went ashore and did not return.

On August 17, the seven-ton motorboat *Jenny T.* was alongside the *Tom August,* taking aboard a load of liquor. When she cast off, bound for the shore, she was carrying 528 cases of Scotch. She had proceeded only a short distance when an engine began to malfunction, and her skipper was forced to work her back to the *August;* just before he got there, there was an engine-room explosion, but he did get alongside the schooner and made fast.

Three of his crew were badly burned and were put aboard the New London motorboat *Alice,* which took them ashore; all three were hospitalized. Meanwhile, the Coast Guard cutter *Seneca* steamed up and her master wanted to know who owned the liquor-laden *Jenny T.* Somebody aboard the *Tom August* said the boat belonged to Captain Whitburn, but when no foreign papers could be produced to prove that she was other than an American boat, the

Coast Guard seized her, liquor and all, and had her towed ashore.

Subsequent events proved that one of the burned men was a transient crew member of the *Jenny T*. Hans Beyer was a stowaway; he had hidden aboard the *Tom August* in Bremen and whether he was being put ashore or had requested to go ashore, the records do not show.

Captain Whitburn sailed from the anchorage off Montauk Point on August 22, bound for Halifax, and he said, "I came around with four hands short on my complement, namely, first mate, bosun, assistant engineer, and one sailor out of our eleven hands, myself having to be on deck all the time for 3½ days and we arrived in the face of a hurricane."

Whitburn submitted to Godman "a true and unbiased statement to be the best of my belief of how the whisky cargo of the M.S. *Tom August* was disposed of in Rum Row." Essentially, it stated that of the 16,048 cases, 12,270 had been disposed of by Baker-Pell. The matter became somewhat complicated because Baker-Pell reported to the investors in Europe that the whole cargo had been stolen.

On October 20, the *Tom August* arrived at Whitehaven, England, and Whitburn fired off a letter to Schooners Associated: "I am now enclosing an amount of money due to each man and if they are kept waiting any longer, they will claim a day's pay for every day. . . . Them that deserted, their wages have to be deposited with the shipping master. H. Pederson, deserted, Bermuda; R. Rohda, deserted, Halifax; H. Whitburn [Author's note: his son], deserted, Rum Row; J. Bidstrup, deserted, Rum Row; H. Boyes, left in hospital; K. Gross, deserted, Rum Row.

The statement regarding the allotments and advances to the crew is very unsatisfactory to me. . . . Have you paid any account for the cook, Wendt; he says that his wife has not had any allotments, and how many allotments have you paid to the others? I know you have not paid my wife, from which I can draw only one conclusion. . . .

At present, the men are pestering me for money. . . . There is no money to give them yet and I cannot tell them when they will get any or where they will be paid off. . . .

The whole matter became increasingly confused; had it involved another kind of business, the principals might have been more eager to go to law for relief. As it was, many of the major questions about who sold what to whom remained unanswered, prompting Whitburn to state his position in the bluntest terms:

I consider that I am in no way to blame in the utter confusion that has been going on as regards the cargo. I may say the blunders, the mistakes, and the cross-purposes and the doublecrossing has [sic] been appalling, and as Mr. Godman tells me there will be a law case about it, I am placing myself in the hands of the Imperial Merchant Service Guild, and they will protect my interest, as I consider and know I have dealt honest and straightforward with a lot of crooks and I will not take any blame as the cargo was placed in the hands of some of the biggest crooks in New York, and I had strict instructions to obey their orders.

At one point, Godman had mentioned to Whitburn that the shippers owed a $5,000 bonus to Schooners Associated "from which it was my intention to give you the sum of $2,000 if the voyage is successful." Whitburn's attorneys sought this bonus, as well as payment for his services as master of the *Tom August;* they soon realized that Schooners Associated was having money troubles, and offered to strike a bargain: "Captain Whitburn authorizes us to say that for an immediate cash settlement, he would accept 400 pounds cash to settle all accounts between him and you, but he will not accept anything less than this amount and this offer is only open for acceptance within the next seven days. . . ."

Schooners Associated responded by saying, "We cannot see that [this] represents any great solution of the difference between Captain Whitburn and ourselves. . . . The last voyage of the Tom August was, of course, the voyage carrying liquor across the Atlantic and we naturally object to the publicity involved in any kind of court action, yet we must have these things settled in a legal manner when we are pushed to extremes by impossible claims. . . . We contend and will prove that Captain Whitburn has no claim to the bonus of $2,000, as our letter to him states that it is subject to the voyage being satisfactory. . . ."

For Schooners Associated, which owned two vessels, the *Tom August* and the *Veronica* — the latter also had been carrying liquor — the end was in sight. By the seventeenth of December, the firm wrote to J. D. Bode of Bremen, from whom it had obtained the *Tom August*'s cargo:

We have to inform you that Schooners Associated Ltd. must be wound up and the following are the reasons:

Tremendous claims have been placed against this firm by the following, among others, Mr. Bidstrup, 1,100 pounds; Captain Whitburn, 1,000 pounds. There are no funds in hand to fight the claims. The Tom August is under writ at Whitehaven and the Veronica is under writ at Halifax. As the matter stands, the sale of both boats will not possibly cover our liabilities, as the best offer we have been able to receive for the Tom August is 2,000 pounds and this does not meet the claims of the captain and mate of that vessel alone. . . .

Obviously, many and probably most, Rum Row operations fared better than did that of the *Tom August,* but her ill-fated voyage illustrates some of the persistent difficulties that plagued those attempting to market illegal booze. The market price fluctuated; it was essential to have well-established shore contacts; the longer it took to sell a cargo, the smaller the profit, and there were, as Captain Whitburn discovered, more than enough unscrupulous people to go around. A Rum Row investment had its risks.

If Godman's claim to "absolute knowledge of the U.S. system of patrols" sounds like braggadocio or the beguiling device of a supersalesman, it was, in any event, supported by one of his former partners who had neither respect nor affection for him.

Sometime in January, 1929, a U.S. Intelligence agent whose code name was "London" went to Hamburg, where he represented himself as agent for some Europeans who owned a consignment of liquor they wanted to sell in the United States. He arranged a contact with the directors of the Deutsche Produkten und Handels A.G. (German Products and Trade Corporation) and "was invited by Mr. Willem Huibers to call upon him at his office, No. 10 Paulstrasse, where [he] had a lengthy conversation with the gentleman."

Huibers was in partnership with Godman for two years, beginning in May, 1925, and they were engaged in the smuggling of liquor from Halifax via St. Pierre to the Atlantic coast of the United States. Huibers's assignment was to go to New York to arrange for the sale of the liquor that they had on hand in Halifax, so he came to know something about that end of the business.

He was highly critical of Godman, whom he described as having "no connections, either in the United States or Canada. He was quite unable to dispose of the [liquor] cargo which I put up and which was mine. I was aboard the Veronica, which carried my cargo, and he gave instructions to the captain of the vessel that not one single case was to be released except upon his, Godman's signature, so that if I wanted a bottle of my own whisky to drink, well, I could not have it, and I was unable to handle my cargo as Godman had assumed possession of it."

Huibers said he was misled by Godman's "talk as to what he can do when actually, he can do nothing. The only item of truth appears to be, and I substantiated this, about this time, he could go into the Barge Office in New York and ascertain the exact position of the government cutters, and this facility naturally enabled him to get thousands of cases ashore. . . ."

He went on to tell the intelligence agent how he had gotten in touch with people in the United States who could handle liquor.

On my return to Halifax, I received a telephone call from a gentleman who, whilst not giving his name, wished me to go and meet him at the post office. I agreed to meet him. He was to carry a newspaper in his left hand.

I met him and he introduced himself as Mr. Caspar. I saw that he knew the bootlegging business from beginning to end. We arranged to ship from Halifax 1,600 cases, of which he was to take one-half of the profits on the sale. He would also put up one-half of the necessary expenses.

This Mr. Caspar knows the business well and also the ins and outs of the Coast Guard routine, as he was at one time in the Coast Guard service of the U.S. Government, so that is a great help. The business is now very difficult and you can only be successful with your schooners if your arrangements on shore work to schedule time, that is, during the relief of one government cutter by another. This is only effective by "grafting," Coast Guard protection. In these days, all the "grafting" is done on shore and not like it used to be, outside the "limit," and that it is why it is so difficult.

The business now is almost impossible and if one can run in, say 2,000 cases per week, then it is very good going. But I personally would like to meet the man who can do it. And furthermore, with all the expenses per case, dollars for this and that, especially for Coast Guard protection, namely, $4 per case, and protection against being hijacked, there is now very little profit in it, although the shore price is about $45 per case, or was when I left a few months ago.

Huibers said he would be willing to "swing several cables to the other side" to pave the way in Canada or the United States for selling a cargo of liquor, adding, "But mind you, whatever happens, your friends are taking their own risk."

The agent "London" also talked to Godman and in a report to Washington dated June 4, 1928, he quoted Godman as saying, "With the aid of an official, I have access to the patrol charts for the vicinity of Staten Island." "London" observed, "How much truth there is in this statement, I am unable to say, but there is very little doubt that in the past, he has been fully informed as to the position of government cutters and so forth in the Staten Island area."

Godman's "secret circular" to his captains warned of the danger of rum pirates. Captain Bill McCoy, who was one of the first group of skippers to go into the business of smuggling liquor — he had never been on the wrong side of the law before and took pride in having his cargo known as "the real McCoy" — had a few words of his own to say about the threat. The fact that McCoy, a highly successful Rum Row salesman, never was robbed of a cargo undoubtedly was due to his constant alertness and defense preparations.

In remembering one night at sea with the liquor fleet, he said,

I went on deck. It had been snowing softly, and the ship stood out white against the black seas. Not a man was to be seen. There was no one at her helm. We were sailing about Rum Row, risking collision with some other ship, square in the lanes of incoming craft, with my entire crew full of Burgundy and sleeping it off below. I got two of the more nearly conscious up on deck and remained on watch the rest of the night myself. We would have been an ideal victim for a rum pirate.

These gentry were becoming troublesome and grew increasingly menacing during the remainder of Rum Row's existence. I had heard of their raids while in Nassau and before coming north on this run had shipped a couple of Lewis machine guns, several Thompson submachine guns, a half-dozen Winchesters, several sawed-off shotguns and a Colt .45 for each member of my crew. While selling liquor on the Row, all of us went armed, and submachine guns were hidden in the furled sails. I also had given orders to my men never to bunch when strangers were on our deck but to keep scattered so that it would be impossible for pirates to hold us all up at once.

Only once did I graze actual trouble with these "go-through men" as the raiders were called, their boast being that whatever job they undertook, they did it and came back with the loot.

Three boats, two men on each, came alongside us one day. I did not like the looks of the visitors and warned my men to be on the alert while they were aboard. I don't think the "go-through men" cared for our looks, either, for we had been at sea a month then, had not shaved since we left port, and each man wore a heavy Colt on his hip. There might have been trouble, but it was averted by the arrival of other customers. They recognized the crooks and told me who they were. I ordered them off my schooner and they went, growling, but obediently enough.

The unprepared did not fare so well.

I talked with a fellow who had sailed with Bill McCoy and he was reflecting on the major changes that had occurred on Rum Row by the middle '20s. First of all, he pointed out, it became more difficult to make a decent profit because more people had to be paid off. He said, "The money was there, buyin' up everybody, and you had to buy the head feller first. But as bad as that was, the pirates were worse.

"There was a Canadian three-masted schooner, the *Eva Caval,* and one gang doublecrossed another and they hijacked everything that was left in her, about half her cargo of liquor. I've even known them to hijack a steamer."

The steamer in question was a classic example of rum piracy. She was the *Mulhouse,* a vessel of about 1,000 tons, of French registry and like many another in the same traffic, shabby and ill kept; some of the European steamers on the Row were so archaic in design and disreputable in appearance that they virtually signaled their business.

The *Mulhouse,* a frequent visitor to the Row, anchored off the New Jersey coast to sell a cargo of liquor — thousands of cases — reportedly worth about a half-million dollars. She had been there a week when she was boarded by a boatload of pirates, thirty of them, armed with guns and knives. Under threats of shooting to kill, they rounded up the *Mulhouse*'s crew and locked them in the forecastle, under guard.

During the following three days, the pirates removed all the liquor from the steamer and stowed it aboard several schooners. They were leisurely about it; they drank a great deal of the cargo themselves, and they sold liquor over the rail to all customers at cut-rate prices. The Coast Guard cutter Gresham patrolled in the area several times while the pirates were in charge but noticed nothing amiss, because there had been no violence, no casualties, and no damage to property.

When the pirates had removed all the liquor, they left the steamer in their respective schooners — the cargo was bound for the New York market. The morning after the pirates left, crew members from other rum vessels — who knew what had been going on — released the *Mulhouse*'s crew from belowdecks and the steamer returned to France, both poorer and lighter.

It was a smooth heist and illustrates why such piracy was tempting: there was no alarm, no chase, no complaint, no prosecution, and no punishment, for all of the obvious reasons — and it was extremely lucrative.

CHAPTER III

OBVIOUSLY, a great many people, including American government officials, knew quite a lot about Rum Row but as with so many aspects of the rum-running business, as visible as it was, it remained a titillating mystery to most of the public. Whether the Row existed and if it did, what it was and where, provided newspaper and magazine writers with an interesting subject. They were handicapped, however, because neither the rumrunners nor the federal agencies involved would give them any information.

In the beginning, law-abiding merchantmen reported sighting vessels offshore, some of them of unusual rig or design, that ran without lights and refused to return signals. The steamer *West Keene,* bound from Pacific ports to New York, sighted a 12,000-ton vessel about sixty miles southeast of Cape Hatteras. The *West Keene*'s master said the stranger had four masts and two funnels, never came closer than four miles, and carried two cargo booms — they are usually snugged down on deck while ships are at sea — rigged to the foremast. An effort to exchange radio messages proved unsuccessful; the unidentified ship refused to answer the *West Keene*.

A few days later, Coast Guard officials received a report from the captain of the American steamer *Lake Arline* that he had sighted a ship with a black hull, showing a crew of thirty on her decks, about a hundred miles southeast of Cape Hatteras. She was described as "rigged in the maritime fashion of twenty years ago. Two large and apparently fast white motorboats were hanging from home-made davits on each side of the main rigging. Astern was a white whaleboat and on a platform built out astern, was a yellow-painted standard fisherman's dory. A lookout platform was attached to each mast and two men were on each side of the platform." The report, forwarded to the Coast Guard via the Navy Department, bore an official comment, "Probably pertinent to theories promulgated as to the disappearance of certain vessels on the high seas. . . ."

So the rumors were fueled, of strange vessels approaching honest freighters "as if prepared to attack . . . ," of an unidentified steamer maneuvering just outside the three-mile limit off Wildwood, New Jersey, of "mysterious ships seen lurking" along the trade lanes of the North Atlantic, and so the sea acquired a new dark drama, at least for coastal people, such as it had not had since eighteenth-century skippers smuggled in tea and molasses. And not all of it was rumor, either. On July 25, 1921, New York newspapers reported, "A tramp steamer cruised saucily outside the three-mile limit off Atlantic City yesterday . . . and taunted federal officials by breaking out pennants saying, 'Lay down your money and come and get it.'

It was the matter of the schooner *Arethusa* and the persistence of the New Bedford *Evening Standard* that placed these mysterious matters in better perspective for the public a couple of weeks later. The *Arethusa,* a lovely vessel to a sailor's eye, already had an impressive reputation. When new, and skippered by Captain Clayton Morrissey, she was the largest knockabout-rigged fisherman afloat, was known as a Gloucester high-liner, and one of the hardest vessels to beat in a stiff breeze. Morrissey was a driver and a sail-carrier; when he was ready to go to sea, he went, defying everything in sight, including a gale.

Alongshore, they still remembered the time, about 1911, when it was almost impossible to obtain bait for a trip for cod on the Grand Banks. Captain Morrissey decided to get bait along the Newfoundland coast and sent most of his crew ashore to do so, in defiance of the laws that prohibited American vessels from getting their supply in this manner. Canadian cutters — three of them — got wind of what he was doing and started for the *Arethusa,* which was standing offshore with only two men aboard, the remaining seventeen of the crew being ashore.

Morrissey set every sail the *Arethusa* carried and went to sea. The cutters chased him fruitlessly over several thousand acres of the North Atlantic until they finally lost him completely in a blizzard so thick that the man at the wheel couldn't see the end of the schooner's bowsprit. When he got ready, Morrissey sailed back to Newfoundland after his crew, paid the libel of $1,000 per man, and put to sea for the Grand Banks.

The New Bedford *Evening Standard* of August 10, 1921, published a story based on the revelations of "a New Bedford man who has been on board the Arethusa, which is lying off Nomansland dispensing refreshment in a truly hospitable manner to all drought-ridden individuals who can sail, row or swim out to the trim-looking fisherman." The master of the *Arethusa* was identified as Captain Bill McCoy, and the schooner was under British registry.

The newspaper reported,

Unlike some of the fashionable resorts of New York, a ticket of admission is not necessary to get on board the Arethusa. Imbued with the democratic ideals of the country off whose shores she is lying, the English vessel welcomes all comers. When the New Bedford man, who paced the deck of the rumrunner only a few days ago, approached the floating bar, he was hailed by the skipper, who met him at the side of the ship and welcomed him on board in the most polite and hospitable manner.

"We transact business here day and night," said the genial captain of the modern pirate craft, "and we manage to supply Block Island, Martha's Vineyard, New Bedford, and Fall River with what the residents of those places seem to want the most. Come out any time you want to; the law can't touch us here, and we'll be very glad to see you."

The *Evening Standard* estimated that the *Arethusa*'s total cargo of liquor when she was fully loaded was worth about $500,000 and that it amounted to 5,000 cases. The story concluded, "At the price of $8 a case in the Bahamas, the cost of the liquor would be about $40,000 which, after deducting $60,000 for ship's and crew expenses, would show a profit in the neighborhood of $400,000, just 1,000 percent of the investment that it took to buy the liquor."

On the next day, the *Evening Standard*'s star reporter, Earle D. Wilson, coaxed a Vineyard fisherman to take him out to the *Arethusa* by concealing the fact that he was a newspaperman and posing as a thirsty customer and entrepreneur "intent on establishing a through route for the cargo from the vessel to New Bedford and other points on the mainland."

Earle, a friend and colleague of many years, related what happened:

We had been out of sight of land for some time and the skipper of the fishing vessel I was on turned to me and said, "If your rum boat is out here, we ought to sight her about 11 o'clock." At 10:45, off to starboard, I spotted first one sail, then another. "There she is," said my skipper.

It had taken us about 4½ hours. Estimating the speed of our vessel at 6½ miles per hour, I figured we were 28 miles out. The Arethusa's skipper said a mouthful when he implied that his location was splendid. Business was rushing when we arrived and we waited for other customers, mostly in swordfishing vessels, to board and be served. Finally, somebody aboard the Arethusa waved to us to come ahead; our vessel hove to, we got into a dory, rowed up to her rail, and we climbed aboard.

The crew resembled as wicked a gang of cutthroats as ever bade a luckless victim walk the plank. All were unshaven, some looking as though their faces had been innocent of the influence of a razor stroke for the nearly four weeks they had been out there. Nobody said anything, so I piped up, "How's chances of getting a drink?" I am not a drinking man, never have been, never will be, but I had to buy something in order to stay aboard and have a look around.

The man I took to be the mate said in startlingly good Yankee, "Anything from a drink to a barrel. What'll you have?"

"Got any scotch?" I countered.

"Sure, we've got everything, but we can't break a case."

"Well, let's see it."

He conducted me below decks, and my view on what constitutes a large quantity of illicit booze — previously based on peeks at piles of confiscated liquor in police headquarters — underwent a decided change. The liquor aboard the Arethusa was divided into sections according to brand and kind. One section held nothing but champagne, another nothing but brandy, another nothing but gin, and so on.

I was in the whisky compartment, where I presume the greatest volume of business had been done. As a rough estimate, I would say the room was about 20 feet wide, 10 feet the other way, and perhaps 12 feet high. It was literally packed full of whisky sewed up in gunny sacks. When the sailor-bartender ripped open one of the sacks, I saw that it contained five quart bottles. The sacks were jammed in just as tight as they could be crammed and reached from floor to ceiling, the entire width of the room. A large closet adjoining was likewise full. Perhaps two or three feet into the room had been cleared out, presumably, by previous sales.

I asked if I could get four quarts — I didn't have any more money than that anyway — and he agreed to it. He handed me two quarts of what I later found to be Calvert's whisky, distilled, bottled, and bonded in Baltimore, according to the labels. This nailed the rumor that only English or other foreign goods were handled by the schooner. The other two bottles were Cedar Brook, likewise an American whisky, and likewise marked 100 proof. I paid him $5 a quart, $20 for the four bottles.

He urged me to purchase more, stating the length of time they would remain there was uncertain, but I wasn't looking for booze, but news, and I didn't.

I took a walk around the deck when we came up, to see what I could see. It was covered with cases under canvas and big barrels and kegs. They were lined about the deck. There was scant room to move. "How much for one of those barrels?" I hazarded. "Two dollars," answered one of the unshaven thugs nearest me. "What!" I demanded, astonished. The crew came as near laughing as I imagine they can. "You can have any one of them for $2," said the mate. "They're all empty."

Yes, business aboard the Arethusa had been good and stuff had been lugged off in something else besides bottles and cases, I took it. I squirmed between two barrels, behind a stack of cases, and made my way to our dory. "Come again and often," shouted the sailor-bartender as we shoved off.

I got a fine opportunity to give the Arethusa the once-over as we rowed back to the fishing vessel. She drifted leisurely, her lines were graceful, she had been hove to in that spot for days and required hardly any attention from the crew to stay there; she made a mighty impressive picture.

In gold letters on her stern was painted "Arethusa, N.P."

I said to myself as we boarded the fishing vessel for the trip back, "Water, water everywhere, and all you want to drink — at the Arethusa, sixty miles from New Bedford and well beyond the three-mile limit."

Wilson's story of the liquor purchase, which was given handsome Page 1 attention in the *Evening Standard*, proved to be something of a bombshell. In Boston, Wilfred Lufkin, collector of customs, said he was "frank to state" that, regardless of newspaper stories, the federal government lacked proof of the smuggling that was reported. He added that he and Harold B. Wilson, federal director of the Prohibition agents in Massachusetts, had agents in New Bedford and vicinity "intent on preventing and apprehending persons smuggling liquor from the rum-running schooner Arethusa to the mainland," if indeed there were any such.

By the thirteenth of August, the *Arethusa* was gone from the area off Nomansland, a victim of the publicity. The news stories first discouraged her customers, then apparently thwarted an attempt by the schooner's crew to land 140 cases of liquor on Martha's Vineyard, and finally "brought federal agents tumbling over each other to reach New Bedford. News of the attention the enterprise was receiving ashore was carried to the Britisher at sea." George and Linus Eldridge, Mattapoisett swordfishermen, who had passed under the schooner's stern on Monday of that week, came ashore on Thursday and reported she was no longer visible anywhere, not even from the masthead.

The *Evening Standard* editorialized,

Though the news of the Arethusa's departure may mean disappointment to bibulous New Bedford men, it will be greeted with delight by Prohibition agents and customs men from Collector Lufkin's office, who have been wandering around New Bedford in much embarrassment for 48 hours. . . .

The collector of the Port of Boston, Mr. Lufkin, thinks the Arethusa story is much exaggerated. He could not find that her skipper landed in New Bedford and deposited money here. He could not find anybody who had brought liquor ashore. He could not find the Arethusa herself, when he went looking for her. . . .

It is impossible to escape the impression that the whole affair has been bungled.

The key figure in all this, Captain Bill McCoy, had been living at Gay Head, on Martha's Vineyard, having fled there from New London, just a skip and a jump ahead of Treasury agents. His recollections of how the *Evening Standard*'s page 1 story affected his operation supply the missing pieces of the puzzle.

McCoy recalled that many of the residents of Gay Head were Indian, and he added,

Indians are ideal people for a rumrunner to live among. They don't ask questions. They don't talk to strangers. They haven't any particular use for law or the government. . . . I stayed with them several weeks. The Arethusa still jogged about No Man's Land, and each night, we discharged more cargo, the bulk of it going into New Bedford escorted by Indians or in fishermen's craft. The Arethusa was the first rum ship to work off the Massachusetts coast.

The government people had no idea what had become of me and ran in circles trying to pick up my trail, while rumors kept floating in about the "mystery ship" that was hanging offshore. The Prohibition authorities turned on the collector of the Port of Boston, demanding that a cutter track down the Arethusa. The cutter tried but couldn't find her, for my schooner went far out to sea before daybreak and did not creep in again till nightfall.

Then scandal broke. A New Bedford newspaper reporter disguised himself as a fisherman, chartered a boat and went out one Saturday to find the Arethusa. He succeeded where the cutter had failed, boarded her, talked with the crew, bought some liquor, and spread the story of his exploit over an entire page.

He certainly laid on the color. There was some excuse for the reporter. My crew all were American citizens who hoped sometime to return to their native land. To avoid recognition when their reprehensible past was behind them, they all grew beards of untamed luxuriance, and, since the schooner had been out a long time and fresh water was scarce, they rarely washed. They looked like Airedales and smelled like camels.

When I saw that yarn, I knew it was time to move again. I could almost hear the outraged squawk it was certain to draw from the authorities. The protest that poured in upon the collector of the Port of Boston almost drove him out of his mind. He was compelled to issue a statement, denying the presence of any rum ship off the coast and saying the reporter had probably encountered some Canadian schooner that had sold him a few bottles.

But he sent the cutter Acushnet after me again. I felt in my bones that it was time to say good-bye to Gay Head. . . . That afternoon, while we were in our upstairs room in an Indian's cottage, strangers drove up to the door, thick, husky men whose appearance yelled "detective." I heard them ask our host where we were. They explained quite glibly that they were friends we had invited to go on a fishing trip with us. Our old Indian answered, quite as glibly, that there never had been any such persons as they described on Gay Head. The strangers left. Ten minutes later, we did, too.

My first thought was for my schooner. . . . I chartered the fastest fish launch in Gay Head and because my luck still was in, found the Arethusa. I told Captain Gott to make a wide circle out to sea, coming in at the end of three days to a point twenty miles southeast of the Cape Ann whistling buoy. If I didn't show up in a few days thereafter, he was to go back to Nassau.

On my way back to Gay Head, I crossed the bows of the cutter Acushnet, coming down coast under a full head of steam and looking like a fussy old lady trying to find a runaway child. She ran up alongside a little swordfisherman, hailed her, and then foamed away on her course. I drew up under the schooner's lee.

"What did the cutter want?" I bawled to her master. He was a lean New Englander, salt and dry as a split cod, and he spat over the rail before shouting back:

"Wanted to know where Bill McCoy and the Arethusa was."

I waited. He spat again.

"Told him I never heard of neither of ye," he roared. "Dinged fool!"

They don't breed squealers among those New England fishermen.

It might well have been that if the federal government had encouraged a few responsible newspaper writers such as Mr. Wilson, rather than considering them as adversaries, Washington's task would have been eased. The spotlight of accurate publicity would have kept the vessels of Rum Row on the move and off balance and the American public's intense desire to know more about what was going on would have been responded to reliably, rather than romantically. It must be remembered that the business of rum-running had a great grip on the mind of the average citizen — especially if he lived near the coast — and that this interest was often further stimulated by personal experiences that concealed more than they revealed.

The family of one woman to whom I talked lived near the shore. She recalled, "One night, when I wasn't very old, there was a knock at the door and my father answered it. A man came in and he was bleeding all over the floor. He had been shot and he wanted to use the telephone. I never forgot it."

Another woman was a nurse in a children's hospital located in Dartmouth, Massachusetts, not far from the water. She said, "I had night duty. We had orders not to let anybody in who wanted to use the telephone. We knew what was going on down there on the beach nights and every time it got dark, I used to wonder what I would do to protect the children if anything happened."

The children of one family grew up to respond to the cry, "There goes the horse again," and they would all run to the front windows of the house, which faced a country road. There was no horse, but the reference was to a motorized horse van, which was used regularly to haul booze from the beach to nearby barns. "We always joked about that being the most-traveled horse in the United States," one of the family recalled.

And the countryside, from New Jersey to Maine, was dotted with barns, garages, and sheds that by night were vaguely silhouetted by dim lights, largely unexplained and uninvestigated, and by day, were full of liquor — and everybody knew it, and largely said nothing.

So the public wanted very much to know more about the business than it knew. But the government, in effect, continued to say no. In a memorandum dated January 25, 1923, Assistant Secretary Edward Clifford of the Treasury Department advised, "My recommendations are, first, that Prohibition officials . . . be requested not to talk to newspapermen, in fact, to give no publicity whatever as to what they are doing.

"I will see to it that the Customs Service and Coast Guard officials say nothing. This matter cannot be handled successfully by giving out information to the press."

In an effort to satisfy reader demand, there were published many newspaper and magazine articles, all long on generality and short on fact, but the classic example of dramatic reporting was an August 15, 1924, copyright story that appeared in the New York *Herald Tribune*. The author, Sanford Jarrell, electrified readers, hungry to know what was going on offshore, when he recounted these experiences:

Fifteen miles off Fire Island, on the south side of Long Island, beyond the pale of the law, is anchored a floating bar and cabaret which is the playground of the rich and fast. It is a large ship of more than 17,000 tons. On board are silverware and other fittings marked with the name of Friedrich der Grosse, a former North German liner.

A jazz orchestra furnishes the music with which millionaires, flappers, and chorus girls out of work whirl on a waxed floor with the tang of salt sea air dancing through their lungs. A heavily manned bar serves both men and women. An excellent cuisine lends tone. Drinks of every conceivable character may be obtained at prices that dwindle the fat wallets of the customers. Revels de luxe are in vogue, especially at the weekend.

The dancing was highly respectable at the early hour; although drinks were served in a fashion fast and furious, the effect was not such as to rock the boat until after midnight. On deck, here and there, were comfortable canvas chairs where one could sip drinks in tall thin glasses, listen to the clink of the ice, the pounding of the waves, gaze upon the rays of the moon playing on the water, and make love marvelously.

At the bar, women as well as men stood up there ordering various drinks and dishing out to each other bright utterances on the literature, scandal, and sensational murders of the day. The bar was equipped with a modern cash register, which was overworked, if ever a cash register was.

There is a democracy induced by alcohol which can be had no other way. Some of the guests aboard the boat came in their own yachts, four of which were anchored nearby Thursday night, but they did not ask for the social status of the others. Aristocracy, nouveaux riches, young women whose conversation smacked of the stage door, a red-haired girl, and others fraternized pleasantly. The hours were whiled away in a manner which would not have amused advocates of the 18th Amendment. . . .

After midnight, the merriment increased. On some nights, they had motion pictures at this hour, showing "The Thief of Baghdad" only a week or two ago. . . . There were no drinks on the house. Now and then, however, some philanthropic gentleman would order a round for all present and thus enrich by $100 or more the coffers of the enterprising bootleg syndicate which owns the ship. The Negro jazz orchestra, we are told, was something new that had only recently been imported.

Efforts to learn, by subtle questions, the identity of the owner or owners of the vessel were flat failures. Even those guests who had been there before were ignorant of this. The general impression, backed by some of the fittings, was that the ship was the old Friedrich der Grosse. The former North German Lloyd liner was subsequently used in the transport service as the Lake Huron. After that, the United States Shipping Board renovated her, sold part of the fixtures, and leased the boat to the Munson Line, which operated her. . . . It is probable that a syndicate of wealthy Englishmen bought her and decided to take a quiet flier in the American bootlegging game.

Boatmen in Bay Shore and other points on Great South Bay who are reticent about explaining their activities on the ocean know her as "that German liner." Certain yachtsmen, they say, are more familiar with her location, which varies to some extent. . . . It took me two days to find the boat and I had the unenviable experience of drifting helplessly in an open boat for two hours, ten miles from shore. There were no questions asked when we clambered aboard the vessel. Each guest had to fork over to a man with a London accent a five-dollar bill, which might be jotted down on the expense account of the tired businessman on the cover charge. Those of us who desired staterooms were assigned to them, and the rate was $5 up, depending on the size.

We could hear from the main dining room the strains of "What'll I Do?" Five minutes later, I was in the ballroom. There were there, and on the promenade deck, some sixty persons in all. The men were obviously wealthy . . . their women companions ranged from sedate old ladies with gray hair and silver monogrammed cigarette holders to young girls who quite likely will return to finishing school in the fall.

Jarrell found the food "quite reasonable and very good" and served in an efficient fashion but the drinks were sold "at exorbitant prices," ranging from Scotch highballs at $1 to mint juleps at $2.50. Of the latter, he concluded that "the chief advantage of buying a mint julep at sea is to be able to assure oneself that civilization is still with us. Mint juleps are rarely seen in the city these days and those concocted by the bartenders of the floating cabaret are really quite commendable."

He said that at midnight it was customary for guests aboard to gather on the steamer's poop deck, where there was a "somewhat dismal" reproduction of the Statue of Liberty, to which toasts were tendered. He concluded by reporting, "At 4 a.m. today, I went to sleep in a neat little stateroom. . . . At 6 o'clock, I was awakened by a steward who informed me that the launch was leaving in half an hour for the neighborhood of Sandy Hook. Only three of the twelve who came out on the rumrunner returned. . . . Even Irene, the red-haired beauty, remained behind. She may be there yet, if her bankroll holds out."

Not long after this issue of the *Herald Tribune* hit the streets, the Coast Guard cutter *Seneca* was storming down the coast from Montauk Point to the Delaware River looking for the boozy liner. Other newspapers, including the Washington *Post,* reprinted the *Herald Tribune* story. Even as official search failed to turn up the German ship, the *Herald Tribune* published an additional account stating that "a fast rumrunner sped out" to the floating cabaret with copies of its Jarrell story and implying that, as a result, it had changed location. The *Herald Tribune* suggested, "It was regarded last night as barely possible that the cabaret ship, to avoid trouble, might have dropped anchor thirty or forty miles out."

However, on August 23, even while excitement over the story remained at an extraordinary level, the newspaper which had started it all reported glumly: "The New York Herald Tribune regrets to state that a story which appeared in its columns on the morning of August 15 under the headline 'New Yorkers Drink Sumptuously on 17,000-ton Floating Cafe at Anchor 15 Miles off Fire Island' was false.

"As the result of investigation begun several days ago by The Herald Tribune, Sanford Jarrell, who wrote the article, was compelled late yesterday afternoon to confess that it was untrue. He has been dismissed from the staff of this newspaper."

Still it is doubtful that this episode created any great credibility gap, because it was, in fact, possible to believe almost anything about rumrunners. In the same month, U.S. Attorney Robert O. Harris in Boston said he had been informed that a big German submarine of commercial type was operating off Cape Cod and "flooding" the Cape area with foreign beer, ale, and wine. The story coincided with reports by airplane pilots in the New York area of unidentified submarines lying in the Hudson. However, *The New York Times* put all of this back on page 6 with a small headline, which suggests something.

And nine days later, customs agents at Mystic seized a former government one-man torpedo boat valued at $100,000. This craft, capable of carrying 400 cases of liquor and maintaining a speed of 33 knots, had 60 dabs of fresh gray paint covering dents in her armor that resembled bullet marks. It was believed that she was the vessel that two weeks before had tried to ram and sink the customs cutter *Shark* off Montauk. In the chase, the *Shark* had fired 800 machine-gun bullets at the craft she was pursuing.

SONG OF THE RUMRUNNER

Yo ho! for the schooner, low and black
That slips through the sea at night
Yo ho! for the rebuilt fishing smack
For the sliding joints in the steamer's stack
That changes her outline quite.

Yo ho! for the cruiser running in
That slips 'neath the black smoke screen
Yo ho! for the doors in the vessel's skin
The hollow bulkhead lined with tin
Coal scows and the submarine.

Yo ho! for the sea fog, white and dense,
That shelters the landing crew
Yo ho! for the tip to the fed'ral gents
That points to the spot where the trails commence
The trails of the faulty clue.

Yo ho! for the tricks of the ancient craft
Revived once again today
Yo ho! for the lights and the floating raft
The game of driving the agents daft
By leading them all astray.

Yo ho! for the dollars as in they come
The harvest of gold we reap
Yo ho! for the split of the rousing sum
Fill up again with the red, red rum
Drink hearty, my lads, and deep.

—Joseph C. Allen
1922

CHAPTER IV

WHAT ACTUALLY WAS GOING on offshore bore little resemblance to Sanford Jarrell's version; it was far less romantic, but much more dramatic, and of broader scale. On a typical day in 1923, for example, the Rum Row fleet ten miles or more from Ambrose Lightship consisted of two small cargo steamers, one steam yacht, and twelve fisherman-type down-East schooners, including the *Dorothy M. Smart,* of Digby, Nova Scotia, plus the steamer *Vaudreuil* of Montreal.

A former officer on one of the Nova Scotia schooners with whom I talked said, "At night on Rum Row, you would think it was a city out there, off Jones Inlet, near the ship lane, or maybe twelve miles off Highland Light. It was like going to a supermarket. We had a good reputation and lots of customers. They would carry your mail ashore and bring you anything you wanted. Three weeks in the winter time was an average trip. It depended on your connections ashore. It might take no more than a week or even three-four nights if the cargo was bought ashore ahead, if you had good connections."

By the middle 1920s, a businesslike pattern was developed that formed the basis for Rum Row. Federal figures revealed that during a twelve-month period, 332 foreign-flag vessels had been engaged in "wholesale and organized efforts" to smuggle liquor into the United States. Of this number, 307 flew the British flag, ten the Norwegian, and four the French. The chief British bases were Halifax, Lunenburg, Sydney, and Yarmouth, in Nova Scotia, and St. John's, Newfoundland. Virtually all the vessels selling liquor off the American coast sailed on fraudulent clearance papers.

Between May 27 and June 11, 1925, nine vessels "from the high seas" arrived with cargoes of liquor at St. Pierre and Miquelon, which offers an idea of the intensity of the traffic. Nova Scotia vessels — such as *Accuracy, Apohaqui, Malbo, Selma K., Good Luck, Placentia, Shamalian, George and Earle, Dream Girl, Game Cock, South Wind,* and *Tatamagouche* — ran the liquor from the French islands to Rum Row.

The American government recognized the need for obtaining information on the movements of Nova Scotia rum carriers early in the game, and some of this was achieved through informers. In hiring such a civilian agent, a standard form was used, which read in part: "For the consideration of $2 per day and no per diem in lieu of subsistence, I agree to furnish the [blank] or his authorized agent with information of violations of the National Prohibition Act for a period of [blank] days, beginning [blank] and ending at the close of business, subject to the conditions indicated below. . . ." The conditions related to observing all laws and regulations governing conduct of federal officers, obeying instructions given by authorized persons, and rendering reports. The document was signed by the commissioner of Prohibition and approved by the Secretary of the Treasury.

Two dollars a day was not much money considering the risk involved. Prohibition was unpopular in the Province of Nova Scotia and the Prohibition enforcement equipment utterly inadequate. The only two revenue cutters of any size, the *Margaret* and the *Cartier,* were stationed at Quebec, leaving to two or three small craft the hopeless task of patrolling the deeply indented coastline of Nova Scotia. On land, enforcement of the law was equally difficult because witnesses were mostly uncooperative and the courts would not convict except on overwhelming evidence. In some localities, the feeling was so strong that agents who took any action were in danger of their lives, and in other places, zeal on the part of an enforcement officer was promptly rewarded by transfer to another post.

Still, the information acquired by Coast Guard headquarters in Washington through diplomatic and informant sources was extensive, as the following samples of vessel traffic monitoring reveal:

June 24, 1925: The American consul general at Halifax reports the departure of the Walter Holken, with a cargo of liquor for the high seas and the arrival from the high seas with a cargo of liquor of the Integral.

The American consul at Yarmouth, Nova Scotia reports the departure with a cargo of 12,000 cases of liquor of the schooner Ocean Maid.

The American consul at Sydney, Nova Scotia reports the departure of the schooner Loyola for St. Pierre Miquelon, with a cargo of assorted liquors.

January 16, 1926: The American consul in Halifax reports the departure for St. Pierre Miquelon of the Hohenlinden with a cargo of liquor and the arrival from the high seas of the Over The Top with a cargo of liquor.

This message, dated Yarmouth, Nova Scotia, November 30, 1931, was based on information provided by an undercover agent:

Good Luck, Captain Charles Donovan, will leave Liverpool (N.S.) today for Long Island. Cargo consists of 129 fifteen-gallon kegs malt whisky. Good Luck is fitted with concealed tanks from which cargo is pumped. Vessel will be in approximately same place where Game Cock was taken on the 15th. Good Luck was accompanying Game Cock on 15th and landed cargo directly on the wharf. Position of landing, near Race below Block Island and north shore of Long Island. [Signed] H.

But even with some knowledge of how and where the rum fleet was operating, the U.S. Coast Guard had been handed a formidable task in being assigned to halt the smuggling of liquor from Rum Row into the United States. Especially in the early years, their equipment was inadequate; as individuals, their attitude toward Prohibition was at least as divided as was the nation's; the temptation of highly rewarding collaboration with the rumrunners was ever-present; the kind of hound-and-hare game they were obliged to play always gave the advantage to the smugglers and — even though their men and vessels were already stretched to the limit — they were also expected to provide all of their regular services of rescue and assistance at sea.

Top-ranking Coast Guard officials knew from the beginning that this new role thrust upon them would inevitably cost them much of the traditional popularity and respect that the service had enjoyed up to that time.

In 1927, Rear Admiral Frederick C. Billard, commandant of the Coast Guard, summed up his feelings about the assignment:

The Coast Guard has been given the task. . . . They don't know the motives or views of each of the 48 states, they don't know the various phases of this social experiment in all its ramifications.

They go out to do the work with which they have been charged, to uphold the power and dignity and Constitution of the United States, and ask no questions. The fight against liquor smuggling is one of the most complex naval operations ever executed; thousands of miles of coast have to be patrolled. The Coast Guard has to fight a system of enemy espionage and propaganda, yet these young men continue their hazardous work fraught with peril and hardship, regardless of the theories of international relations, and ask no questions.

The Coast Guard was already performing a large number of important and arduous duties that carried more of an appeal than apprehending rumrunners. It was perfectly apparent that the task meant a very difficult and perplexing sea problem. For all the complex administrative problems incident to creating and operating an enlarged fleet, there were only 200 regular commissioned officers in the Coast Guard and there are only 286 such officers today. Marked enthusiasm for the elimination of this particular source of liquor supply could not be expected on the part of the average old-time sailorman.

Anyhow, the Coast Guard was given the task and it did not discuss it or argue about it, it simply answered, "Aye, aye, sir" and sailed into the job.

The patterns of interaction between the Coast Guard and the vessels on Rum Row were varied; most commonly, they involved picketing and trailing, in an effort to make it more difficult for the offshore craft to transfer their liquor cargoes to small boats assigned to carry the booze ashore. On occasion, however, Coast Guardsmen in civilian clothes manned a captured rum launch, went out to Rum Row and purchased liquor, thus establishing proof of the offshore vessel's intent to land its cargo illegally in the United States.

A successful instance of this strategy occurred on October 9, 1924, slightly more than twenty miles off the New York Harbor entrance. The Norwegian steamer *Sagatind* cleared from Antwerp for St. Pierre and Miquelon with a cargo of liquor manifested for delivery at St. Pierre, off the south coast of Newfoundland. On the night of the ninth, she was off New York, transshipping liquor to the British schooner *Diamantina,* which lay alongside. A Coast Guard lieutenant commander and a Secret Service agent, in civilian clothes and manning what the Coast Guard referred to as a "test boat," purchased twenty-five cases of liquor from the *Diamantina.* Although the money was paid to the *Diamantina* for liquor that was scheduled to become part of her cargo, the slingload of bottles actually was passed to the test boat directly from the *Sagatind,* so that it did not have to be handled twice.

The fact that the *Sagatind* was discharging cargo into the *Diamantina* and that a portion of this cargo was passed to the test boat connected both vessels with the delivery of contraband liquor. The Coast Guard's case was that the cargo was not properly manifested, it was being unloaded without a permit and being unloaded between sunset and sunrise without a special permit which was required, and it was being unloaded for delivery into the United States.

Both vessels were seized shortly thereafter, early on the morning of the tenth, by the Coast Guard cutter *Seneca.* With Coast Guard prize crews in command, they steamed under their own power to an anchorage off Bedloe's Island, where the Coast Guardsmen were relieved by customs guards. The right to board, search, and seize such vessels was established under treaties between the United States and both Britain and Norway, as long as the foreign ship was within one hour's steaming time from the coast. Former rumrunners, such as the test boat was, obviously were capable of speeds far greater than twenty miles an hour, thus placing *Diamantina* and *Sagatind* within official reach.

The incident involving the *Sagatind* illustrates graphically the difficulty in distinguishing between rum-running era fact and fiction. In *Rum War at Sea,* by Malcolm F. Willoughby, commander, USCGR (T), published by the Government Printing Office and the closest thing extant to an official Coast Guard history of the period, the author writes:

. . . Seneca ran alongside the slowly drifting Norwegian steamer Sagatind, forty miles offshore. Seneca took the situation in hand and fired three 3-pound shots across her bow, anticipating sudden flight. But there was no response from Sagatind. The cutter hove to and a boarding party went to the silent ship to discover a most sordid condition. They found 43,000 cases of liquor from an original 100,000 cases, $26,000 in cash, and the deck still piled high with cases.

All of Sagatind's crew were stupefied from drink except three whose jaws were broken; one man had a broken leg; many had black eyes. All were herded from the forecastle to the deck, cursing and staggering. The master said fights in the crew had been daily routine since the ship had cleared from Antwerp for St. Pierre. At first, he had tried to prevent the fights, but had given up on reaching Rum Row. Sagatind was the largest rumrunner captured up to that time.

Willoughby, who had the cooperation of Coast Guard officials in the preparation of his book, including several retired officers who were in the service during this era, noted that "many of the incidents were highly dramatic. There is always a temptation to let one's imagination rise above the basic facts to produce an exciting and gripping story. That is not the way of history, and it has been assiduously avoided. . . ."

And yet, in his official report of the affair dated October 17, 1924, Eugene Blake, Jr., commanding officer of the *Seneca*, concluded: "The accounts appearing in the New York papers on the morning of October 13, with respect to the drunken condition of the crew of the *Sagatind* were entirely without foundation." Blake added, "The masters and crews of both vessels offered no resistance to the boarding, search, and seizure of their vessels and were perfectly tractable in every way."

There the matter hangs, and with the passage of more than a half-century, it is virtually impossible to discover the source of the report of drunkenness and violence.

I interviewed an officer of the *Diamantina*, now eighty-two, a down-Easter slightly built and still chipper as a boy. He has spent a lifetime at sea, in everything from sailing coasters to diesel trawlers to oceangoing ships spanning the globe. He remembered the seizure of the two vessels well, relating it as a rather ordinary event, and recalled much else in addition. He said:

I was in the rum-running business for a couple of years, off and on. It was the only dollar you could make; they were only paying $35 to $40 a month in the three-masted coasters. I was in five schooners and some steamers that ran rum. They paid us in wages and bonus. A deckhand got $75 a month and $75 bonus. I was mate and got $150 a month and $150 bonus. The Diamantina was built in Lunenburg; she was a new vessel, had a crew of ten or 11, and would carry 6,000 cases. Really, they weren't cases; there were six bottles to a bag, sewed up in a diamond-shaped burlap package.

In St. Pierre, gin was 25 cents a quart, imported champagne, $1 a bottle, rum, 50 cents a gallon. The rum people owned the warehouses at St. Pierre. The stuff they had was Black and White, White Label, Smugglers, and lots of imported champagne. They used to get the liquor from Europe in wooden cases and they put the stuff in burlap there, because it was easier to stow and handle. There's no wood on St. Pierre and when they got mountains of those wooden liquor boxes, the people there shingled their barns and fish shacks with them and used the stuff for kindling. The rum people built up St. Pierre, warehouses and everything.

We'd get clearance at St. Pierre to go to Nassau, with a load or in ballast. Some boats had their cargoes consigned, but some didn't. There were a lot at it in the peak of the business, maybe a hundred steamers and schooners. Sometimes we'd get a load from a European steamer; those big steamers would carry 60,000 to 70,000 cases and they'd anchor about 30 miles offshore of New York. Intermediate vessels, such as I was on, would go out there and take 5,000 to 6,000 cases and go in to anchor on Rum Row.

We had all kinds of customers. There were lobster traps out there, so the lobstermen would come out from Sheepshead Bay, and the scallopers, too. We used to sell small lots, as well as 600 to 800 cases to a boat. We took cash. Some of them came in speedboats. One boat had false gas tanks in behind the bulwarks; unscrew the covers, the top came off the split tanks and he could take about twenty cases.

Sometimes we carried supercargoes. They would notify the charterers when we left St. Pierre and give us the position to anchor. They'd come off and we'd retail it. Sometimes there would be six or seven to as many as twenty boats alongside. Lobstermen would put down a couple of cases; little fishing boats would carry in two or three. One fellow took two-three cases and he came out every good-weather day and peddled the stuff on a bicycle in Brooklyn.

Some of them weren't even boatmen. They'd come out with an oil hat and oil skins, but wearing dress shoes. They couldn't handle a boat and they'd come at you, bang, head on. They followed the garbage scows out to find us and we'd show them on the compass how to get back. They'd come alongside, ask you what you had — sometimes some of it was on deck — and you'd tell him the price and he'd pay you. Then you give orders to the crew and say, "Give this fellow so many of this, so many of that —"

Once in a while maybe some of the stuff broke in the burlap but I never once saw any go overboard. When you're at it all the time, you get used to it. We were young. We took it off the big ships with a cargo net, but a case is nothing to handle when you're used to it. And when the owners would come, say to get 400 to 500 cases, they'd match their half of a torn playing card wtih our half. Once in a while, if we had liquor in wooden boxes, the customers would put it in sacks themselves if they were going to dump it in the water with a buoy inshore.

Offshore, we'd move around. The Coast Guard was hanging around and we'd watch them. They'd shut off their lights. It was a cutter that took in the Diamantina and the steamer [Sagatind] that we were getting a load from. The way it was, you never knew who you was working for. This fellow was supercargo. He had sold to this boat [the Coast Guard test boat] and they had marked the money. Now if he had burned it or given it to the crew, he would have been all right. But they had bought ten or twenty cases or something like that, and he had to open the safe — he had taken in about $6,000 — and the marked money proved that you had made a connection, you had sold booze.

When we anchored off the Statue of Liberty, the customs fellows came aboard. In no time at all, they wanted to get at the whisky. They told us they could get a good market for it, but we didn't want nothing to do with them. Every evening, they came out with suitcases, one fellow at the head of ten or twelve, the watch at night. They packed their little grips with three or four bottles.

After the hearing was over, we went down to a Brooklyn dock and our fellows would carry three-four bottles ashore, maybe to buy a suitcase or a shirt and when they got to the head of the dock, the guards wouldn't let them out without paying; maybe if they started out with four bottles, they'd get out with one or two.

We had rifles and so on aboard; I had a beautiful repeater shotgun. They just took it and I couldn't get it back. I tried, but I couldn't. They said they were breaking up the whisky; I never saw them break up none, but I saw them take plenty ashore. The ones who made the most money out of it were the customs officers and the policemen, because it never cost them anything.

There was an awful lot of graft going on with the charters, the hijacking, the police and the Coast Guard payoffs. The Coast Guard got to catching the inshore rum boats, then they'd put men aboard, and come offshore to buy from us. That's how they got the Diamantina. Once, we saw them catch a boat in the daytime. By and by, when it got dark, we had a customer alongside; we had the tarpaulins up, and the first two tiers in — we had loaded about 400 cases aboard him and he was trying to beat me out. He was saying he didn't have as many cases as I knew he had. So I jumped aboard him; we had covered his stuff with canvas because otherwise the cases would show, and I was down there counting the cases.

Well, along came these Coast Guard fellows with the rum boat they had caught in the daytime. They jumped right aboard our customer, but they fell when they landed and that gave me a chance to get back aboard our vessel.

We paid those Coast Guards $1,500. I thought at first that was just to let our boat go. But they waited around while we finished loading it. They were cursing us up in the clouds while we loaded and they kept saying, "How long is it going to take you to load this damned thing?" I said, "You got yours; what's your complaint?" So they said the ship they were off had gone to Fire Island and would come back before daylight. For the $1,500, they were willing to give our boat safe passage in to the beach, but they had to get back out before their ship came back and they were afraid we wouldn't get through in time.

Was he ever fired on? "Just once," he said.

We were anchored, with our lights on, near Jones Inlet. There were a lot of us out there and a lot of passenger boats, coming and going, because it was near the ship lanes. The fellows in the inshore rum boats used us as shields. They were cute and they knew enough to keep for the ships going into New York.

Well, there was this boat going like hell, must be fifty miles an hour and too much speed for the cutter that was chasing him. The rum boat got on the other side of us from the cutter, used us as a shield and the cutter fired high through our rigging, figuring that would make him stop. But it didn't. After he used us for a shield, he got on the other side of a big vessel going into New York and by that time, the Coast Guard couldn't catch him anyhow.

Eventually, in mid-May of 1925, the federal government decided to present to the public an idea of what was going on offshore. At that time, 385 foreign rum-running vessels, representing what Washington described as a "billion-dollar combine," was being combatted by $30 million worth of Coast Guard floating equipment. The Coast Guard fleet consisted of an authorized fleet of 20 converted destroyers, 16 cutters, 204 patrol boats, and 103 picket boats.

The principal centers of rum-running activity were New York, New Jersey, and New England, essentially because of their population density. Coast Guard strategy at this time called for establishment of a rum blockade, the picketing of "every rum boat that comes within striking distance of shore and the continued patrolling of all waterways leading from the sea to the shore bootlegger bases."

The government announced that

a state of war — a war of patient attrition — virtually exists on the seas off New York, New Jersey, Rhode Island, and a portion of Massachusetts. All movements against the beleaguered rummies are transmitted in code by wireless to the Coast Guard headquarters in Washington. The Coast Guardsmen are getting little shore liberty.

53

Crews and members of crews are being shifted constantly to offset attempts of the "enemy" to frustrate the blockade by bribery, intimidation, and sabotage.

It was believed that the Coast Guard could so tightly ring the offshore smugglers with small, heavily armed boats as virtually to stop the flow of liquor. At the time of its announcement, Washington was realizing certain successes; with the blockade less than two weeks old, it claimed to have forced more than 70 smuggling vessels to abandon Rum Row and "scuttle to sea." To emphasize the effectiveness of its strategy, the Coast Guard invited a group of newspapermen to take a four-day inspection cruise of what Lieutenant Commander Stephen S. Yeandle, aide to the commandant, called "the national shame," the ocean end of the rum-running business.

The cruise, aboard the cutter *Pequod,* ranged from Nantucket Lightship on the north to Atlantic City on the west. Twenty-five miles off Montauk Point, at dusk, the *Pequod* came upon the schooner *General Pau,* out of Liverpool, Nova Scotia. A reporter, shouting through a megaphone, held an hour-long ship-to-ship interview across a narrow strip of the gray Atlantic between the two vessels. The *General Pau*'s supercargo, standing in the glare of a searchlight, bandied jests with his interviewer; he stood surrounded by wooden cases and declared, not too solemnly, that the vessel's cargo was fish, principally hake, and added that "there isn't no booze aboard."

What did he think of the Coast Guard and would he receive any newspapermen aboard? He laughed, and ducked the first half of the question. "No, no," he drawled, "I'd like to oblige you, but I can't."

"What do you think of the blockade?"

"Time will tell."

"How are you getting on? Plenty of water, food, and other things?"

"Oh, not so bad, not so bad."

"Drinking the water aboard?"

"Hope to tell you we're not."

A number of flashlights then were focused on the schooner and the supercargo and crew were asked to pose for the motion-picture-camera newsman. They did, most agreeably, and the interview continued, the supercargo readily launching into a discussion of Broadway, the night life, and cabarets. He wasn't going to leave the area of the blockade until he was "good and ready," he said.

Asked how much "stuff" he had sold since his vessel was picketed, he replied, "What do you mean, 'stuff'? Fish?" At this point, a member of the schooner's crew handed him something and he held it up in the light. It was, in fact, a fish and everybody on both vessels laughed.

"Half the country's going blind," a reporter yelled.

"What from," asked the supercargo, "drinking wood alcohol?"

"No," said the reporter, "from eating dead fish."

There was a final hint, however, that the blockade was interfering with the *General Pau*'s activities. Asked if he was getting rid of "any of that fish aboard," the supercargo replied, with a sweep of his arm in the direction of the Coast Guard vessel, "What, with all that fandango around me?"

At the end of the cruise, four of the newspapermen decided to test the efficiency of the Coast Guard picket boats — the inshore line of defense. By paying an exorbitant price, they persuaded the skipper of a rum launch, temporarily idled by the blockade, to run the gauntlet with them aboard.

One of them related,

Our hired boat was capable of about 35 miles an hour, but as it skirted among the fishing nets and clam diggers, the throttle was down to about 20 miles. This was about the fastest speed most of the picket boats are capable of. Their engines are smaller than the rumrunners' and the construction of the vessels is not so recent.

As the rumrunner loafed along, a picket boat spied him. Only a few hundred yards separated the craft. The picket boat blew its siren — a signal all the fishermen in that area understand. It means that the craft so signaled must draw alongside the government boat for examination.

The rumrunner, at the instigation of the reporters, refused to heed the signal. The picket boat then came along over the water at its best speed, but made no appreciable gain on the rumrunner. Then some of the government crew took up their service rifles and began to blaze away. Their range was slightly off but it was close enough to send the reporters to the bottom of the boat, leaving only the pilot exposed to the gunfire.

He didn't stay that way for long. When the first bullet skipped along the surf within his range of vision, he pulled on the throttle. The motor gave instant response and the flat bottom of the launch began to spank the waves. It jumped from one to the other at its fastest speed. The government picket boat was left far behind.

Coast Guard reaction to this experiment was candid. An officer commented,

We have a few sea sleds that can equal the best the rumrunners have, but most of our picket boats are too small. They do the best they can, as we have done the best we could with the money given us for law enforcement, but it isn't enough. That is why we had to establish the blockade. If we don't cut off the flow of liquor at its source offshore, we can't cut it off at all. If the rumrunners get their cargo, the chances are good that they will land it.

Why these fishermen know their inlets so well that they can lead a pursuing vessel right into their fishing nets. They have even been known to throw nets over behind them to get tangled in the screws of the picket boat. It is piracy of a perfected sort.

The blockade was certainly being felt by the rumrunners. On May 20, the *Tern, Maria S. Howes,* and *Captain Merriam,* all loaded with liquor, anchored in the stream at Halifax and reported they had been chased from the Row by the activities of the Coast Guard. A large number of vessels in similar situation were already there and several more were at Lunenburg. The Halifax *Morning Chronicle* commented gloomily,

If the activity continues against the rumrunners, a vast amount of money which is invested in the vessels and their cargoes will be lost.

A number of Nova Scotia schooners have been chartered to Americans and their crews are mostly made up of Nova Scotians. The money involved in provisioning the vessels and paying the crews has all been spent in the province and has been no small factor in the prosperity of the province. The charters which have been paid for such schooners have been very large, some at the rate of $2,000 to $6,000 a month, and the crews have been paid wages commensurate with the risks involved.

The provisioning of a schooner for a trip to the Row has cost several thousand dollars each trip, which has contributed in great measure to the greatly increased trade of both Halifax and Lunenburg, and other South Shore ports down to Yarmouth.

Within a few months, the gloom had also settled upon St. Pierre and Miquelon, which were whisky-logged. Four hundred thousand gallons of liquor, chiefly Scotch, valued at $3.75 million, had been landed there by rumrunners who could not dodge the Coast Guard and put it ashore in the United States.

But the liquor traffic was lucrative, the rumrunner was persistent, the demand was heavy, and the smugglers — who publicly claimed that they could hold out as long as the U.S. government — counted on a divided American Congress to hold down Coast Guard appropriations enough to keep them in business. And the Coast Guard was deeply concerned about the same possibility.

CHAPTER V

I F YOU WEREN'T THERE, it's hard to imagine what it was
like," a former Nova Scotia rumrunner said to me of
his Rum Row experiences, and the same comment might
well have been made by a Coast Guard officer of the offshore blockade. Because the principals on both sides were
men of the sea, they brought to what was essentially a
lonely, often boring, sometimes demanding and dangerous
life that durability which is common to the deep-water
sailor. Their problems differed, of course; they were "enemies," to use the government's own word for the smuggler,
but they both had problems that would have discouraged
lesser breeds.

The Coast Guard's task was made more difficult by factors ranging from the necessity of having to patrol in heavy

weather, faulty equipment, lack of sufficient manpower and vessels, various smugglers' ruses and tactics, and some differences within its own ranks as to how to make the best use of its floating forces. Examples of these persisting frustrations may be found in hundreds of pages of the official records and as laconic as these tend to be, even at this distance in time, the emotions of the men who wrote them may be felt.

Early in February, 1926, the destroyer *Terry* was bound offshore to relieve another Coast Guard vessel, which was picketing a rumrunner 33 miles southwest of Montauk. First she struck a snow squall, which required slowing to six knots and sounding the fog whistle because visibility was virtually zero. At one in the morning, the destroyer arrived at the reported position of the rumrunner and having heard nothing from the picketing vessel and being unable to sight either craft, the skipper, Commander E. A. Coffin, headed the *Terry* into the wind and sea to await clearing conditions. It did not clear. Instead, seven hours later, the wind was blowing 90 miles at hour, accompanied by very rough sea and continuous snow. The destroyer was proceeding at dead slow speed; she was laboring, floundering and virtually helpless in the heavy seas, all of her deck gear was badly iced up, and her pilothouse windows were frozen over. At about that time, she took a monstrous sea over the forecastle head, which bent down the deck 1½ inches and buckled the center stanchion in the cabin compartment. Coffin requested permission to seek shelter and headed inshore.

After several days of examination and repair at New London, the *Terry* prepared to go to sea again, but this time, the deterrent was mechanical. Coffin wrote:

Started heaving in [the anchor]. Found windlass working worse than usual, chain coming in in jerks an inch at a time and sticking on dead center. I wish to note here that this is one of the most worthless of windlass engines I have ever seen. Even in its prime, right after overhaul at the Philadelphia yard, it was too weak to heave in a chain if a light breeze was blowing.

Finally managed after 40 minutes to heave in 24 fathoms of chain, leaving the anchor dragging on the bottom, and then the windlass quit altogether. Drifted broadside down the river, dragging the anchor. . . . At 5:20 p.m., gave up attempt to get under way today and anchored below Fort Trumbull. Engineer continues to repair windlass engine.

The master of the destroyer *Conyngham,* on a December patrol off Cape Ann, reported, "At 4 A.M., the thermometer in the officers' quarters registered 40 degrees, with steam in every radiator." Another destroyer skipper noted that "the vessel's bridge vibrates so badly at 15 or more knots that the filaments in the two 500-watt spotlights were broken during the last patrol." Henry Coyle, aboard the *Jouett,* reported a leaky boiler and complained of its fittings, on which "the bolts were frozen, badly corroded and twisted off." He also objected to removal of an arc light aft on the destroyer, which had been replaced by a 1,000-watt bulb. Coyle wrote, "There is no comparison between the ray of the arc light and that of the present bulb. It is just as necessary to have a light aft of excellent power as forward. When a black circles the ship, it is most essential, especially if it is at all hazy."

The term *black* for rumrunner was commonly used by the Coast Guard.

Coast Guard vessels picketed and trailed the offshore rum fleet, cruising thousands of miles in an effort to prevent transfer of liquor to the inshore boats. The harassment certainly bothered the Rum Row fleet, it interfered with their activities, yet many Coast Guardsmen found the government's effort against the smugglers less than satisfactory.

"We trail and retrail them to the limits of an area, and beyond these limits, only to trail them again, and all at vast expense to the taxpayers," wrote C. H. Dench, commanding officer of the destroyer *Downes.*

We have done much to reduce the maritime rum trade, but we could do far more at measurably less cost if we might seize the rum vessels on sight.

The men in this business are renegades whom no foreign countries are likely to defend or uphold and against whom the United States should adopt some policies with the flavor of severity in them. The Coast Guard, in my opinion, should fight might and main, not for greater personnel and material, but for the right to fight the enemy with a BIG STICK.

The commander of the destroyer force, H. G. Hamlet, was moved to comment on these remarks: "[Such] sentiments are those of an officer with but one task to perform in connection with the vast problems which confront the Coast Guard. Mr. Dench seems to lose sight of the fact that 'greater personnel and material' is a very BIG STICK which we advocate."

After trailing the rumrunner *Dorothy Earl* for about twelve hours and then losing her near Nantucket Lightship because of poor searchlights, the skipper of the destroyer *Shaw,* obviously somewhat discouraged, suggested a new strategy. R. L. Jack concluded, "The woods were full of rummies on the last patrol and none of them that were sighted were able to do any damage, but only a few of them were sighted. That there are a number of rummies that leave port and are never sighted must indicate to us that we must search more assiduously and this we cannot do if we are forced to spend large periods trailing."

Jack suggested mobilizing a number of smaller trailing vessels under the supervision of a "mother ship" cutter, leaving all the destroyers free to "sweep day after day and keep the area clear." He added, "It is pretty evident that the article in the New York Daily News was not entirely without foundation and unless we can utilize our destroyers as 'eyes' instead of 'hands,' we may be compelled to acknowledge defeat." The article in question had pointed out the obvious, that most rumrunners were eventually successful in landing most of their cargoes.

61

Hamlet responded in the best tradition of the service, giving the only possible reply in behalf of an organization that was determined to carry out its assignment: "It is regrettable that an officer of the ability and character of Commander Jack would pay any attention to such fake propaganda as was published recently in the Daily News. . . . It is probable that our weak point is our trailing facilities, but these are being brought up to standard as rapidly as possible. The Force Commander has not the slightest idea that the Coast Guard will ever be compelled to accept defeat on any project."

Yet a year and a half later, James Pine, commanding officer of the destroyer *Wainwright,* expressed concern because "the reluctance of the active blacks to leave the area where found and their apparent willingness to await a period of fog when their escape is comparatively easy . . . diverts the destroyers from their primary function, that is, as scouts, to a minor role, that of trailers," which is precisely what had bothered Jack.

Certain patterns of operation emerged, for both the Coast Guard and the rumrunners. For example, the smugglers' areas for contact with shore vessels became fairly well established; it was typical that within a 15-mile square southeast of Montauk Point, the rumrunners *Lucky Strike, Good Luck,* and *Josephine K.* were sighted repeatedly by patrol craft, which could trail, but not seize "the foreign blacks."

The offshore rum vessels, whose names became as familiar to the Coast Guardsmen as their own, also discovered a certain advantage in numbers. So it was that a destroyer patrol reported: "Fifteen blacks were sighted. They included all of the usuals, the Bear Cat, Mavis Barbara, Frederick H. II, Rio, Silver Arrow, Yamaska, Apohaqui, Accuracy, which was formerly the Mazel Tov; Vanaheim, Doctor, and Malbo. As the number of blacks was more than double the number of destroyers, it was evident that some of these blacks, such as the Vanaheim, were merely decoy vessels to keep the destroyers offshore."

At about this time, mid-1928, at least some of the patrolling destroyers followed a pattern of locating the regular blacks as early in the day as possible, trailing them, and dropping them in the afternoon when they appeared to be bound offshore and in a position to be out of effective operating range for the coming night. Then the destroyers withdrew to establish a blockade approximately sixteen miles outside the line between Montauk and Nomansland, which they maintained until daybreak. Guarding this line undoubtedly interfered with the blacks' contacts and was certainly more effective than having the destroyers on trails more than sixty miles offshore. Further, trailing was a one-on-one proposition and no more blacks could be trailed than there were destroyers, leaving the remaining rumrunners free to operate.

Whether or not trailing with destroyers was effective, it provided one of the most dramatic and dangerous aspects of the deep-water patrol. Surely in all the annals of intricate ship handling what one observer wryly called "the booze ballet" remains unique — and it caused concern at several levels of government, from the bridge of the patrol vessel to the office of Secretary of State.

In attempting to elude their trailers at nightfall, the smugglers adopted a practice of darkening ship abruptly, extinguishing all navigational lights, and changing course, very often directly across the bow of the trailing vessel. An instance of this tactic occurred when the destroyer *McCall* was trailing the British schooner *Mary, Mother of Elizabeth*. The schooner suddenly doused sail and lights and doubled on her course; before the destroyer could turn, the rumrunner was under her stern and had escaped successfully, aided by severe weather. In the maneuver, the smuggler barely missed ramming the *McCall* on the starboard quarter and was then nearly hit by the overhang of the destroyer's starboard bow.

The incident prompted Seymour Lowman, Assistant

Secretary of the Treasury, to protest to the Secretary of State: "The practice of foreign vessels engaged in the smuggling trade of running at night at high speed without the required running lights is not only a violation of the international rules of the road, but may eventually lead to one of them being rammed and badly damaged or sunk. I have to suggest that you consider whether these vessels should be reported to the nations whose flags the vessels fly."

Mostly, serious collisions were avoided in these jousts, largely because of the excellent seamanship of the Coast Guardsmen. The destroyer *Jouett* was headed south from Vineyard Sound Light Vessel and at ten in the morning of Monday, February 16, 1931, sighted a black identified as the British oil screw *Yamaska;* her hailing port had been painted out. *Jouett* began picketing her, in part because, as Coyle, the destroyer's skipper, said, "She had eluded [us] twice under circumstances that did not satisfy me as to her superiority and ability."

At about six-thirty P.M., when it was dark, *Yamaska* got under way with lights on and attempted to escape by cutting under the destroyer's stern and running in circles. A half-hour later, these maneuvers having been unsuccessful, the rumrunner put out all lights. She then turned and ran in various directions, periodically circling in the direction of *Jouett*'s quarter, heading for the destroyer's stern; the Coast Guard vessel, several times shifting her rudder from hard right to hard left to respond to or anticipate the black's moves, continued to hold *Yamaska* in her high-intensity arc light.

Coyle said,

At 1965, the black settled down for four minutes and gave us a chance to change the carbons in the arc light. At 2020, the black turned on her lights. At 2030, she turned them out again and started circling and running on various courses to escape. At 2120, the black yielded, after a three-hour continuous attempt to escape, put on her lights but showed no stern light. She steadied on course 100 mag., speed ten knots. At 2350, the black stopped and drifted. At 2365, the black got under way, put on her lights and attempted to escape.

Tuesday, 17 February: at 0010, the black steadied on course 106 mag., at 12 knots. 0150, black stopped. They do this to gain a distinct advantage. Unless almost constant watch is kept with glasses, the wash will not be seen to have stopped, a sure indication that they have slowed and the black will be overrun before the vessel can be stopped.

At 0205, black under way. 0306, sighted Nantucket Light vessel. 0335, black headed for the light vessel. 0400, black commenced to maneuver to escape, using smoke screen. 0417, black faded out of sight. Ran down the bearing with 125 mag. and picked her up, dead ahead. 0440, black circled Nantucket Light vessel. Fired two blank one-pounder shots as a registration of protest and disapproval by the United States because the black was endangering through risk of collision, in trying to escape, light vessel personnel and the light vessel itself, placed there by our government for the use of our vessels, and those of other nations that follow the sea, as a navigational beacon.

This warning had the desired effect; she did not circle it again, but drew off and continued efforts to escape in the vicinity. Steamer traffic was going by. 0500, black stopped and drifted. 0510, black under way, commencing maneuvers to escape again. 0545, put out our searchlight as black was visible in our Zeiss binoculars. 0558, black realized escape was hopeless for the night, due to approaching daylight; stopped and put on her lights. 1000, black stopped and drifted.

At 1806, black under way attempting to escape, attempting to cut circles under our stern. 1830, black started smoke screen and turned out all lights. 1840, black started to back down at full speed. We backed, too. She finally went ahead full speed, cutting towards our stern. We went ahead full speed with rudder turning the ship away from her. We were turning well before she realized what was happening. We had to shift our light to the other quarter. This broke her advantage completely.

At about 2100, it commenced to get thick and started to snow. Lost black as she circled to escape, range of searchlight being cut by elements. We ran down the bearing and picked her up again, headed to the right on our starboard bow. Headed over toward her, but not directly for her. It was supposed she was going ahead full; instead, she was backing full speed astern.

When the light finally showed this, it looked as if we were going to be rammed by her. It is believed that she deliberately tried to back into us at right angles. It was a question of whether to ram her to save ourselves or at least come hard right to present the bow as sharply as we could and let fate take its course, or take the chance of getting rammed at right angles amidships. I thought perhaps they would go ahead and prevent a collision.

It was quickly decided that by going ahead full speed with rudder amidships, we might get by. This was done and as soon as the bow was by the black's stern, full right was given. She was still a few yards away and backing full speed. We blew the danger signal on our whistle and displayed our searchlight along our starboard side to show the exact situation. He still backed at full speed. She missed our stern by about ten feet. It was rapidly falling off in the right direction. I feel convinced that he felt he might put us out of commission even though he wrecked his own stern doing it. A little closer and our propeller guard would have torn his stern off, without injury to the Jouett. At 2130, black stopped and drifted.

2367, strong breeze had shifted to the east. It was quite thick weather and a deluge of rain. Eventually, on Wednesday, 18 February, the Jouett stopped trailing the Yamaska, feeling that we had accomplished our mission because easterly gales were predicted and we didn't think the black could make a contact anyway. I wanted no misunderstanding in the minds of those on board the Yamaska of the fact that we were dropping them and not otherwise. I think they have a more wholesome respect for the ability of the destroyers and are less impressed with their own merits on the sea. I trust they will remember the 13 on our bow for some time to come. . . .

This whole series of events does not contribute to the morale of those on board [the black]. It is a fair sample of what can be done to make these smugglers on our coast realize that the game is not an easy one. I cannot but feel that we are accomplishing more by getting after one boat if we have to trail her than by watching contact areas. This system gets at the personnel; it impresses them with the element of danger of being lost at sea. The skipper may not mind, but the crew do not like to have a destroyer go roaring by with blowers wide open at full speed so close aboard. The more experienced men we can drive out, the less effective becomes their operation by new men.

Obviously, the skipper of the *Jouett* disagreed with those who thought trailing rumrunners with destroyers was a misuse of personnel and equipment. Nor is it provable that this kind of harassment actually frightened any great number of "experienced men" out of the smuggling business. Undoubtedly, they did not like it and it angered them because it cost them time, which was money. But as the mate of the *Diamantina* pointed out, the crews of these vessels had no other opportunity for making a good dollar so easily. Furthermore, the initiative for playing these dangerous games afloat rested with them; they could resort to other tactics any time they chose. And perhaps most important, "the element of danger of being lost at sea" — while obviously present — was minimized by the Coast Guard's own exceptional competence.

Collisions between government craft and rum vessels in these midnight maneuverings were rare and, as far as I am aware, without exception, the fault of the rumrunner. And even when they occurred, the Coast Guard immediately shifted from the role of law enforcer to rescuer and assisted the vessel it had been trailing. After four hours of standard escape tactics — dousing lights, changing courses, backing down abruptly and attempting to use other vessels as shields — the black *Shubenacadia* tried to cross the bow of the destroyer *Davis*. Both craft were making 10 knots.

When it became obvious that the *Shubenacadia* could not make it, both craft attempted to back down at full speed, but the rumrunner struck bow-on against the starboard side of the *Davis,* abreast No. 1 waist gun. The black's bow was badly smashed; her master and nine men abandoned ship in three dories and went aboard the Coast Guard cutter *Marion,* and two hours later, she began to settle on even keel, and sank.

On occasion, a rumrunner's maneuverings to escape his trailer were not only unsuccessful but incomprehensibly unimaginative. The cutter *Sebago* was picketing the smuggler *Bear Cat*, which tried various devices to get away, and finally took a position off the Coast Guard vessel's port quarter. In this relative position, with the *Bear Cat* going ahead at full speed with rudder hard left and *Sebago* at 12 knots, with rudder hard left, the two craft continued to turn for nearly two hours, making twenty-two complete turns without altering rudder or speed.

H. R. Searles, commanding officer of the *Sebago*, said, "The only excuse apparent for such utterly dumb maneuvering might be that Bear Cat wished to be able to show in her log that she had tried to escape."

The rumrunners did other things in an effort to get rid of their Coast Guard harassers, including trying to disable pursuing government vessels, sending in plain language radio messages intended to deceive, transmitting phony distress signals to lure government craft away from certain areas, masquerading as fishermen, and using planes, both for spotting patrol craft and picking up booze.

At about eleven at night, the patrol boat *Cahoone*, operating off Long Island, sighted a Canadian rum vessel lying dark, with two contact boats nearby, waiting to load. The *Cahoone* waited for one of the speedboats to run alongside the mother vessel, tie up, and begin taking aboard liquor. Then the Coast Guard vessel ran up at full speed, being sighted at about five hundred yards off; the speedboat cast off and got under way. *Cahoone* threw her searchlight on the fleeing craft, blew her whistle, and fired a machine-gun burst across the bow of the contact boat without stopping her or causing her to show lights. The patrol boat then fired into her with a machine gun and lobbed three three-inch 23-caliber shots at her, but was unable to stop her and she disappeared in the dark.

Meanwhile, the mother vessel showed lights and ran off to the eastward; *Cahoone* pursued, but the Canadian had more speed and also was lost sight of. The patrol boat stayed in the area, sensing that this was the contact point and that both rum vessels very likely would return to it. During the next day, the Canadian vessel showed up again and proved to be the three-masted schooner *John Manning* of Parrsboro; *Cahoone* picketed her all through the second day and into that evening.

The Coast Guard skipper said, "At about 10:50 p.m., *Shemalian,* a black, made contact with *John Manning* and placed aboard the schooner what appeared to be fresh provisions from shore and from the conversation, there also appeared to be mail. Someone on *Shemalian* called to *John Manning* and asked what boat we were. The reply was '*Cahoone.*' Someone on *Shemalian* said, 'She is the one who fired on us last night.' "

Just before noon on the third day, the *Manning* got under way; it became immediately evident that *Cahoone*'s continued picketing was getting under the skin of the rum vessel's master. As the patrol boat proceeded to follow, a steel cable several hundred yards in length was trailed astern of *Manning,* obviously a deliberate attempt to foul the propellers of the patrol boat.

Cahoone's skipper said, "Handling the machine gun myself, I attempted to cut the steel cable with gun fire. All fire of the machine gun was well clear of Manning and no wild flourishes or bursts were used. The cable was then drawn on board Manning, a tattered British ensign was shown at the gaff and no more difficulty was experienced."

The rumrunners' use of the fake distress signal was effective because the Coast Guard's principal mission remained the providing of assistance to mariners in trouble. Even though the signals raised doubts as to their authenticity, they could not be ignored.

At 1:25 on the morning of March 28, 1931, H. R. Searles, commanding officer of the cutter *Sebago,* received from the shore station at Rockaway a report of an SOS —

a vessel in distress about thirty miles southeast of Barnegat Light Vessel. Various contradictory positions were given in subsequent messages and the crew was reported to have abandoned ship. *Sebago* stood for the general area at full speed.

Meanwhile, the destroyer *Hunt* had intercepted the message to *Sebago* and even though her master concluded it was "garbled and open to doubt," he reacted swiftly to the information that "crew and passengers of vessel in distress were taking to boats."

The *Hunt,* laid up for ten years and recently overhauled extensively, did herself proud in steaming to the search area. At 1:32 A.M., she had worked up to 25 knots and preparations were made to cut in the reserve fireroom for a full-speed run to the search area, because the report of people in open boats in darkness in seas that were already rough contained the ingredients of emergency. At 3:15 A.M., Hunt had warmed up to 32 knots and by 6:20 A.M., to 36.4 knots; she covered one hundred miles in 3.5 hours, her lookouts doubled, heaving spray over her bows and rolling heavily.

Simultaneously, a sizable fleet of Coast Guard destroyers, cutters, and patrol boats was converging on the scene, now pinpointed at forty miles south-southeast of the light vessel. The destroyers arrived shortly after daylight and, because of poor visibility, could have accomplished nothing had they gotten there sooner. *Sebago, Hunt,* the destroyer *Upshur,* the patrol boats *Pulaski* and *Cuyahoga,* several patrol craft from Base 9, and Coast Guard district boats conducted a wide search for boats or wreckage. A Base 9 aircraft flew over the area for two hours.

At 9 in the morning of the twenty-ninth, the *Hunt* reported "a queer assortment of floating debris, not enough to have been a cargo from a vessel of any size" about ten miles off Atlantic City. The flotsam included about one hundred new oil lanterns, with red glass and green base and marked "I.A. Company," many paper drinking cups and brooms, and one large barrel labeled "ACL Crystals, Lot 137." Several fishermen in the vicinity, hailed by the *Hunt,* said they had not heard anything about a wreck. The search was finally called off at seven that night, releasing the various Coast Guard units to their regular patrol duty.

Searles concluded,

I am now of the opinion that the SOS call of last night was a fake. . . . The Sebago did not hear the SOS, nor did any radio station except Manasquam. The steamer Pan American heard the call but from a direction whose radio bearings placed the distressed vessel near Hoboken. . . . And though every effort was made, at no time was any radio call letter given to identify the vessel in distress.

What this means is that some of these patrol vessels were tied up for as long as twelve hours because they arrived at the scene at 0700. . . .

Furthermore, if you count running time, the *Hunt* at least was diverted from her patrol responsibilities for an additional five and a half hours. From the rumrunners' point of view, the diversionary tactic must have been deemed eminently successful.

It was common practice for "inshore" rum boats to attempt to masquerade as fishermen, and often the transparency of this device affronted common sense, moving Coast Guard officers to try to find some reason to take the boats into custody. Similarly, stated destinations of the offshore vessels and their actual locations were so much at variance as to provide official frustration.

Southeast of Ambrose Lightship, cruising in an early-afternoon haze, the destroyer *Ericsson* observed a white wake moving at high speed to the westward; because of the poor visibility, the craft making it could not be seen. After a spurt of fifteen minutes at twenty-two knots, the destroyer began to close in on what proved to be the American auxiliary sloop *Goose*. Observing that they were being overhauled, the *Goose* slowed down, dumped over a trawl and began towing it, as if she were fishing. The *Ericsson* came up to her and sent a boarding party to the *Goose*. Her fishing gear was brand new and unused. She was spick-and-span, unmarred by dirt or wear, except on her port side, which was discolored by paint not her own. The Coast Guard watched for this particular condition very carefully; it usually indicated lying alongside another vessel at sea, as the inshore rumrunners had to do when loading.

There were a half-dozen scallops on the *Goose*'s deck, the only fish aboard, and her hold was empty. The master of the *Ericsson* concluded that she was in the vicinity of a contact point, awaiting darkness so that she could take aboard a load of liquor from an offshore vessel. Accordingly, the sloop was "gone over thoroughly in order to find some reason for taking her into port to prevent contact." Finally, it was discovered that she had six men on board whereas her license called for only four, and "there being no means of identification of the extra men, it was considered advisable to take [her] into port to determine whether the extra men were aliens being smuggled into the country."

Having turned the *Goose* over to a patrol boat, the *Ericsson* searched the area, using the sloop's position as a center, to look for the craft that was scheduled to load her. After a high-speed chase to the eastward, the destroyer overhauled and began to trail the British oil screw *Good Luck* of Shelburne, Nova Scotia. During the night, word was received from ashore that the Coast Guard believed the *Good Luck* was sailing under false papers; *Ericsson* was directed to investigate.

The skipper of the destroyer advised the *Good Luck*'s master that he was sending a boarding party to examine his papers. The latter replied that the American Coast Guard would do nothing of the sort, whereupon the deeply-laden black got under way at her best speed, on a course east.

Aboard the *Ericsson,* the gunners fired two warning

shots and three solid shots across *Good Luck*'s bow, the third one falling close on her stem. A fourth one had just been ordered to be fired into her hawsepipe when it was noticed that she was slowing down. The destroyer ceased firing.

[I] lowered a boat and sent over a boarding party to examine the papers [the Ericsson's master said] but they were found to be in proper order, except that the vessel had cleared . . . from Yarmouth, Nova Scotia, for Saint John's, Newfoundland, in ballast. The clearance was presented as being her last clearance.

Instead of being in ballast, it was evident that she was well loaded, only about five inches of the red boot topping of her waterline being visible. She was well out of the course from Yarmouth to Saint John's, and was not proceeding on that course, but was lying to in the vicinity of New York.

. . . I sent a message to Commander, Destroyer Force, recommending bringing the Good Luck into our waters pending complaint to Ottawa, because of the hovering of this vessel so contrary to her clearance, but I was advised there was no cause for this procedure.

In Coast Guard intelligence files of this period, there is a memorandum on lined yellow paper, written in longhand, and signed by initials that look like "N. B. H." It concludes, "When Coast Guard *boats* obtain 100 percent perfection and control, the smugglers will use *planes* exclusively. Improvement of surface equipment brings air smuggling nearer." The Coast Guard vessels never did "obtain 100 percent perfection and control," but there was nevertheless some limited use of planes by rumrunners. At least one of these got in trouble and the smugglers had, of course, to turn to the Coast Guard for help.

At nine in the morning of October 5, 1932, Lieutenant Commander L. V. Kielhorn, commanding officer of the destroyer *Semmes,* received instructions to look for a disabled seaplane seventeen miles south of Shinnecock Lighthouse. Three hours later, two small objects were sighted on the water, close together. They proved to be a disabled Sikorsky amphibian and the British vessel *Bear Cat,* the latter making off and disappearing to the southward as soon as the *Semmes* was sighted.

The weather was nasty — lashing rain squalls, wind between 20 and 30 knots, and a rather rough sea. It was decided to remove the crew of the aircraft immediately and to pass a towline to the plane if possible. The *Semmes* was maneuvered into a favorable position, lowered a boat, and shot a line to the plane. Because the *Bear Cat* was a known black and the position of the plane was at a known contact point, the Coast Guard boarding party searched the aircraft while removing its three-man crew. There was no liquor aboard, but papers in the possession of one of the three, who first gave an alias and then recanted, indicated that the plane "was to be used in violation of the smuggling laws."

It was discovered that the plane had been in the water more than twelve hours; it had been seriously damaged by the seas, some struts being badly bent and one pontoon having filled with water. Even while its crew was being removed to the *Semmes,* the damaged pontoon dropped off. Nevertheless, a towline was made fast from ship to aircraft and the destroyer got under way slowly, at no more than 3 knots.

Crippled as it was, the plane could not straighten out with the towline; the hawser caught over one of the wings and the aircraft slowly turned turtle, capsizing and sinking within fifteen minutes — the ship meanwhile having been stopped altogether, when it was realized that towing was impossible.

Putting the pieces together, Kielhorn decided that the plane had left Atlantic City the afternoon before, established radio contact with the *Bear Cat,* landed on the water at the rendezvous, and tried to take a load of liquor, but was prevented by the deteriorating weather. When the aircraft attempted to take off, it was already too late; she struck a heavy sea, which badly bent a strut and loosened the stays. When the sea filled the forward cockpit and one of the pontoons began to fill, it became impossible for her to taxi or even to drift safely. *Bear Cat* notified the rumrunner shore station, which forwarded the call for help, anonymously, to the Coast Guard.

Slightly less than a month later, between 7:15 and 9:30 at night, Coast Guard vessels in the Montauk Point area observed several flares drop from an aircraft and heard the plane's engines, which were described as "hitting perfectly," thus eliminating the possibility that it was in difficulty. The flares were dropped variously in the area of Gardiner's Island, Bartlett's Reef Light Vessel, Watch Hill, and Fisher's Island.

A report from the area to the Coast Guard commandant notes,

It is well known that one ring of rumrunners is using planes to transport liquor, scout out our forces at sea, direct speedboats to offshore contact boats, scout out our patrol boats at shore bases in the afternoon, to observe the number of boats missing.

The plane recently contacted by the destroyer Semmes . . . was a rummy plane; a notorious rumrunner was found on board. This is the Java crowd, working the Bear Cat and others of that group. These flares serve two purposes; at least they illuminate our night patrols in the area they are most interested in, for observation by the plane. They also illuminate and silhouette the whole area for the observers on the incoming speedboats. The flares are very bright and burn about two minutes.

Because so much time has passed and because it never was *my* job to bring the offshore rumrunner to book or at least make his life miserable, I have a tendency to take notice that inevitably, some of them were caught inside the twelve-mile limit and that when they were, some of the masters were candid and friendly and some even more than that, poignant in their downfall. Nor is this surprising; these down-East sailors had a heritage of hardship and hard work, of simple lives and sacrifice, of persistent separation from family, because this is the way of the seagoing. They were largely men more silent than talkative, fiercely industrious, exceptionally unafraid, generally unlettered, unassuming, more often than not. They became smugglers not because they were essentially devious or because they possessed any other qualifications for lawbreaking but because they were in the right place at the right time, possessed of the right skills, and they were short of cash. So they took the risks and when they were caught — after banging about offshore in a cat-and-mouse game that forced them into what was essentially a trying, vexatious, and even sad life — they were not very devious, being poor liars, and sometimes there is close to a hint of tears in the record.

Late on a July afternoon, R. E. Hunter, skipper of the destroyer *Henley*, sighted a suspicious-looking vessel west of Georges Bank, in low visibility. She was a subchaser type; a swing around her stern identified her as the rum-runner *Mareuilendole*, out of Weymouth, Nova Scotia; she immediately began to head offshore rapidly.

There was good reason for this. Hunter secured radio bearings from North Truro and Surfside, and they put his position inside the ten-mile limit from Pamet River Coast Guard Station, which checked with his soundings. Being sure of the *Mareuilendole*'s position when he first sighted her, Hunter chased her, came close aboard, and ordered her to heave to. It was found that she had a cargo of liquor and a fraudulent manifest; Hunter himself boarded her to interview her master, Watson Wagner.

Wagner talked very freely. He made no mention of being bound for a particular port, seeming to take it for granted that the master of the destroyer knew why he was off the American coast. He said he had taken soundings that placed him outside the twelve-mile limit and he admitted that he knew he was subject to seizure if inside that limit. His manifest called for "general cargo," but it was all liquor and there was no question but that a large amount of it had been disposed of. His chart also showed activities off Boston, revealed by pencil marks, erasures, or pinpricks indicating where recent positions had been plotted.

He discussed without hesitation the method of delivering his cargo, saying that they did not sell for cash over the side unless fifty miles or more off the coast, in accordance with orders from his owners, and that he delivered his cargo only upon orders. Wagner mentioned various rum vessels he had been on and said that he personally had had the *I'm Alone* built but that, after several years of running, had sold it.

The two-masted schooner *I'm Alone*, built at Lunenberg in 1924, operated for four years between Gloucester and the Virginia Capes as a rumrunner and reportedly earned more than $3 million for her owners. The year before Wagner was picked up in the *Mareuilendole*, *I'm Alone* was sold and under the new owners operated in the Gulf of Mexico, where she was eventually sunk by Coast Guard gunfire when she refused to heave to — an incident that had serious repercussions in British, Canadian, and Washington diplomatic circles.

Wagner also said he knew that the penalty for a rum carrier having a radio transmitter aboard was a fine of $7,000 and a sentence of five years in prison for the operator. He said that he did not have a transmitter aboard, which was an artless falsehood; the *Henley*'s chief radioman found it and discovered that it had recently been tampered with, presumably to support a claim that it was inoperable.

Additional evidence further implicated *Mareuilendole*. Two days preceding her seizure, there had been a liquor landing at Rye Harbor, New Hampshire, which was frustrated by Coast Guardsmen who seized 139 sacks of liquor and a dory. The seized liquor was "exactly similar" to that found aboard *Mareuilendole*. Further, *Mareuilendole* was carrying two brand-new dories when the *Henley* caught her. These boats were marked "Zwicker-Lunenberg" and an attempt had been made to efface this mark by scratching it with a sharp instrument. The dory that was found on the shore at Rye Harbor with the liquor was exactly the same in appearance, also brand-new, and bore the same marks of effacement.

To cap it, a memorandum found in the possession of Gerald Lewis, supercargo on the *Mareuilendole,* indicated that 1,200 "packages" of liquor had been placed aboard the vessel at St. Pierre and Miquelon. Examination of the cargo holds indicated that in the main hatchway, cargo had been removed and that "approximately 475 cases of liquor had been unladen and . . . apparently smuggled ashore in the vicinity of Rye Harbor. . . ."

The Halifax *Evening Mail* saw fit to acknowledge what had happened to the friendly Captain Wagner and his vessel, a note in slightly minor key in an otherwise rather ebullient account of what was going on on Rum Row. The *Mail* observed,

Conservative estimates made on the waterfront this morning [July 16, 1929] placed the amount of liquor landed on the American coast during the past few weeks by four rum craft here for supplies in the vicinity of 20,000 cases. Daily, as the moon grows fuller, the fleet is increasing. The moon will be full on July 22 and when it wanes, heralding the dark nights, these boats will sail for St. Pierre to load fresh cargoes.

One of the fleet which makes monthly visits here will not return on schedule, for, pending a decision of the Federal Court at Boston, she is being held there. This motor vessel, the Mareuilendole, skippered by Captain Watson Wagner of Lunenburg, was seized last week with a cargo of 14,400 bottles of liquor and was alleged to have been taken inside the ten-mile limit.

While visiting American tourists complain of the drought in the United States on account of the Jones law, the rum-running fraternity deny this, stating it is no hindrance to them. Empty holds on their arrival here bear out this testimony.

Yet the Rum Row stint for the down-East sailor was simultaneously boring and risky, and if he lost the game, he lost a lot; mostly, under such circumstances, only his intimates knew how he felt, but there is at least one exception. Captain William J. Breen was master/owner of the schooner *Carrie L. Hirtle* when she was boarded off the Maine coast by crew members of the patrol boat *Antietam*.

When asked for the ship's papers, Breen produced a register and a manifest certified by the customs at St. Pierre, which showed that when certified, the vessel was about to depart in ballast. Her destination was shown to be Meteghan, Nova Scotia. The manifest had been altered to show that the schooner had a hundred gallons of liquor on board; this entry was made in ink that differed from all other writing on the document.

Breen confessed that he had altered the paper himself. Search of the vessel revealed that instead of being in ballast, she actually had on board 518 cases of alcohol, six gallons to a case; 187 sacks of assorted liquors, containing 12 bottles each, and two kegs of rum.

While Breen was showing to the Coast Guardsmen a chart on which he had fixed what he said was the *Hirtle*'s position — well offshore — a letter dropped out of the folded chart. He picked it up, and started up the cabin ladder to the deck, tearing up the letter quickly. As soon as he reached the rail, he threw the pieces overboard. They were recovered immediately by the Coast Guard prize crew.

Apart from the fact that the letter, once pieced together, contained certain implications of guilt — and that is what the government was after — there is a poignancy about it, even now, with more than a half-century intervening. It says something about what the rumrunner's life was like, what the men were like, for the master of the *Hirtle* was undoubtedly not that different from many another in the Rum Row trade:

My dear pal, just a line, old sweetheart. Thought you might be getting a little uneasy, but I have had a little hard luck. The cutter pulled me in from off Machias, Seal Island. I was fifteen miles off at the time but he said I was nine. I laid their [sic] becalmed and couldn't get off. How I did wish I had the Engine in while I was praying for wind but none came.

Instead, when the fog glened up along comes a bran [sic] new Patrol Boat what you see their picture in the Motor Boat magazine just out on his first trip, luck for him I supposed, but Hell for me. He wouldn't listen to no reasons as their Skipper was a Square Head and he thought he owned the world with his five or six armed men with him.

However he says your only nine miles off and I'm going to tow you in. I told him we was fifteen but he wouldn't listen, so here he brought me. They don't know just yet if they will proceed to Boston or leave me here. I hope Boston because I think I can get a better deal in a Boston court than you can in the state of Maine.

If that dam Nelson had of been on his Job, if he had of had boats enough to cleaned me up, there would have been nothing to it and I would now have been in Meteghan. Nelson didn't get his half off.

One thing I know, vessel is seized and the balance of the cargo is gone. I've only taken in $2,000 of my own as yet. I stand to lose $5,000 more. I guess al [sic] they can do is to take the Vessel but thats bad with a Capital B. Bad enough at that. I cant write much at present as I dont know who I can trust to mail this letter.

Only just dont worry no matter what turns up. Ile be in a better position tomorrow to know what they are going to do but for a sure Bet I know Vessel and Cargo will be held and perhaps forfeited. However, don't worry Old Pal, as I aint worrying much. I Think I have a pretty good case as regards getting off, and have a clearance from Meteghan and a bill of health and as they saw no boats near me or don't know I unloaded any, I don't think they got any cause to hold me.

Now then Ile close and don't you worry one Bit and Keep well and perhaps Ile go home and stay with you and pick berries all summer. I'm getting so now I hate to stay away from you overnight. Well goodbye for now Dear Pal. Ile write more particulars as soon as I get the information.

CHAPTER VI

ON OCCASION, Coast Guard and customs officials had to deal directly with deep-water rum ships when those vessels bypassed the usual smuggling method of transferring their cargo to inshore boats at sea and chose instead to come into principal U.S. ports themselves. A combination of bribery, subterfuge, and luck occasionally made this worth trying — it was timesaving — but when law and big-ship smuggler met, the results made headlines.

The mate of the *Diamantina* had had firsthand experience in this kind of traffic. "I was on the towboat Metec from Montreal," he said,

and we went into New York and tied up to a dock. You could heave a rock to the Brooklyn Bridge. The wharf was all full of carts and they had a gang there to unload us. All that front street at the head of the wharf was blocked off; cops were keeping everybody off the wharf. We unloaded several hundred cases.

There was a fellow I knew well who had a Canadian-registered steamer. He sailed from Pierre Miquelon with two clearances, one for Nassau, loaded, and one for Nassau, light. When he went into New York with a load, he was purposely short of coal so he could say that was why he had to come in.

He took the load of liquor in on a Saturday night; daylight come [sic] on and he never got out, because they were slow unloading him. The law people come on board; they said, "You are a dam' smart man, coming in short of coal, but we've got you, because you passed quarantine without stopping."

So they lifted his ship's papers and ordered him to report for a hearing at nine on Monday morning. They put two cops in a little house at the head of the dock. This fellow paid them off and they let him go. . . . So then he got coal in Brooklyn and he was gone by Sunday night for Halifax. He sailed without his papers. When he got offshore, a four-stacker came by and he just hoisted his union jack and kept on going.

Others fared differently, including *Taboga,* a nineteenth-century steamer with two masts and a tall, pencil-thin stack. *Taboga* had once seen service as a U.S. Navy supply ship with the fleet at Manila in the Spanish-American War. A waterfront reporter for the New Bedford *Morning Mercury* described her emergence from the past to begin what proved to be a colorful rum-fleet career:

"One day in 1922, a strange steamship came into New Bedford Harbor and tied up at a dock in Fairhaven. Those aboard disclaimed any knowledge of the purpose of the visit or where the vessel was bound. The Taboga remained at the wharf for months, during which time more or less fitting out was done."

At dusk on February 3, 1923, the steamer put to sea. At the last minute before sailing, Captain Mark L. Gilbert came aboard and took the place of the man who had ostensibly been in command. Gilbert was known in the area; he had attempted unsuccessfully to operate a dry dock and shipbuilding company in Fairhaven during World War I. With the order, "Let everything go!" Gilbert assumed authority; *Taboga*'s lines were cast off and she was under way.

An eyewitness commented, "The ship's company included Chinese and a crew so rough it might have been believed the devil himself would not care to go to sea with them." The papers taken out at the Custom House showed a provisional Panama registry, issued by the consul general of Panama in New York, and the steamer flew the Panama flag. She had aboard "a wireless operator," wrote the *Mercury* reporter; "the ship was very dirty and rusty and as she went down the harbor, she carried a heavy list."

Slightly more than a year later, they were describing *Taboga* as the "will-o'-the-wisp" rumrunner; she had just landed part of her cargo at Gloucester and some of it had been seized by police on an island in the Annisquam River, but the steamer was elusive. She was reported variously off Boston and in the vicinity of Martha's Vineyard; the Coast Guard intensified its efforts to find her and broadcast a message to all ships and shore stations to "look for the vessel and report her at once."

About sixty days later, in June, 1924, *Taboga* actually was located and detained. Described as "the most elusive rumrunner along the New England coast," she was picked up fifteen miles from the whistling buoy off Nomansland for having changed to Panamanian registry without authority. There was a small amount of liquor aboard, and the Coast Guard cutter *Acushnet* towed her into Boston Harbor. Jubilant Prohibition officials announced that they had removed one of their "chief irritants from Rum Row." They had not removed it for long.

By February of 1925, *Taboga,* still skippered by Gilbert, had been renamed *Homestead,* flew the flag of Costa Rica, and was back in the liquor business. Gilbert had been declared a fugitive from justice by federal officials in connection with a liquor conspiracy indictment brought against him. Secret instructions were sent to the Coast Guard destroyer force commander at New London to seize the *Homestead* if she was found on the high seas. The unusual precautions of secrecy were taken because of apprehension over international complications; there were reports that Gilbert claimed British citizenry.

Homestead was located at anchor, 24 miles south of Montauk Point, by the destroyer *Jouett,* on the afternoon of February 4, 1925. The *Jouett* requested the assistance of the cutter *Redwing* to assist in towing the steamer to New York. Thus began a dramatic series of events handled with extraordinary tact and delicacy — and effectiveness — by Commander W. H. Munter, force commander, who was aboard the *Redwing.*

Gilbert's steamer, which proved to have aboard about 2,000 cases of liquor — all that was left unsold of her 40,000- to 50,000-case capacity — was still lying at anchor when *Redwing* arrived at 2:45 P.M., February 5, having proceeded to the scene at full speed. The cutter lowered her port surfboat, with Ensign (T) J. J. Buskin in charge, intending to put a prize crew aboard the *Homestead.* Gilbert, well aware of what was intended, frustrated the action by getting his vessel under way before the boat could get alongside; he executed this maneuver so rapidly that he was still dragging his anchor when he gave the "all ahead" signal from the bridge.

Redwing retrieved its boat, hoisted it in the davits, started in pursuit, and easily overtook the rumrunner. The cutter hailed Gilbert, informing him that all Coast Guard vessels had orders to board his steamer, wherever found, and to take her into New York. He was ordered to stop his ship to permit a Coast Guard officer to board. *Homestead* kept on her way; Gilbert yelled back that he refused to allow anyone to board him and that he would resist any attempt made to do so.

The cutter's skipper then informed him — twice — that if he did not stop, he would be fired on. Gilbert also was ordered to head about and set his course for New York. The master of the *Homestead* replied that he was a British subject, that he was on the high seas, and flying the flag of a nation friendly to the United States, and that he did not have to submit to being boarded by any vessel of the United States. He added that he had no intention of going into New York, that he was on his way to Havana, and, with a certain amount of profanity, he declared, "I am going there or sink!"

At 3:08 P.M., *Redwing* fired three warning shots from a one-pounder, with sufficient intervals between to make certain *Homestead* had not stopped her engines in response. She had not; the rum vessel was on a southeasterly course and continued steaming out to sea. The cutter's command again spoke to Gilbert and warned that he could blame only himself for any damage that might be done or loss of life that might result from gunfire if he continued to refuse to obey orders.

Six minutes later, the cutter fired a warning shot from a three-inch gun, hoping that the larger caliber might make more impression on the *Homestead*'s captain. *Homestead* continued on her course. *Redwing* ranged up fairly close alongside for more accurate shooting and let go another three-inch shell close on the bow of the rumrunner. Gilbert responded with "a lot of profanity," but otherwise the situation did not change.

The cruise report of the *Redwing* notes that "the Costa Rican colors were now hoisted at the flagstaff aft. Passed to the other side of the ship by the stern and close to, and attempted to disable his rudder by firing a second shot into his stern. The captain of the Homestead lowered one of his lifeboats to the rail and placed what appeared to be a sick or wounded man on a mattress into the boat. Also, shortly after this, the Costa Rican colors were half-masted.

"Thinking it possible that someone had been injured on board the Homestead as a result of this gunfire, a radio was sent to Coast Guard Headquarters, Washington, stating that the captain of the Homestead resisted being boarded after a show of force by the Redwing. A reply was received in answer to this message which stated in substance to bring Homestead to New York City regardless of protests or resistance."

At 7:31 P.M., shortly after receiving this response from headquarters, *Redwing* again came within easy speaking distance of the rumrunner and her skipper hailed Gilbert, telling him he would be forced to stop his ship unless Gilbert did so voluntarily or set a course for New York. The latter made no response; *Homestead* continued heading to sea and on the cutter, orders were given to shoot to hit the *Homestead*.

It was dark now, and with searchlights playing on Gilbert's steamer, *Redwing* fired nine shots from about 300 yards, one of which struck the port side of the pilothouse, exploded, and wrecked the interior, including the steering compass and wheel. *Homestead*'s engines were stopped. Gilbert yelled through a megaphone that his steering gear was disabled. He still refused to be boarded or take a towline. He said he would resist any boarding and considered the Coast Guardsmen "pirates on the high seas."

Crew members on the rum steamer could be seen preparing to lower boats, and someone aboard the *Homestead* signaled with a flashlight that she was slowly sinking. Shortly after this, boats were lowered with men in them; the port lifeboat pulled off the port quarter about fifty yards and lay to, later returning to the *Homestead*. The starboard boat did not leave the ship's side.

During the night, the *Redwing* stood by, with her searchlights on the steamer; everything aboard the *Homestead* appeared to be quiet and orderly and there was no sign that she was sinking. Several times, the cutter's skipper demanded that Gilbert accept a towline and make it fast; the latter continued to refuse. At nine on the morning of the sixth, *Redwing* sent an armed boat's crew to board the rumrunner so that they could take a towline, but the *Homestead*'s master refused to put over a line or sea ladder so that they could get aboard. A moderate swell made it impractical — even unsafe — for the cutter to go alongside the rum steamer and board her in that manner, although it was now obvious that was what would have to be done eventually.

The cutter *Seminole* was on her way to assist, if necessary, and she arrived on the scene at noon, by which time, the brisk westerly wind had died down and the swell had subsided considerably. The two Coast Guard skippers plotted their strategy and it was decided that *Redwing* would go alongside *Homestead* "with a show of force and seize the vessel. This was done accordingly. No physical resistance was made by anyone on board the *Homestead*. The seizure took place at 2:30 P.M., February 6, 72 nautical miles from Montauk Point Lighthouse." At three P.M., *Redwing* had the rum steamer in tow and started for New York.

The statement that "no physical resistance was made by anyone on board the Homestead" is from the official cruise report of the *Redwing*. Newspapers reported differently. The New York *Herald Tribune*'s Washington bureau stated,

Details of the thirty-six hour running battle between the rumrunner Homestead, sought for almost two years as the boldest plyer of the illicit trade in the Atlantic, and the Red Wing and Seminole of the Coast Guard patrol, which resulted in the capture of the liquor carrier . . . were disclosed by Rear Admiral Frederick C. Billard, commandant of the Coast Guard. . . .

Defiant, even after his rudder and steering gear had been shot away and his pilothouse riddled with one-pound shot, Mark L. Gilbert, captain of the Homestead and his crew of 28 were taken only after the Redwing's rails were lashed to those of the Homestead and the latter subdued in a fight which raged over the decks of both ships.

The New Bedford *Evening Standard* and other newspapers referred to "a free-for-all, hand-to-hand battle," which occurred after "the Redwing wallowed alongside, tied fast, and her crew poured over the rails."

Perhaps the most miraculous aspect of the incident is that no one aboard the *Homestead* was killed or injured by gunfire, not even by the shot that hit the pilothouse.

Name-changing, to make rum ships harder to identify, as Gilbert did with the *Taboga-Homestead*, was frequently practiced. The *Diamantina* became the *Mousmee*. The 135-foot British steam trawler *Hohenlinden* of Montreal, another offshore vessel that came into port to discharge liquor, employed even cruder devices.

The *Hohenlinden* berthed at the old Union Dock in Bay Way, New Jersey, on the night of October 1, 1926. She was seized by federal officials at 5:50 the next afternoon; her cargo was liquor and her crew was engaged in unloading it. Those aboard fled and were pursued and fired upon by the Coast Guard, but they had too much of a head start and escaped.

Staten Island Coast Guard officials forwarded to Washington four photographs of the vessel, noting, "Attention is called to the coils of rope hanging over the name on the stern and on the bow of this vessel, evidence of concealing this name. On the bow and on the stern, the first two letters 'HO' and the last three letters 'DEN' had been painted over with gray paint, leaving the name to appear as 'HEN-LIN.'"

Sometimes, the use of double identities was more sophisticated; in one instance, it involved a trick to get the Coast Guard cutter *Manning* away from the Virginia Capes so that a rum boat with a load could sneak into Chesapeake Bay.

Off Diamond Shoals, the British steamship *Rowan Park* sighted an auxiliary schooner displaying a distress signal. The *Park* approached her and the schooner's master identified his vessel as the *Leader;* he said that he had lost his rudder and was doing the best he could to steer her by manipulating her sails. The captain and crew of the *Leader* said they did not want to leave the vessel — although the *Park* offered to take them aboard — but they asked the steamer's skipper to radio for a Coast Guard cutter to come to their aid. The *Park* did so, and proceeded on its way.

Knowing that the *Manning,* which ordinarily patrolled the area, was steaming out to sea looking for the disabled *Leader,* the skipper of the schooner headed in for the coast. In fact, his vessel was the *Julito,* of Honduran registry; there was nothing wrong with his rudder, and his cargo was 2,000 cases of alcohol, champagne, and gin. *Julito* did, in fact, get by the Capes unobserved and steamed as far up Chesapeake Bay as the Pouquoson River, but here the scheme fell apart.

Although she had successfully dodged the offshore Coast Guard patrol, *Julito* was spotted by somebody in the bay who reported her presence to customs. Customs alerted two Coast Guard patrol boats, which took off in hot pursuit, resulting in a seizure and a mystery. When the vessel was overtaken, there was no one on board. A dog was running up and down the deck. There was a fire in the galley stove and bacon and eggs were sizzling in a frying pan. Obviously, the crew had been gone only a very short time.

However, the schooner was about two miles from shore. It would have been necessary for her crew to row that distance in a small boat to escape the patrol craft. Yet no small boat was in sight nor was any member of her crew, and I am not aware that this riddle was ever solved.

Probably the most spectacular big-ship name-changing occurred in 1933. On May 3 of that year, the State Department informed New York port authorities that the steamer *Holmewood* had landed several cargoes of liquor in the vicinity of the Brooklyn Bridge, the most recent on the evening of January 25. Customs and Coast Guard forces were alerted.

Five months later, Customs Agents Gordon H. Pike and William J. Finck, working out of the office of Collector of Customs, New York City, provided the next information. Shortly before four o'clock on the afternoon of October 2, the phone rang in their office. It was an anonymous informant; he said that a big steamer was coming in that night from the north, that it would be picked up by a tug in the vicinity of Red Hook and proceed into New York, or up the North River, with a cargo of approximately 25,000 cases of liquor.

At 10:15 that evening, Customs Inspector Michael Guilfoyle, in charge of Patrol Boat No. 546, hailed a ship in the North River, off Weehawken, New Jersey, asking her to stop for boarding and identification. From the darkened steamer's bridge above, the answer came that she was the *Texas Ranger,* bound for Albany, and could not stop because of the tide. Port authorities were, in fact, expecting the arrival of either the *Texas Ranger* or the *Texas Shipper* — both owned by the same line — that night. Because of this, the vessel hailed by Guilfoyle had already passed one checkpoint successfully; she had signaled to the tower observer at Sandy Hook that she was the *Texas Ranger* and he did not challenge her. Guilfoyle did not know that the vessel had informed Sandy Hook that she was bound, not for Albany, but for Erie Basin, Brooklyn, "for minor repairs." He allowed her to proceed.

But customs was double-checking. Agent J. W. Roberts got in touch with the president of the Newtex Corporation, owners of the *Texas Ranger,* and asked him where the ship was. She had been delayed; neither the *Texas Ranger* nor the *Texas Shipper* was in the New York area — they were loading cargoes in Virginia and Texas respectively. That information touched off the alarm. If the ship in the night was *not* the *Texas Ranger,* what vessel was it? What was she doing and where did she go?

90

Pike and Finck were ordered to drive along the east shore of the Hudson looking for the steamer that Guilfoyle had hailed the night before.

At 2:05 that afternoon, Coast Guard Radioman First Class B. E. Howell of the Intelligence Unit at New York intercepted a code cipher message. It was in one of several rumrunner codes that the Intelligence Office had succeeded in breaking and it read, "Heave your anchor immediately and get under way. Stand up the river toward Albany." This information was phoned immediately to all Coast Guard and customs patrols in the area.

Howell remained on the alert for something more and an hour later, his persistence was rewarded. From the same rummy shore station, he intercepted a plain-language transmission: "Anchor the boat in good place immediately. Take all men off in one of the lifeboats. Hide the lifeboat if possible. Come ashore on New York side. Try not to attract any attention. Call MIT when you come ashore. PA Code."

The ship answered, "OK" and inquired, "Shall I ditch the gear?" The shore instructed the ship to "destroy tuning settings, also take out receiver coils and so forth." There followed a discussion as to whether they should "change name" — evidently of the ship — and some talk concerning the names and nationalities the men and officers were to assume. It was decided "Don't change name. All off. Raise anchor lights." The last transmission by the ship that Howell heard was at 3:55 P.M., when she signed off in answer to the shore's urgent order to "Get off at once. Tear up all papers at once. Get off."

Because of the nature of the instructions and the further fact that the use of code had been abandoned, apparently because it would have taken more time, it seemed clear that something had frightened the shore station operators into ordering the abandonment of a rum ship somewhere at anchor in the Hudson. The mention of "one of the lifeboats" suggested that she was a large vessel. The instruction to "Come ashore on New York side" indicated that she was not far up the river.

Lieutenant Frank M. Meals, Coast Guard Intelligence officer at New York, said, "Just what frightened them, I do not know. I speculated as to whether the information telephoned by [my] office concerning the 2:05 P.M. interception could have reached the rumrunners so quickly and accurately as to inform them of the government's activities and the fact that the approximate location of their vessel was known to government agents. There [was] grave possibility of a leak somewhere, although every precaution was used by this office to supply the information over private phones to responsible officers."

At 4:20 P.M., Howell intercepted another plain-English transmission from the shore station: "I don't understand your claim you are past City Island. If you are proceeding up the sound, if nobody follows, will unload you at Port Jefferson tonight." There was no answer from the ship.

Coast Guard Intelligence thought the affair was beginning "to take on a fishy look." The 2:05 P.M. message was in code and quite in accord with the rummy practice if the principals were still unsuspecting and thought they could land their cargo somewhere up the Hudson. The 3:05 P.M. transmission in plain English was understandable if it was considered that the rumrunners were now aware that their plans were endangered; they were forced to abandon the greater security of code in order to make a quick getaway.

But the 4:20 P.M. transmission seemed too good to be true, especially coming from a rum-running group that had been extremely cautious and reticent in their radio activity for the entire previous year during which Intelligence had been monitoring their traffic. This message might be intended as a decoy, perhaps to cause the withdrawal of Coast Guard and customs patrol boats from the Hudson. But there was also the possibility that the rum ship had disregarded instructions and gone up the East River. And the excitement over supposed abandonment of the ship might also explain the shore station's continued use of plain English.

It was decided to overlook no bets and the 4:20 P.M. message was forwarded to all government units concerned with the warning that it might be intended to deceive.

Meanwhile, Customs Agents Pike and Finck were driving north, surveying the river at various points. The break came at Croton-on-Hudson, where they discovered a steamer at anchor between Grassy Point and Haverstraw, about a mile off the west shore, and near some deserted brickyards. It was obvious from her waterline that she was loaded; smoke was coming from her funnel.

They commandeered a launch and went out to look at her. The name "Texas Ranger" was painted, in some instances, obviously freshly painted, on her bows, bridge, lifeboats, and life rafts. On her stern, which read "Texas Ranger, New York," a painter's scaffold hung from the rail, precisely at the level of the letters. The ship's hull, superstructure, and boats were painted in the Newtex Line colors and were "identical to the most minute detail with [those] of the real Texas Ranger."

Pike and Finck steamed around the vessel's stern — it was now about 6:30 P.M. — just in time to see two men in a lifeboat pulling away from the steamer and heading for the shore, near one of the brickyards. Anticipating that they might have to go ashore to catch their quarry, the customs agents jumped into a rowboat being towed by their launch and pursued the lifeboat — successfully. Their two prisoners proved to be the chief steward and an oiler from the steamer; they said they had left the ship in the afternoon with the remainder of the crew and had been ordered to return to make certain that the vessel was properly protected with anchor lights.

Pike and Finck returned to the *Texas Ranger* with their prisoners and boarded the steamer with other customs and Coast Guard officials who had arrived by that time. No members of the crew were aboard. One of the boarding party recalled, "All four hatches were battened down and all of the turnbuckle fastenings were sealed with twine secured with lead seals bearing the imprint of the St. Pierre Miquelon Customs. [We] observed by looking through the ventilators that all of the hatches contained cases or bags of liquor, which were plainly discernible." The final tally revealed that the cargo was 25,000 cases of Canadian liquor, "valued conservatively at $1,000,000."

A search of the officers' cabins and chartroom indicated that every effort had been made to conceal the true identity of the ship and the names of the captain and every other member of the crew. Names had been cut from blueprints, charts, and books and torn out of the clothing that had been left. Little remained in the way of documentary evidence.

However, there were found papers indicating that the steamer had had several names. She was first the *Canadian Pathfinder,* then the *Navadoc,* and next, the *Holmewood,* whose home port was initially West Hartlepool, England, and later, Glasgow, Scotland. In the chartroom were also found metal stencils that were identical to the letters stenciled on the bow and stern of the ship and that bore smudges of white paint — the color used in painting the name "Texas Ranger" on the vessel.

Ashore in Haverstraw, town police had been informed that shortly after three P.M., six or seven men carrying suitcases had asked for directions to the railroad station and that they had left for New York. Thus alerted, authorities picked up seventeen members of the crew of the *Texas Ranger,* all aliens. They were interviewed, but no crew member was very talkative.

Several said that they had signed on at Louisburg, Nova Scotia, that they knew the cargo was liquor, and that they had left the ship in the afternoon on orders of their officers. Vincent Walsh, who said he had joined the steamer at North Sydney, Nova Scotia, added that he did not see the name "Texas Ranger" painted on her but knew that two or three days out of New York, the name had been changed and the smokestack repainted. He said that the vessel proceeded up the Hudson, anchored first off Ossining and, on the following day, anchored where she was seized. He was in his bunk asleep, off Haverstraw, when someone shouted, "Get your clothes on and get ashore!" With others, he "piled into one of the lifeboats." No one had given him any money or tickets to proceed farther.

Samuel McDonald, another crew member, said he had helped to repaint the stack under orders from the boatswain, whose name he could not or would not give. Victor Batcher, seaman, declined to answer any questions about the movement or operations of the steamer but he acknowledged that the liquor had been taken on at St. Pierre and that all of the painting had been done "in one watch, three or four days out of New York."

The *Texas Ranger* incident attracted understandable public attention, even though few of the details were known, except to government officials; it was derring-do in the best tradition. *The New York Times* observed, "Only the last-minute timidity of the smuggler's captain, who had averted detection on two nerve-wracking occasions, resulted in capture of the crew and failure of the most audacious smuggling plot in the memory of Customs men. . . .

"No one knows just why the captain suddenly lost his nerve and abandoned the vessel. It is believed he thought he had gone aground, so he went over the side and rowed ashore alone."

Given the advantage of more information than was available to the *Times,* it is possible to come up with a more plausible theory. The appearance in Haverstraw of "six or seven men carrying suitcases," who took a train for New York, suggests that the captain did not row ashore alone, but that the ship's master and officers left together. The fact that the second intercepted radio message ordered the captain to "anchor the boat in good place immediately" would seem to indicate that the ship was maneuverable immediately prior to abandonment and therefore, not aground. Nor was there any ship conversation in the radio traffic to suggest that the skipper thought he was aground.

When one considers that customs received a telephone tip on the *Texas Ranger* from someone who knew not only when she was due to arrive in New York but precisely how many cases of liquor she was carrying, it seems reasonable to conclude that those managing the operation learned that it had been compromised, either from within or by rival smugglers. Not knowing to what degree or how soon the law might find the ship, they abandoned the effort in haste.

The volume of big-ship traffic landing liquor directly in major East Coast ports is difficult to pinpoint, especially because it was always highly controversial; law enforcers tended to claim that it was lower than the rumrunners maintained. Still, some clue may be provided by Michael J. Long, former wireless operator on the British rum-running steamer *Clackamas,* and later, a federal Prohibition agent. On September 27, 1927, Long said that Canadian rumrunners had sent nineteen ships loaded with liquor into U.S. ports within the past twelve months and that all but two had succeeded in landing their cargoes, valued at "millions of dollars."

One of the two ships frustrated in the smuggling effort was the *Clackamas,* and Long, a thirty-five-year-old Australian, who described himself as being virtually a prisoner aboard the vessel, brought about the seizure of the vessel and the arrest of her crew.

In early February, 1927, the *Clackamas* was at Port Mulgrave, Nova Scotia, loading a cargo of pulpwood. Long said that she cleared Port Mulgrave on February 8, her cargo destined "for any consignee south of Latitude 60 degrees," a line, incidentally, which runs approximately through Julianehåb, Greenland. He added that many of the crew were shanghaied, brought aboard drunk or drugged, and came to to find themselves miles at sea.

"Our destination, I did not know," said Long.

I shipped as wireless operator and there was something peculiarly wrong about our wireless outfit from the start. I could receive messages, but in some manner, I could not transmit.

Two days after sailing, I was awakened by the ringing of the ship's telegraph from the bridge to the engine room. Our engines were stopped. I looked out of my porthole and saw a ship in the distance flying an international distress signal. It was the Beatrice, from St. Pierre Miquelon. She was flying the French flag. The French schooner came quite close and the captains of both vessels engaged in conversation.

The captain of the French vessel said he was waterlogged and in distress. He came aboard our vessel. As he was passing me, I heard him say, "I suppose all the crew are your friends?"

Later, the captain of our boat came to me in the wireless room and told me the schooner was waterlogged and in distress and that she had a cargo of liquor aboard. He said he did not know what to do and that he was salvaging the liquor and that he was going into the United States with it under bond. He said that everything was legal and right.

On our ship, some of the pulpwood was hove overboard to make room for the liquor, which I found out amounted to 5,000 cases of champagne, 5,000 cases of whisky, and some barreled goods. The captain commanded me to leave the wireless room and give the boys a hand in transferring the liquor from the schooner to the Clackamas. They were unloading the liquor from the schooner by means of slings and placing it 'tween decks of our ship. Both crews were doing the unloading. I took particular notice of the cases as it was my duty to see that the crew did not pillage any of the liquor.

The champagne cases were marked "Heidsieck, Rheims, France," the whisky cases were marked "Peter Dawson," "Usher's Green Stripe," "Buchanan's Black and White," "Johnny Walker," and other labels. On further examination of the cases, I found them to be stenciled "Antwerp," "S. Pierre." We also took aboard about 250 barrels of liquor, which I presumed to be whisky.

After the unloading, a man came aboard our ship from the Beatrice and I noticed that he had tallied the cargo as it was being unloaded. He was introduced to me as Mr. McEacharn. He was known to most of the other crew as supercargo.

We reached Nantucket Lightship about 10 a.m., February 22. Our ship stopped alongside the lightship and our captain delivered a verbal [sic] message to the captain of the lightship. The light keeper repeated the message back and after the captain of our ship said O.K., we proceeded on our voyage again.

About 3 o'clock that afternoon, we arrived at Quarantine, New York. We passed through Quarantine, customs and immigration and proceeded on our way. We then passed through a large jackknife bridge without any tugs or assistance and proceeding further, we grounded three times. The last time we grounded rather heavily on a sand bank and the ship nearly turned over. She gradually slid off the bank, however.

We arrived at the municipal dock at Port Newark, New Jersey about 10:45 p.m., Sunday, February 13. There was a severe snow storm at the time. The first question that a person on shore asked was "Is Mr. Murphy aboard?" This man turned out to be our supercargo. He immediately went ashore and conversed with the man who called him.

There were a great many men on the dock and about sixty large trucks. Everything was in total darkness — the ship's electric lights were cut off, and the lights on the trucks were out. The men on shore took some lumber and placed it alongside our ship to be used as skids. The unloading finished about 7 the next morning.

I knew all along that the laws of the United States were being violated and I determined to inform the proper authorities the first chance I got. There was no use of me protesting while I was aboard the ship as I was under the captain's orders. I saw my chance while the ship was coaling and slipped aboard a barge and came ashore and told the Customs authorities.

The *Clackamas* was at Philadelphia when Long succeeded in leaving her and a contemporary account confirms that ". . . he escaped in a coal barge when the watch was relaxed while the vessel was loading in mid-stream, off Girard Point. He then gave Customs authorities information resulting in the arrest of his shipmates. His tale was corroborated by Elias Toirer, a seaman aboard the

Clackamas, who admitted the truth of the story after being confronted with Long's statement in the office of U.S. Marshal W. Frank Mathues."

At Newark, Colonel Ira L. Reeves, state Prohibition administrator, branded as "poppycock" Long's story that 10,000 cases of liquor had been landed at Port Newark. It would be almost impossible for that amount of liquor to be landed in Newark and hauled away without agents learning of it, Reeves said. However, on March 29, essentially on the strength of Long's testimony, the master of the *Clackamas* and twenty-five members of the crew were indicted by a federal grand jury on charges of unlawfully possessing and transporting liquor, fraud in importing the cargo, and conspiracy to violate the National Prohibition Act.

A singular instance of courage in combatting the major-port liquor landings by deep-water vessels involved Coast Guard Ensign Charles L. Duke, skipper of the 33-foot launch *C.G. 2327*. Duke had a crew of two and his armament consisted of his five-shot revolver. A former Navy enlisted man and later a reporter for the Washington *Star,* he had had only two years of Coast Guard experience when he made a single-handed ship seizure on the night of July 3, 1927. High-ranking Coast Guard officers hailed it as "the most heroic exploit" since the service had begun chasing rumrunners.

Duke was patrolling in New York Harbor; the wind was fresh and the night black, the stars blotted out by clouds. About nine P.M., he observed a German liner anchored off Quarantine, its lights outlining the big hull sharply against the Brooklyn shore. The liner had halted customs inspection but another vessel behind it — using the German ship for cover, he thought — did not stop. The second ship, with only two dim lights visible, passed Quarantine and headed up the Narrows, toward the Upper Bay.

Ensign Duke, immediately suspicious, set out in pursuit,

at better than twenty knots, and quickly closed the gap between his launch and the darkened steamer. As he came up into her wake and flashed a light on her, the ship's name was visible on the stern: *Economy;* she was a run-down, weather-worn European freighter.

The ensign maneuvered his boat close alongside in the heavy chop and spray; he hailed the *Economy* and ordered her to heave to, but she remained under way and did not respond to his command. Because of the zigzag course the steamer was taking, past Bay Ridge and then across to New Jersey, Duke concluded that whoever was in charge on the bridge did not know New York Harbor. He hailed the *Economy* again and this time received a reply. "I'm going to dock at Greenville," someone called down from the darkened ship. "If you want me, you can find me there at Greenville. I don't intend to stop now."

Duke pulled his launch up alongside the steamer until the two were about stem to stem, proceeding at equal speed. He fired two warning shots from his revolver, as a signal for the *Economy* to stop. The freighter, her two lights flickering dimly, did not reduce speed at all.

By now, because of the speed and weather conditions, the Coast Guard launch was poking her nose into every sea, sending a shower of drenching spray over herself every time she rose to meet the next crest. Already soaking wet and cold, Ensign Duke went forward in his craft and hung on, while his helmsman maneuvered closer to the rapidly moving steamer. It was a ticklish job; the launch pitched and wallowed, and once came close to being battered against the rusty steel side of the steamer.

The ensign knew he could not prolong this kind of danger to his own command or to the personnel for whom he was responsible. As ship and launch once more came close together, narrowing the gap of black water between them, he reached out, grabbed the freighter's rail, and pulled himself aboard the steamer. He knew precisely how defenseless he was; he had a flashlight and three cartridges remaining in his revolver. He had no way of knowing how many men or weapons he faced. In one last magnificent gesture, he yelled from the steamer's deck to Chief Boatswain's Mate Madsen, who was at the wheel of the launch — obviously hoping those aboard the *Economy* would hear him — "If I'm not out of that pilothouse in two minutes, turn the machine gun on them." Madsen, well aware that the launch had no machine gun, played the game, and shouted back "Aye, aye, sir!"

Flashlight in hand, Ensign Duke groped his way to the deckhouse. He was stopped by a burly seaman, who demanded, "Where do you think you're going?" Duke did not reply, but cracked the man on the head with his revolver butt; the sailor staggered backward and went sprawling to the deck. The ensign shone his light upward; there was the ladder to the bridge, and he was anxious to get there. Every turn of the propeller thrust the steamer nearer to the New Jersey shore, and if it reached a pier, the crew could easily jump ashore, scatter, and escape in the darkness.

The wind blew hard as he reached the ship's bridge. In the distance, the Statue of Liberty's torch shone coldly in the blackness. Duke burst into the wheelhouse, flashlight in one hand and gun in the other, as soon as he got inside; there were six men there, including one who obviously was master of the vessel.

"You stop this ship or I'll pull the trigger," Duke said to the captain, and pressed his revolver against the latter's ribs. The master was pleasant enough, but stubborn. He signaled to stop his engines, but he argued. He said he did not know that he had already passed Quarantine. Duke asked him where his customs stamp was and why the ship reeked of alcohol. No answer.

He ordered the master to change course so as to anchor off the Statue of Liberty, to permit boarding of the steamer by Prohibition authorities. The captain demurred, even though the revolver was poked into his ribs. Duke knew he had to take additional action, and in a hurry. The steamer still had way on and, abruptly, the Coast Guard ensign spun the untended ship's wheel, swinging her around. In seconds, there was a sharp jolt; the *Economy* was stuck fast on the mud of Robbins' Reef in ten feet of water. That completed Part One of the ensign's task — preventing the crew from getting ashore.

Then he herded the six on the bridge together and ordered them below at gunpoint, telling them that he did not want them running about the deck. He hailed his two men in the Coast Guard launch, which was standing by, shouting, "Hotfoot it to the Statue of Liberty and get some help!" Meanwhile, a speedboat, which Duke also found suspicious in both appearance and actions, was circling the *Economy;* he assumed that whoever was aboard it — probably unaware that the steamer was aground — wanted to tell the ship's master where to land his load of liquor.

Aware that help might be some time coming, Duke was looking for some place aboard where he could barricade himself in the event the *Economy*'s crew members decided to offer resistance. At this point, he was approached by a young seaman, smooth-cheeked and boyish, who pleaded with him to be "easy" with the captain. The ensign, well aware of the odds against him — and anxious to keep his distance, for fear of trickery — pushed the sailor away. In so doing, he struck him with the flashlight. It blackened the seaman's eye, gashed his forehead, and smashed the flashlight beyond repair, which left Duke without a valuable aid on the unlighted ship.

Meanwhile, the two Coast Guardsmen in the launch were under way at best possible speed for the Army barracks on Bedloe's Island. They reached the Statue of Liberty at 12:30 A.M., but, for some reason, the soldiers there refused to let them use the telephone, so they had to cross to the Barge Office to ask for reinforcements for the ensign. Help was dispatched at once. However, instead of going to Robbins' Reef, at least some of the additional

Coast Guard units went to Weehawken and had to work their way down the west shore until they found the *Economy*.

The cutter *Calumet* arrived on the scene at about two A.M., but could not get close because of the shallow water. Patrol boat *C.G. 122* went aground on the mud flats and patrol boat *C.G. 143* came perilously close to grounding. It was not until six o'clock in the morning that the first help got to Ensign Duke aboard the seized vessel. He did not get off the *Economy* until ten A.M. — thirteen hours after he had first sighted her — when a guard was posted to watch over the steamer and her crew.

An hour later, he walked into the floating Coast Guard headquarters at Stapleton to report to Lieutenant Commander E. D. Jones, his senior officer. Jones said, "Duke looked as unruffled as if he were just coming down to breakfast after a sound sleep. His uniform was bedraggled from salt water and he needed a shave, but you would never have imagined that that man had been on duty continuously for twenty-six hours." Jones told him to go to bed at once and permitted no one to wake him until five o'clock in the afternoon.

When he awoke and was discussing the episode, Duke — six feet tall, twenty-seven years old, and with a soft southern accent — said, "I had a hunch that the rumrunners might try to slip by over the [holiday] weekend. This steamer had that rumrunner look. You'd think they would be wise and paint their boats, but they always pick out the worst old tubs for their rum ships. I can tell one almost every time."

Of the young man whom he struck with the flashlight, he said "We got together on our differences later. I was a little sorry for what I had done. He was a nice boy and he didn't mean any harm. The skipper must have been good to him on the voyage and he wanted me to be good to the skipper if I could."

Mrs. Duke, to whom he had been married only fifteen

months, remarked, "I wish he wouldn't do things like that. It's kind of risky jumping on boats like that all alone."

Investigation revealed that the *Economy* carried 3,000 drums of alcohol containing fifty gallons apiece and worth at bootleggers' prices a total of $500,000. Nor was she actually the *Economy*. She proved to be the *Greypoint*, 793 tons, owned by the Kirkwood Line, Ltd., of Belfast. She had cleared from Antwerp with her liquor cargo consigned to the British West Indies, apparently stopped in Halifax to take aboard her Nova Scotia crew and, en route from that port, had her name changed for the entry into New York.

Jones, commanding officer of Section Base 2, said,

The seizure was quite a stunt, for which Duke is entitled to great credit. The case is different from others in which we have had an accurate description and everyone was set to make the grab.

In this case, we had nothing to work on. Duke was on duty and went out on the picket boat on his own initiative to check up on the Narrows patrol, to look over suspected boats in Gravesend, and on the general idea that the rummies might pick a holiday period to pull one off. It was a good hunch. Duke played his part perfectly. The night was very dark, it was blowing hard, and the picket boat was throughly drenched.

Obviously, despite valiant efforts of the overworked Coast Guard and the vigilance of customs and Prohibition agents, the rummies were moving a lot of rum. The general situation prompted nationally beloved newspaper cartoonist Tad to have one of his dancing stick figures comment — only a few weeks after Duke's dramatic exploit — "If there is no Hades, where has Prohibition gone to?"

And at the outset of that same year, in January, 1927, Miss Charlotte Molyneux Holloway, special industrial investigator for the Connecticut Department of Labor, concluded that bootlegging in Connecticut was more reliable than in other states. Miss Holloway so stated in her biennial report, which was submitted on or about January

14, to Labor Commissioner Harry MacKenzie. She wrote, "Connecticut industries rank high, have worldwide renown and even its bootlegging industry is credited with greater reliability and more reasonable prices than that of other states."

CHAPTER VII

T HE COAST GUARD was frequently, often painfully, reminded of the smugglers' successes and its own complex difficulties in attempting to combat a popular traffic whose entrepreneurs had money enough to buy whoever and whatever had to be bought, whose principals had the sympathy of perhaps every other man in the street, and whose most militant activists shared the government's view that law enforcer and rumrunner were "enemies" and that this was war.

Sometimes, they were reminded of these successes by their informers, some of whom were not so articulate, others very much so. On November 12, 1928, an informer at Oyster Bay, Long Island, wrote to his contact with the Coast Guard,

Dear Jim, I had to work tonight driving the boss out, so could not get any information for you. I was in East Norwich about two weeks ago in ——— ———'s bar one night and one of the guys went out of there with rubber boots and a coil of inch rope. He said he was expecting a boat in. That place does a big business. When I say big, I mean thousands of dollars worth.

Nearly every night, they get a truckload. I see a dark-haired man come in their [sic] one night, he was an Italian with a big black mustache and he collected $1,300. Another night, I see him get a big roll. They do so much in there the cash register does not hold the money. They keep an iron box on a shelf in back of the bar. That box has six or eight compartments in it and I seen so much I felt sick.

They have a big pull with someone. One night, I seen eight big chaps drinking and eating, and I said to the bartender, some Huskies. He said State Troopers. When any rich family wants a few cases all they have to do is give them a ring and the stuff is delivered.

I think those birds know when and where most of the stuff is being used in this section. They have always used me good. I am not telling you this because of a grudge. Please burn this letter after you read it.

Obviously, "Jim" did not burn it; it was transmitted to Coast Guard national headquarters in Washington.

The following letter was dated October 26, 1923; it was sent to Treasury Secretary Andrew W. Mellon, and was written by a New York businessman whose identity I know. Its historic value lies less in the undocumented allegations — although corruption of law-enforcement agencies went hand-in-hand with implementation of the Eighteenth Amendment — than in the widespread pattern of citizen concern of which it is a symbol. Many believed that if this law could not be enforced, more law and more ethics would be eroded as a result. The businessman observed:

Atlantic Highlands, New Jersey, together with the adjoining borough of Highlands, is commonly referred to as a "free port of entry" for the rum fleet and I have occasion to hear a great deal about the illicit importation of liquor. What I say is not based on legal evidence but upon what would be strictly called hearsay, but which are matters of such common knowledge and told so frequently and coming from the bootleggers who talk freely with their friends, that we who live in that neck of the woods believe it to be true.

We believe the lack of enforcement of the Prohibition law is due more to a lack of morale than to the lack of numbers of men employed. It is a matter of common repute that your Coast Guard is paid a per case fee of $3 for all liquor landed at Highlands and Atlantic Highlands. It is also understood that the inland Prohibition officers receive $1 per case and that the local police receive another $1 per case. Recently, there has come into existence a well-organized band of hijackers who prey on the bootleggers and who demand another $1 per case for protection. We have had in Atlantic Highlands and vicinity in the last five or six weeks at least four shooting matches between bootleggers and hijackers. Last Saturday night, one was shot near the railroad station and taken to the hospital and I have since been informed that he died.

Some months ago, a lawyer who has defended a number of bootleggers told me he ate dinner at one of the hotels at Highlands a few days before I had the conversation with him and that he counted eight automatics and revolvers lying on tables and chairs while the owners ate their dinners. He said they carried them in holsters in true Wild Western style. In this same conversation, I asked him why that was done so publicly and why Prohibition agents did not get them.

He said there is a Prohibition agent walking the streets down there every day, but he does not see anything. And he said further, "If you were in his place and got $500 per week for looking the other way, would you see anything?"

It is reported that Coast Guard offshore, in return for the tribute which they collect from the bootleggers, let them alone at night and only interfere with them during the daytime. It is also reported that lights are displayed at night and signals by day, notifying bootleggers when your fast boats are either present or away, so that the bootleggers may know when it is safe to go out and when not to. The booze running is so flagrant and open that we cannot believe the Government agents do not know it, and when the bootleggers themselves tell their friends that they have to pay tribute, and how much they pay, we feel bound to believe it is so.

The lack of enforcement of the law and the open violation of it have caused contempt and disregard and disrespect for the law greater than has ever existed before. Young men in our community who have been brought up to lead fairly upright lives have seen so much of the violation of the law and have seen so much money made by its violation that many of them have yielded to temptation and fallen a victim.

It is only a few mornings ago that I stopped in a local garage and while having my tires blown up, listened to a conversation between the garage man and a young man of the town who was getting gas a few feet from me. He told the garage man, in a tone which would be heard by anyone in the vicinity and without seemingly any fear whatsoever of being overheard, that he was out all night and he delivered twelve cases to a place some miles away, and went on to say that he has several customers in that vicinity. He did not say what the cases contained, but neither the garage man nor myself needed any explanation to satisfy our own understandings. This is only one of a number of instances which I might relate.

Another thing that enters into the case is the small punishment meted out to the bootlegger, even when caught redhanded and apprehended. An attorney for some bootleggers recently told me of some of them being fined $250 and $500 and then said, "They can make that up in one trip." If the judges could be induced to give jail sentences, and long ones, there would be less bootlegging.

If these suggestions are of any consequence, I shall be glad that I wrote this letter. If they are of no value, you will pardon me for taking up your time. This letter, however, is not intended for publication, as I am not yet ready to be a mark for the gunmen, nor do I care to sell my house to the insurance company.

On January 17, 1924, Secretary Mellon replied to the letter, the terseness of his response in itself indicative of the uphill nature of the task with which he, and the Coast Guard, had been charged. The secretary observed, "The Department is fully alive to the opportunities which the coast of New Jersey and other coasts offer for the transaction of this illicit business and is doing what it can with its limited and inadequate facilities toward suppressing the traffic."

Coincidentally, this period — the beginning of 1924 — marked something of a turning point for the Coast Guard, which found itself about to expand considerably after nearly three years of struggle with antismuggling responsibilities far beyond its capacity. A few statistics make the picture clear.

At this time, approximately 160 rum vessels were operating in waters adjacent to the American coasts. These were complemented by the inshore smuggler fleet of several hundred powerboats of various sizes and speeds. The federal government estimated that 100,000 cases of liquor a month were coming into East Coast areas from a half-dozen countries.

Until 1924, the Coast Guard had had twenty-nine steam cutters for deep-water work and a fleet of inshore craft with which to combat the smugglers and carry out its regular task of assistance to mariners as well. Since the beginning of its involvement in blockading the coast and intercepting smugglers, it had seized nearly 150 vessels, mostly small craft. By its own estimates, it had been able to intercept only about 5 percent of the liquor entering the United States from the sea — something like 30,000 cases to this date. Government officials also figured that rumrunners being pursued had jettisoned 20,000 cases of liquor.

Early in 1924, President Coolidge asked for — and Congress subsequently approved — the appropriation of $13,853,989 for increasing the equipment and personnel of the Coast Guard. These funds provided for the transfer of 20 laid-up destroyers from the Navy to the Coast Guard, and reconditioning and equipping them; the acquisition of approximately 300 additional large and small vessels, and the recruiting of nearly 5,000 more officers and men. Up to that time, Coast Guard personnel had included 209 commissioned officers, 396 warrant officers, and 4,051 enlisted persons.

It was encouraging to the service. Even if the destroyers were aged, even if the rumrunners did have a "bribery fund," with which they were liberal, and even if the new recruits — some in on one-year enlistments — were of varying quality and variously susceptible, at least the national government had acknowledged that the Coast Guard needed help.

In part, the action by the Coolidge administration and the Congress reflected strongly voiced public concern. On October 15, 1924, Gilbert J. Raynor, a member of the Long Island Committee of Public Safety in East Moriches, Suffolk County, New York, forwarded a petition to Washington bearing the signatures of several hundred Long Islanders. It requested that the Coast Guard assign several picket boats at the east end of the island — as had been done at Fire Island and Jones Inlet — "for the purpose of preventing smuggling of liquor."

A week later, Rear Admiral F. C. Billard, Coast Guard commandant, informed Mr. Raynor that a "substantial" increase in boats for use in that area was contemplated "and there [was] good prospe that they [would] be ready within the next few weeks."

More vessels, money, and manpower were not, of course, the whole answer. Coast Guard officials were sensitive to the fact that the success of the liquor traffickers might be — as Secretary Mellon's correspondent had suggested — "due more to a lack of morale than to the lack of numbers of men employed," at least in some cases. Accordingly, the service made continuing efforts to find out whether Coast Guard personnel were performing their antismuggling assignments properly.

On April 6, 1924, the Coast Guard seized the motorboat *J-1013* at the entrance to Block Island Sound, about four miles east of Montauk Point. There were two men aboard and, questioned separately, one said they had left Noank at midnight on a pleasure trip and the second said they had left Mystic at midnight on a pleasure trip. One had in his possession $1,914, letters bearing Canadian stamps, "clearly intended for delivery to a person in the rum fleet and one letter received from a person in the rum fleet for mailing in the States." There were also aboard the boat a .30 caliber Winchester repeating rifle, a .30 caliber Army pistol, and ammunition for both.

It was decided within the next couple of days to put a Coast Guard officer aboard the *J-1013,* whose markings and appearance were not altered in any way, and assign him to surveillance of both the rum fleet and Coast Guard operations. The assignment was given to Lieutenant R. B. Hall, who was to operate in cooperation with the cutter *Seminole,* temporarily commanded by Lieutenant Commander Clarence H. Dench. Hall was ordered to visit Point Judith Harbor of Refuge, board all boats there; proceed to Great Salt Pond, Block Island, board all boats there; confer with the officer in charge, New Shoreham Station, Block Island; survey Block Island Sound, and rejoin *Seminole* at a specified hour off Block Island.

When the *J-1013* did not arrive at the rendezvous as scheduled, Commander Dench, both with the ship's launch and the cutter itself, endeavored to check on Hall's whereabouts. The *Seminole*'s skipper found the information that he was given by Coast Guard personnel, compared with Hall's own account when he rejoined the cutter, disturbing.

The surfman on watch at New Shoreham said that neither Hall nor the *J-1013* had been in Great Salt Pond. Hall had, in fact, gone into Great Salt Pond and had conferred with the officer in charge at the New Shoreham station.

At Point Judith station, the chief petty officer said that the *J-1013* had not been inside the harbor of refuge there on the previous day. She not only had been there, but Hall had boarded a vessel just outside the breakwater, taking about ten minutes, and evidently was not observed by the station watch.

Hall concluded that Block Island was being used as a halfway point in the transfer of liquor between the offshore rum fleet and the mainland. Of his surveillance trip, he said,

When I approached the wharf at New Harbor, Great Salt Pond, a truck backed up to the dock and awaited our landing; the boat, being a seized rumrunner, displayed no flag to indicate it was being operated by other than rumrunners. The truck hastily departed when the men on the dock saw men in uniform aboard. Three men remained on the dock and appeared much concerned about something and wanted to know how long we were going to stay there.

I believe that the efficiency of the Coast Guard would be greatly increased in this vicinity if a regular crew were assigned to both stations on Block Island and the stations put in charge of keepers who are not related either by marriage or birth to the inhabitants. . . . With reliable crews on a small island such as Block Island is, it should be impossible to land liquor at either of the two accessible landings. But if liquor is landed, evidence could be obtained, provided, of course, the fear of incriminating relatives is removed.

Commander Dench observed,

It has been suspected that some Coast Guard stations are doing little or nothing toward the prevention of rumrunning. . . . There are various indications coming from various sources which lead one to suspect that some stations are in collusion with the rumrunners or connive at their activities.

As everyone knows, nothing ever happens on the beaches without the men at the stations hearing about it. In common with all isolated places and small communities, the surfmen know and can scarcely help knowing, the details of their neighbors' affairs.

How then is it possible that we get no information concerning rumrunners from them? No information has been received from any of the Coast Guard stations in any of the territory past which or through which liquor is being transported from the Montauk rum fleet, yet from the master of a rum-running motorboat operating out of Ford Pond Bay, information was gained (under pressure, to be sure) as to the location of liquor warehouses on Montauk Point. To anyone who knows that area, it is inconceivable that the three Coast Guard stations in that vicinity do not possess the same knowledge.

While in New London, a fisherman, resident of Block Island, said the following, in my hearing: "A Coast Guard captain on Block Island is getting his. I don't mind saying it, even if he is a relative of mine." Then he went on to tell of seeing early one morning sixty cases of liquor standing on the wharf at Block Island Harbor about 800 yards from the Coast Guard station. He said this liquor was moved from the wharf in broad daylight.

The chief petty officer at the Point Judith station, when asked about rum-running activities, said, in effect, that "Things are pretty quiet." I consider this an unsatisfactory statement. Probably, he knows much more.

Dench recommended transferring the boatswains and the station crews "well away from the baleful influence of their rum-running relatives and friends; their loyalty to their relatives is all too likely to exceed their loyalty to the Government." He also suggested discontinuing the employment of temporary surfmen in all stations within the sphere of rum-running operations because they "are very likely to be of the rum-running fraternity who take the job to let their colleagues in the fast motorboats go by unmolested. Men captured in rum-running boats have often asked members of the Seminole's crew as to how to get into the service."

Finally, the commander concluded, "If they are intimidated by the overwhelming numbers of the rum-running gentry, our land force should at least have the courage to write an official letter to that effect, whereupon the stations should be strengthened by what might be called small garrisons."

Nor were such difficulties within the service restricted to

a single area. In the mid-1920s, Coast Guard Commander John B. Littlefield was assigned to conduct an investigation into the "alleged dereliction of duty among Coast Guardsmen in Southern New England stations." Of this inquiry, the Providence *Journal* reported, "Charges against enlisted men at two stations include, it was learned on highest authority, failure to hold regular drills, and falsification of log entries. Unofficially, it was reported that liquor parties ashore and afloat, in which women participated, also were investigated. Coast Guardsmen likewise are said to have attended boxing bouts in New Bedford when they were supposed to have been on duty."

R. L. Raney, commander of Section Base 14 at Block Island, on a scouting trip in Narragansett Bay, found the Brenton Point picket boat *C.G. 2343* tied up to the rum-runner *Marge* at Tiverton, at 8:30 P.M. No Coast Guardsmen were aboard or locatable, although he checked the local poolroom, at the suggestion of some fishermen who said they thought "the boys were up there." After a thirty-minute search, Raney returned to the dock and found the crew aboard the picket boat. He said, "During their absence, it would have been possible for anyone to run away with the boat or for civilians passing by the bridge to think the Coast Guard men were having a conference with the rumrunners."

Further, in the Coast Guard files, there is an unsigned memorandum dated August 27, 1927, and directed to Commander (Charles S.) Root of Coast Guard Intelligence. It is titled "Smuggling In and About the Eastern Division," and notes,

Mr. A. D. of Boston, whose information is considered entirely reliable, advises me that liquor discharges are an almost nightly occurrence in and about the fish wharves of Boston from fishing schooners which receive their cargoes from blacks hovering along the Northeastern shorelines. It is hardly likely that the blacks have been neglecting such an excellent market as Boston and it is hard to believe in the face of all the recent seizures in New York that the blacks would still continue to neglect Boston, an almost virgin field so far as seizures are concerned.

To my knowledge, this service has never seized a major vessel in Boston Harbor. . . Base 7 seems to be the only base that has made seizures. Base 5 and Base 16 have done little or nothing to justify their existence.

Commander Dench had suggested the possibility of strengthening the shore stations "by what might be called small garrisons." There were sound reasons for taking such action in several areas. From the beginning, the Coast Guard was made aware of the hostility toward its anti-smuggling effort; this feeling mounted as the volume of liquor traffic and the number of dollars involved increased. Its intensity ranged from the exasperation of the fisherman trying to make extra grocery and rent money in lean times to organized harassment of service personnel and, in some cases, to threats of bodily harm, violence, and murder.

Early in 1922, the commander of the Eastern Division, G. C. Carmine, noted that shore stations had been given small arms, but no ammunition. He pointed out that the illicit liquor traffic "is generally handled by men of desperate character who will stop at nothing," emphasized that the surfmen had to be provided with means of self-protection, and recommended that they be given "suitable arms and ammunition to meet these dangerous conditions."

Thirteen days later, William J. Wheeler, commanding officer of the cutter *Tampa,* reported "indications of the landing of liquor in the vicinity of Coast Guard Station 22." He added, "It is understood that this and other stations have no revolver ammunition and that the recent experience of a surfman near Gurnet in being horribly beaten and almost drowned by smugglers has discouraged further efforts by the unarmed surfmen."

The commanding officer of the *Seminole* praised the

"spirit, energy, and activity of the special agents on patrol at the eastern entrance to Long Island Sound." But he warned, "These men should be better armed. They should be supplied with U.S. magazine rifles and an abundance of ammunition, for the men they operate against are efficiently armed and I have no doubt will not hesitate to use arms against small patrol boats when there is a chance of getting away by so doing. On the Vereign, there was a 401 rifle loaded with dumdum bullets."

Vereign, previously named *Sovereign,* and before that, *Little Sovereign,* was a steam yacht with a crew of thirteen, skippered by a former World War I Naval Reserve lieutenant commander. Bound in with $100,000 worth of champagne, whisky, and alcohol stacked so high that only her engine room and pilothouse were clear, she refused to stop until *Seminole* lobbed a solid shot through her wheelhouse, variously wounding three men.

At Scituate, Massachusetts, an attempt was made to club Joseph Dabue, a surfman, and his attacker threatened to kill John Glynn, who was in charge of the Coast Guard station there. Dabue was patrolling the beach at North Scituate when a man stepped out of the darkness, wielding a club, and aimed a blow at him. "We're going to kill you first and then we're going to kill Captain Glynn," he threatened as he swung his club again. Dabue struck his attacker's arm and the club flew from the man's hand. As the latter fled up the beach, the surfman drew his revolver and fired two shots at him.

The attack took place in an area called "The Glades," which had been known for some time as a rumrunners' paradise because of the amount of liquor they had been able to land there. When Glynn tightened surveillance of the area, seized a boatload of 200 cases of liquor, and arrested thirteen men, he and his station crew received threats of retaliation. The attack followed.

The conflict between serviceman and smuggler became spasmodically ugly in those areas where the liquor traffic was heaviest. Shortly after eight P.M. on January 17, 1925, the Coast Guard patrol boat *2319,* commanded by Urban B. Kilbride, sighted a launch — later identified as the *K-11599* — off Sandy Hook. Kilbride hailed the launch and ordered her to heave to; somebody aboard the *K-11599* laughed derisively, and her speed was increased. The patrol boat took up the pursuit and Kilbride ordered Motor Machinist's Mate James C. Moore to fire a warning shot across the bow of the fleeing launch. It did not stop her. Two more shots were fired, the launch slowed down, and someone aboard her called out, "You've hit one of us!"

There were two men aboard, one bleeding profusely, and thirty-five cases of whisky. Following the surrender of the launch crew, the trip ashore was made as quickly as possible and Moore took the wounded man and the second prisoner directly to the Army hospital at Sandy Hook. First aid was given there, but the Army doctors said the injured man might die from loss of blood and that Moore could not keep his prisoners there overnight. The uninjured prisoner requested permission to telephone the Long Branch hospital for transportation there for his wounded colleague. Moore agreed.

Soon an automobile appeared, and Moore and the two men started, as he believed, for the Long Branch hospital. They had gone several miles and were in Belford when the driver remarked that he had inadvertently passed the crossroad leading to the hospital. He stopped the car.

Moore recalled, "Six men leaped out of another car and attacked me, took my weapons, and hit me over the head with a blackjack. I fell in a lump, pretending I was dead. They threw me into the snow and hurried away." The Coast Guardsman said he was convinced that his assailants intended to beat him to death and, when they drove off at high speed with his two prisoners, were certain that they had done so.

In a letter of commendation to Moore, Admiral Billard,

Coast Guard commandant, called the assault "outrageous." It was assumed that the uninjured prisoner had arranged for the attack when he made his phone call.

About two and a half months later, Chief Boatswain's Mate Carl Gustafson was at the wheel of *C.G. 237,* on patrol duty off Race Rock Lighthouse, Long Island Sound; it was in the early hours of the morning. Someone in a boat that approached "stealthily and without lights" opened up on his pilothouse with a machine gun and killed the Coast Guardsman as he stood there. The murderers were never apprehended.

In the same year, openly defying the law forces of government, bootleggers and their sympathizers on land and sea virtually laid siege to the Coast Guard "mother ship" *Argus,* which was anchored in Rockaway Bay, Long Island. The *Argus,* more of an ark than a seagoing vessel, was incapable of moving under its own power; aboard were 125 recruits.

The hostility of the civilians toward the ship and her personnel was first manifested by threats and minor disturbances when members of the *Argus'* company went ashore. Words soon led to actions, producing an alarming situation, and an observer said,

Attempts to go ashore in small boats have been frustrated by the rumrunners and mail destined for the Argus, brought from shore in launches, has been seized and rifled.

At night, parties of bootleggers drive automobiles to the shore and boldly fire upon the Argus. In the day, residents of the neighborhood crowd the beaches and revile seamen working aboard the vessel. Hostile craft, full of jeering men, steam about the ship, hurling insults at the crew.

Argus is a marooned vessel, a floating island in the midst of an enemy country, a target for bootleggers' bullets, and the abuse of the Long Island countryside. Every means has been adopted to harass her crew.

At that time, *Argus* personnel were awaiting the return of cutters that were patrolling off the coast, assuming that with their return, "the disorder [would] subside to sullen mutterings, the bullying motorboats [would] disperse, and the seamen [would] be taken ashore under escort."

At one point, it was revealed that Captain W. V. E. Jacobs, commander of the New York division of the Coast Guard, had received a letter from the rumrunners threatening his life. Other officers also were told they would be killed if pressure on the smugglers was not relaxed, and bootleggers informed the Coast Guard it was their intention to blow up the Barge Office headquarters at the foot of Manhattan near the Battery.

Certain emphasis was lent to these threats by an incident that occurred on the same day they were made public. Off the New Jersey shore, near Cape May, a patrol boat opened fire on a rumrunner. The bootlegger returned the fire, and more than four hundred shots were exchanged before the faster rum boat, fearing capture, dumped overboard 100 cases of liquor and escaped.

Such experiences had their effect on Coast Guard morale. On June 2, 1925, nine members of the service attached to Base 2, Staten Island, chose not to reenlist when their two-year hitches were up, and it was predicted that another hundred would leave on July 1 under similar circumstances. Some said they were leaving because of insufficient time ashore — they said they had received only forty-eight hours' shore leave after twenty-one days at sea. But others, especially those who had served on small boats, said their lives had been jeopardized by machine-gun fire from rumrunners and that they had had to chase smuggler craft into shoal water where there was serious risk of running ashore.

Then there was bribery. The Coast Guard had to be constantly alert to its dangers, as well as to the possibility that its personnel might be in collusion with the rumrunners or even sell seized liquor themselves.

There is a report from the commanding officer of the cutter *Seminole* datelined Stapleton, Staten Island, New

York, December 28, 1923; this may well have been written by then-Commander Philip H. Scott. Scott was described by one who knew him as "the kind of man one would expect to meet as commander of a cutter. A Southern gentleman with a Virginia accent, he was a beloved skipper, an expert seaman, and a terror to the rumrunners. For relaxation, he studied the Latin and other classics from original texts, and eighteenth-century books in English."

The *Seminole*'s skipper noted,

About 4:20 p.m. today, the quartermaster on watch informed me that a Captain Q—— was at the gangway and wanted to see me. At the gangway stood two middle-aged men, apparently well-dressed, substantial looking. The nearer one was dark, short, and stout, and said he was Captain Q. The other man gave me the impression of being older, more of a blond type, and several inches taller than Q. I asked them into my cabin and showed them seats, and stood by a chair myself, most of the time they were in the cabin.

Q. began by saying that I was not the captain he had expected to see. I suggested perhaps he had come to the wrong ship. He said no, it was the captain of the Seminole, but he was a short, stout man who always went ashore in a very light suit. Then I told him I had not been in command very long, that Captain Addison had preceded me, and that he was stout and not very tall, but as I remembered him only in uniform, I had no idea what sort of suit he went ashore in.

I said Lieutenant Ahern had been in command for two months during the summer and he was short, but by no means stout. He seemed unable to recall either name, but said he had seen him about the middle of September. I said then it was undoubtedly Addison they wished to see, for he was in command at that time. Here, the conversation lagged, so I asked if it was a personal matter or ship's business that he wanted to see the captain of the Seminole about. He made some evasive reply which I do not recall and, after a few moments, asked, "How is the rum business?" I said, "Thriving, I presume. Plenty of it outside, at least, plenty of ships."

"That's what I came to see you about," he said. "I want to get in a couple of loads. How about —."

I presume my changing expression stopped what he was about to say. I was so astounded that I was momentarily dumbfounded. Then, rising and stepping over to his chair — for I had taken a seat at my desk shortly before this — I said, "You get out of that chair, out of this cabin, and off this ship as quick as God will let you, or I'll throw you in irons." And I used other words not in my vocabulary, which I do not now recall, but then apt, fit, and fully justified, and demanded by the occasion.

At the gangway, I demanded his name and address, which he gave as H—— Q——, Jersey City.

Efforts to pay off Coast Guard petty officers at Staten Island resulted in the seizure of the rum-running schooner *Madeline E. Adams.* Early in April, 1925, Motor Machinist 1st Class Elmer D. Barber, in charge of cabin picket boat *C.G. 2325,* was approached by two men and offered $8 per case if he would go to Rum Row with the *2325* and bring in a load of whisky. Barber reported the incident to Lieutenant Commander J. I. Bryan, commanding officer of Section Base 2, and was instructed to negotiate with the two men and to try to get them to agree to use a patrol boat instead of a picket boat, the former being larger and therefore better for offshore work.

After further negotiations, Boatswain Augustus F. Pitman, skipper of patrol boat *C.G. 203,* was introduced to the two men on April 8 and arrangements were made to use Pitman's boat to bring in a load.

Pitman said,

I was to pick up two men who were the agents [of the two with whom he had negotiated] at a point in Ambrose channel at Buoy No. 10 on Thursday evening, April 9, at about 5:30 p.m. These men were to be transferred from one of their boats to the 203. We were then to proceed to the rum fleet and to a schooner named the Madeline E. Adams, then anchored about eighteen miles off the coast of New Jersey and there, through these agents whom we had on board, to procure a cargo of liquor from the Adams.

This whisky was then to be brought into New York Harbor and to a point near Bayonne, New Jersey, near the Elco motor boat works, and it was then to be transferred from the 203 to one of their boats, which would be waiting for us. One of the agents whom we took with us, who gave the name of J. C. Maloney, was to act as pilot. After the transfer of the whisky to the waiting boat, Barber and myself were to receive payment for our services at the rate of $8 for each case of whisky brought in. The 203 was then supposed to return to her patrol at sea as if nothing had happened.

Rough weather delayed the plan, but on Friday morning, April 10, Pitman was able to put the two men aboard the *Adams*. The sea was still running too high to permit loading liquor aboard the patrol boat, but he agreed to come back to the schooner when the weather moderated.

Pitman said,

At 2:45 p.m., April 11, I left the base, in charge of the 203, and proceeded to the Adams, arriving at her at about 5:55 p.m. The two agents greeted us and had the whisky on the deck of the schooner all ready for loading. We started immediately to load the whisky on board the 203 and the crew of the schooner assisted us in doing so. We were supposed to take on 500 cases, 300 of which was to be champagne and 200, Scotch whisky.

We finished loading about 7 p.m., April 11, and immediately shoved off. The agents both accompanied us on the 203 and immediately upon arriving inside the territorial waters of the United States, I placed them under arrest. I headed for Scotland Light vessel and upon arriving there at 9:05 p.m., spoke to the C.G. 180, Ensign J. F. Kennaly in charge, and informed him that I had accomplished my mission. I reported to him the position of the schooner Madeline Adams.

What happened then was that the cutter *Seminole* went after the *Adams*. After a twelve-hour chase, during which the schooner had all of her sails set and her auxiliary engine hooked up to full speed — officers of the cutter said she was capable of making eighteen knots — the *Seminole* captured the rumrunner. The Coast Guard ship fired several shots during the chase and finally seized the vessel at three P.M. on April 13, twenty-one miles off Fire Island.

The British schooner had aboard 3,000 cases of whisky, wine, and alcohol, valued at $250,000 to $450,000, and the worth of the vessel itself was set at $75,000.

Sometimes, in addition to steadfastness against corruption, both singular courage and shrewdness were demanded of Coast Guard personnel who found themselves in potentially dangerous situations without immediate hope of assistance.

Albert W. Johnson, boatswain's mate 1st class, was in charge of the patrol boat *C.G. 2277*, based at East Boston. At 1:30 on a bleak morning in January, he had secured his craft to a dock at Commercial Point in Dorchester Bay, where he could watch for rum-running activity.

A boat running without lights came down the channel.

Johnson recalled,

I waited until she got abeam of us and then used the searchlight on her. Then I sent up a flare signal, which illuminated the area and I identified the boat as the Mary of Boston. We started our engines, cast off, and proceeded to overhaul her.

The Mary at once turned to the right and was beached right off Commercial Point. We secured alongside the Mary; her engine was still running and the crew missing. I told L. A. Leavitt, motor machinist's mate, 1st class, to shut off her engines.

Several men, apparently the crew of the Mary, were near some buildings ashore; we could see them in our searchlight. When they abandoned the boat, they had opened the sea cocks in the engine room and there was about four feet of water there.

One of the crew of the Mary shouted from shore, "How much will you take to let the load go?" Then he shouted, "We will give you $500." Upon receiving no response from us, he shouted again, "We will give you $1,000." I paid no attention. A few minutes later, one of the men ashore wanted to know if we were from the Point Allerton Coast Guard station. I made no response to this.

Sizing up the situation we were in, I decided to notify the base by telephone. The only means I had of doing this was to leave one man aboard the Mary with a Lewis machine gun and plenty of ammunition. I left Seaman 1st Class W. E. Rees aboard, with the gun and a flare signal kit, and instructions to protect the boat and cargo at all costs until I returned.

I got under way with the 2277 and headed for Lawley's shipyard to notify the base. After securing to a shipyard dock, I left Leavitt in charge and ran approximately a half-mile to an office building, where I located a night watchman. At 3:20 a.m., I telephoned the base and notified the officer of the deck of the seizure of the Mary and the situation I was in.

About twenty seconds after I finished telephoning, a sedan drove up in front of the office building with six or seven men and stopped on the opposite side of the street. One man got out of the sedan and came halfway across the street and wanted to know if he could talk business with me. As I was in shadow inside the office building, I told the night watchman, Alexander Octon, to tell him "Nothing doing." The man said "O.K." and then got into the sedan and drove away. As soon as I saw the coast was clear, I left the building and hurried back to the 2277. I did not attempt to capture any of them as I was all alone with the watchman, and only one gun between us.

At 3:50 a.m., we secured again along side the Mary, which was still fast aground. Shortly after that, with our searchlight, we could see two men at the shore end of the dock. One of them shouted, "I am Officer Curtis of Station No. 11 and have a man here who I think is one of the crew of that boat. Will you come ashore and identify him?" Suspecting a ruse, I immediately shouted back, "All right, that being the case, hold him for further investigation."

About fifteen minutes later, six or seven policemen from Station 11 came down to the shore opposite where the Mary was aground and, after identifying them as policemen, I asked them if they had an officer by the name of Curtis attached to the station, and told them the circumstances of the ruse. They shouted back, "No such officer is attached to Station 11."

At 4:30 A.M., *C.G. 178* from the East Boston base arrived to assist Johnson. A half-hour later, Coast Guardsmen had pumped the water out of the *Mary*'s engine room and floated her; her cargo consisted of 1,093 sacks.

On occasion, the rumrunners' ample funds were applied in more indirect manner. Two of twelve Coast Guard converted submarine chasers returned to their Staten Island base after four days of blockade patrol, showing "every evidence" of having been tampered with. One was towed in with a disabled engine and the other had a propeller missing. It was concluded that these mishaps were not the result of accident, but of deliberate design, and they were described as "sabotage made possible through bribery."

Another incident, which may or may not have involved bribery, occurred on December 21, 1925, when rumrunners stole a Coast Guard patrol boat and used it to land liquor under the protection of the official government insignia.

The patrol boat, *C.G. 2325*, had been laid up for repairs. Recaulking of the hull and engine overhaul had just been completed and she had not yet been returned to active duty. Thus, no watch was on board as she lay at Pier 18, Staten Island.

What happened was described in contemporary accounts as "one of the most daring rum-running feats recorded since Rum Row was established." Bootleggers stole the boat and landed 1,500 cases of liquor "under the very noses of Coast Guard cutters and other Government craft. Three times the craft went out to Rum Row, now about fourteen miles at sea, loaded five hundred cases of liquor on each trip and landed the cargo. Coming and going, the bootleggers gaily saluted at least a dozen rum chasers and had the salutation returned."

Some Coast Guardsmen could *not* withstand the temptation of what the rumrunners had to offer from their "bribery fund."

Early in January of 1927, more than a dozen defendants were on trial in federal court in New York City, charged with conspiring to violate the Prohibition law. Three of the government witnesses were former Coast Guardsmen who had served on patrol boats. They testified variously as to how the crew of a patrol boat ran liquor ashore from Rum Row, helped the rum ships do business, set erring rumrunners on their courses, and accepted money and whisky for their services.

One of them, William R. Hughes, a former petty officer, said that his patrol boat frequently went out to Rum Row in the fall of the year before to communicate with the rumrunner *Vincent A. White*, a schooner. He added that on one occasion when there were Coast Guard destroyers about, the one-pounder on his patrol boat was loaded so that it could be fired and thus give the boat the appearance of being in a chase, if interrupted. At the time, he said, they were transporting a smuggler out to the *Vincent A. White*.

Hughes said that later they all went back to Greenport, Long Island, and two members of his patrol boat's crew "went around the docks to see who was moving liquor so they could collect the usual fee paid to the Coast Guard per case. No liquor was coming in and they got nothing."

A second witness who was a former Coast Guardsman, Frank J. Stuart, said he accepted a bribe of $2,000 from one of the defendants for permitting several fishing boats to land liquor in Fort Pond Bay, near Montauk. He also stated that his patrol boat seized a rumrunner, the *Dawn*, on which there were 200 cases of liquor, and attempted to take it in tow, but wind and current were adverse and the *Dawn* grounded. Stuart said that he salvaged the liquor, ordered his crew to fire several shots into the *Dawn* and that she caught fire and sank. He said the patrol boat then ran into Fort Pond Bay, landed the liquor, and the crew disposed of it for $3,000, which was divided among them.

As titillating as these revelations were to the American public, the judicial outcome and the published reaction were at least as interesting historically, insofar as they revealed a national attitude toward Prohibition generally and toward the government's effort to enforce it.

The New York trial lasted more than two weeks. The jury was out twenty-four hours, acquitted eight defendants and reached no agreement on six others. Underlying the jurors' failure to convict was a rejection of the testimony and methods of the government's "undercover" men, and of its principal witnesses, several of whom had confessed to wrongdoing themselves. Hughes, for example, became a member of the government forces after he was discharged from the Coast Guard following his arrest as a member of a rum-running operation.

The New York Times saw fit to editorialize on the outcome of the trial and commented, with respect to the witnesses "of the so-called 'undercover' class,"

They were not merely suspected of being agents provocateurs, but were of so despicable a sort that it is hardly surprising one juror protested that he would stay out until doomsday before voting to convict anybody on the evidence of such witnesses as the government brought forward.

The case may be extreme, but it is, after all, typical. In many parts of the country, it has been found again and again, that jurors simply will not convict in liquor cases. They will even ignore the most positive instructions of the judge as regards the law. This state of mind, constituting as it does, one of the greatest difficulties in the enforcement of the Volstead Act, was plainly foreseen when Prohibition was adopted.

Say what you will, men make a distinction between laws affecting their personal habits and those having to do with the rights of others. Juries are made up of men who do not live apart from their fellows, but understand the common sentiment of the community, and may be expected to frustrate many such trials as the one which has lasted for two weeks in the federal court of this district and ended in a complete fiasco.

Underlying this "common sentiment of the community" were two deeply felt beliefs held by many — the first being that the Prohibition effort was at least futile, if not unreasonable, and the second that the Coast Guard would be much better employed if performing its traditional service of aid to mariners.

Concerning the first, on November 18, 1927, several men were on trial in Salem, Massachusetts, charged with conspiracy to bribe certain public officials and to violate the liquor laws. One of the most interesting items of testimony was that a crowd of three hundred spectators gathered at Salisbury Beach to watch the unloading of a boatload of liquor. Obviously, such a well-attended event — uninterrupted by anyone rushing off to sound an alarm — indicated considerable public acceptance, if not approval, of the activity.

And on October 19, 1932, a New York City editorial writer touched on the second aspect, obviously sensing that it was a matter of concern to many. He commented,

New York newspapers had little space in which to record the recent loss in pursuit of their calling of two Martha's Vineyard fishermen. It has remained for the Vineyard Gazette to set down the details.

In the early hours of October 2, two fishing boats were returning from their grounds off Nomansland, a heavy swell was running, with an occasional breaking sea, when at about 3 o'clock, the leading boat noticed that the other's light had disappeared.

Thinking that their companions were having engine trouble, the men in the first launch immediately went about in search. No trace was found of the boat or the two men in her. Apparently, she had tripped on a sea, filled and sunk.

With daylight, the remaining boat made for the Coast Guard station at Woods Hole, reported what had happened, and got a promise that three cutters would be sent out. She then hastened back to search again. According to her people, one Coast Guard destroyer approached, "made a circle or two and steamed away," while later, a cutter came on the scene. The cutter, however, lay under Nomansland most of the day, finally coming out to hail the searching fishermen and then dash in.

Ultimately, the fishermen gave up. As they came into Woods Hole about 9 o'clock in the evening, the cutters awoke to a sudden activity. According to the fishermen's story, they were followed in, raked with searchlights, a party came on board looking for their papers, and turning "everything upside down," and one Coast Guardsman remarked, "It looks damn funny to see you fellows coming in without any fish."

The feelings of the fishermen, friends of the lost men for whom they had been searching, may be imagined. It is difficult to imagine what they felt a few days later when the two bodies were discovered in a fish net near New Bedford, each wearing a life preserver. They had died, not of drowning, but of exhaustion. They may have lived for many hours, during which a thorough search might have effected their rescue.

Unfortunately, a magnificent service, which has gloried for years in its great record for saving life at sea, appears to have been taught that the apprehension of liquor smugglers is a more important duty, and with the personnel which has come into it since it has acquired this precious new mission, it performs even that duty badly.

As a footnote, I knew the boat that sank. I knew the two men who were drowned, their families, and their friends. I know what the Vineyard reaction to their deaths was. It was bitter and of the kind of bitterness that made unlikely allies of drinker and nondrinker in their rejection of the Coast Guard's antismuggling role.

It is also worthy of note that on occasion — there are at least two recorded instances in which smugglers came to the aid of their pursuers — the rumrunners did something that further enhanced their public image. One such instance moved the Boston *Globe* to editorialize on November 28, 1924:

Early in life, the poet Goethe made a discovery which goes to the roots of human experience and deeper. He said, after a certain searching experience, "Law, custom, mortality, and institutions touch only the merest surface of life." What did he mean? It can be explained by a little incident which happened off our New England coast a few days since.

Three government agents whose duty it is to chase rumrunners on the high seas found themselves in sore straits — gasoline low, compass capricious, drinking water frozen, and food gone. Storm-battered, and well-nigh desperate, they were finally rescued by one of the rum-running law breakers whom they had been sent out to catch.

Here is something older and deeper, more honorable and august, than today's laws or yesterday's customs, something which antedates today's morality and institutions venerable with antiquity, for they are only the clothes of life, but this is life itself. It is the spontaneous spirit of mutual aid welling in the average human nature under stress and bridging, with help and sympathy, the artificial barriers thrown up by society to separate man from man, brother from brother.

Disbelieve in it as we will, this element does work. It will not down. Thwarted here, it springs up somewhere else, for the life principle is in it. Sages know this. They all try to utter it. But the truth of this bedrock, Mother Earth sweetness and soundness of human nature lies so much deeper than any words that all sages can do in speaking of it is stammer a few broken syllables. But there is a way in which it can be uttered, and that is in action. It is a truth which, to be known, must be lived.

The rumrunner lived it.

CHAPTER VIII

THE HIGH-RISK PART of the total rum-running opera-tion, of course, and its mainstay, involved the load-ing of the inshore craft on Rum Row and running the gauntlet of government vessels constantly patrolling be-tween the Row and the ports and beaches. In several ways, the rumrunner did what he could to minimize this risk, the first involving night visibility.

There is a chart in Coast Guard files titled "Prevalence of blacks with reference to phases of moon" — "blacks" being the government's code word for rumrunners — and dots on it indicate a consistent pattern of twelve to fifteen offshore rum supply vessels in the North Atlantic area in dark-of-the-moon periods during September, October, and November. The peak month was October, with 26 vessels;

there were 22 each in January and September, and May was the thin month, with only 7, presumably because the weather was too good. When the weather deteriorated and there was less moonlight, the figures went up; in the dark of the moon, the rumrunner was more comfortable and more active.

Sailings of liquor-laden vessels from Canadian ports were similarly related to phases of the moon. Some idea of the volume and frequently of this traffic is indicated by figures for the year ending January 31, 1930: the *Mareuilendole* was sighted a total of six times off the North Atlantic coast, and seized in July. The *Mary Mother of Elizabeth* was sighted four times and seized in November; the *Vinces* was sighted twelve times and seized in September; the *Flor del Mar* was sighted four times and seized in December, and the *James B.* was sighted four times and sunk in October. The total number of different blacks sighted in this area during the year was fifty-two.

Especially in the earlier years, the rumrunner also relied on ingenuity in moving his illegal cargo through the inshore waters. The patrol boat *C.G. 124,* skippered by T. C. Losch, was on duty in the Race, Long Island Sound, and sighted the fishing schooner *Marianne* shortly before eight in the evening. This vessel was believed to be a liquor carrier and she had been the subject of a confidential memorandum issued by the section base commander nine days before.

Losch hailed the schooner, boarded her, was informed that she was en route to New York from New Bedford, and he made a thorough search of her quarters and hull. He found no liquor. However, there was one thing wrong — although the *Marianne* had aboard only a small quantity of fish, she was down by the head, and this aroused his suspicions.

He radioed his base at New London for instructions and was ordered to take the vessel there for search "if believed justifiable." Losch replied, "Believed not justifiable, only two bins of fish. No indications of concealed contraband unless in secret compartments." But somebody at the base, possessing unusual strength of conviction or an irresistible hunch, nevertheless replied, "Bring in Marianne for examination."

When the *Marianne* arrived at New London, Boatswain Alexander C. Cornell began to search her at 2:30 in the morning. One and a half hours later, he gave up, and reported finding no liquor aboard. Lieutenant R. C. Jewell, for some reason not satisfied, took over the search himself and also found nothing; by 9:30 A.M., he was almost prepared to release the vessel. Almost, but not quite; in a final burst of inspiration, he took the draft of the vessel and measured the depth of the hold. There proved to be a difference of about seven feet. *Marianne* was not about to be released until the discrepancy was resolved.

Jewell began by assuming that perhaps his figures were wrong, that he had made the error. He called a diving party and had the depth of the keel measured precisely. There was still a difference of about five feet between the draft and the depth of the hold. Coast Guardsmen drilled through what proved to be double false bottoms in the hold, drove metal rods through the holes until they hit something solid below and then withdrew them. The rods smelled of whisky.

Marianne was seized and her crew placed under arrest. Jewell related that the schooner had "a false bottom, false keelson, and a hatch concealed by cement which had been poured over the false bottom. When the investigators broke through the cement, they discovered the large liquor cargo stowed in the area below. The hatch, which was sealed by cement, was between her two masts, just abaft the foremast. Ordinarily, they had fish and ice on top of the whole business, resting on planks and it was below the planks that the cement-concealed hatch was located."

The destroyer *Cummings* was about twenty miles south of Great South Bay, Long Island, early one afternoon and came upon two vessels lying close together — the *Mary* of New Bedford, a fisherman, and the fully loaded British rum ship *Temescouda*. J. A. Starr, commanding officer of the *Cummings,* boarded the *Mary* and confirmed that she was scalloping. He also confirmed that she had a deck built in the hold extending forward from the engine room about ⟋3½ feet above the keel. The only entrance to the hold below this deck was through a hatch on which the mainmast stood. The portion of the mainmast below the main deck was hinged; when swung forward, it prevented the opening of this hatch and tended to conceal it. Starr concluded, "No doubt that this vessel was there intending to load liquor from the Temescouda or another rummy in the vicinity. A marker buoy was anchored near, with a red pennant and red flag, on which a lantern was hung during the night."

A couple of vessels built along conventional fishing-boat lines, the *Etta K.* and the *Moonlight,* had double hulls. The *Etta K.* had concealed trapdoors on deck and a hull within a hull about two feet apart — just big enough to accommodate a case of liquor — that went down as far as the turn of the bilge. The inner hull had planks and timbers just like the outer hull. I do not think she was ever caught. After Prohibition, she was taken to a boatyard and the inner hull was stripped out; I talked to one of the men who helped do this job and he said, "We were working on her, my cousin and I, way up in the lazarette. I heard a tinkle, tinkle and I said to him, 'Hey, what's that?' We found a gallon jug with Bacardi rum in it; we had hit it with something, and it had broken. That was the only thing we found."

Another kind of "disguise" was attempted in the use of unlikely craft to transport liquor, principally towboats and barges, which assumed a certain innocence of purpose by virtue of their leisurely pace. In late January, 1925, an anonymous phone caller informed customs officials that the tug *Lorraine Rita,* operating between Philadelphia and

Atlantic City, was in regular contact with rum vessels off the New Jersey coast and that it was bringing liquor into port, either aboard the tug or the vessel under tow.

Two weeks later, in accordance with general orders to "board and examine the Lorraine Rita wherever found," Boatswain J. M. Vincent, skippering the *C.G. 183,* sighted her, fired one shot to make her heave to, and took her into Atlantic City. The tug was carrying 988 cases of Scotch whisky and 400 cases of Bass ale in the forward hold and 1,612 cases of Scotch in the after hold, the total cargo being valued at between $150,000 and $170,000.

In mid-1932, Thomas Finnegan, deputy collector of U.S. Customs in Boston, listed three tugs and fourteen barges which, "according to reliable information, [were] engaged in smuggling liquor into the city of New York. Owners of the barges [were] said not to be party of the smuggling."

The pattern of operation was simple. The barges carried coal north from Newport News, Virginia, and other South Atlantic ports and on their return voyages, were loaded with rock from Stonington and other Maine ports. On the trip north, they contacted the rum fleet off New Jersey and took aboard liquor while the tows remained under way at about five knots; when they returned south, the same procedure was followed with the rum fleet off Rockland, Maine.

Arriving at New York, the barges would be towed past Sandy Hook and anchored off the Battery, ostensibly for the night, as coastwise tows commonly did. After dark, a harbor tug took the barges to a coal wharf, where the liquor was taken off and loaded in trucks. While it was still dark, the barges were returned to the Battery anchorage and at daybreak, the oceangoing tug picked them up and continued on its way.

But these devices were exceptions and they did not work well enough nor could they handle volume enough. Obviously, what was needed was speed — an inshore boat that could carry a good load and remain fast enough to outrun anything likely to chase it. In the early years, especially in those times when the Coast Guard was short on boats and men and the blockade less effective, the rumrunners picked up such boats as were available and attempted to adapt them. I remember one such instance very well, and what it emphasizes is that, in general, the better a boat was for running rum, the less likely that it could be used effectively for anything else.

The boat in question was a double-ender, and whatever she may have been designed for, it was not fishing. Her owner was a fisherman; he had her because he was poor and could not afford anything else. I do believe he cursed her every day he went to sea, principally because she lacked the bearing and work room aft that a draggerman finds essential. There was no fisherman in the area who would have bought her from him at any price, however low. His colleagues pitied him because this was the craft he had to fish from and when they were all offshore together, those in the other boats kept an eye on him constantly, fearful that he might go over the side in his oilskins because he had to handle his trawl gear in such confined quarters.

But then came the early days of rumrunning, and on a bright fall afternoon, a couple of men came to the dock to see him, he sitting there, knee-booted and cross-legged, mending twine. I didn't really know how it came about, but I knew what happened, so when I got ready to write this book, I went to see his widow. She is a grandmother several times over and was willing to talk to me about it because her husband had trusted me.

"Everybody knew what was going on," she said.

You knew right away when a man stopped fishing and started running rum. In the first place, his family began to eat proper and you could tell by what they bought at the grocery store and whether they had to run up a grub bill all winter.

It was fall then, that first year. The weather had been bad for more'n a week — wet and the wind no'theast — and nobody could fish much inshore and even if you did, the price you got for what you brought in was almost worse than nothing. We had three young ones — I think that was the time they'd all been sick with somethin', one after the other — and we didn't have much coming in, no real money you could count on. Never knew what it would be, one week to the next.

George worked hard. He never let up on himself none, but it just didn't come out to much, the way things were. I darned socks till they was more darn than socks, I tell you. Sometimes we had sweetener to the coffee and sometimes we didn't. Ernest, that was my oldest, went rabbit hunting after school days before he sat down to his homework. That was most of our meat.

Well, George come home one day that fall and he sat down in a kitchen chair. I stood there ironin' and looked at his hands and could of cried, they were so full of salt-water sores because he didn't have no good mittens. Then he dug into his pants pocket and come out with three ten-dollar bills, all wadded up. I like to fell over. He said, "Emily, all you got to know is that I ain't running around. That's all I'm going to tell you."

Of course, I knew what he was saying. I knew where the money come from. Any woman in my place would of known. After that, I thought about it some and it may sound funny now, but I talked to God a little bit about it when I was alone, because I didn't have nobody else to talk to. I knew it was wrong, what he was doin', and I worried about it some, but finally, I said to myself, "Well, day at a time, nothing else to be done about it." Anyway, it was a pretty regular business and mostly I knew when he was going and when he was coming back. He was home a lot more and that was good, and my Lord, how the money did begin to come in.

The thing was, as you said, they cut George in first of all for his boat. They come down to the dock to see him and they wanted to buy her because she was fast and would turn quick and would hold a lot. Well, when George found out what they wanted her for — they didn't come out in so many words, but he knew — he asked 'em for money enough to buy him a good dragger. They didn't quite want to pay that much, and they knew George had got his boat cheap because she wasn't no good for fishing, so they made him an offer to throw in with them, run his own boat for them, and they'd buy him a new injin. Which they did. So the boat got him into it, you might say.

I didn't sleep easy on nights when he was out and after the kids were tucked in, I'd think up things to do. Every other thing, there'd be a story in the papers about somebody got shot at; more'n likely, somebody we knew or a boat we knew. One year, I knitted sweaters for everybody and did it all between nine at night and six in the morning.

However, the reasonably fast makeshift boat was not the ultimate answer, either; what was inevitable in a trade as well heeled as the liquor traffic was the emergence of sophisticated equipment specifically designed for rum-running: capacious, fast — and, of course, expensive, but that did not matter.

A hint of the new direction appeared in *The New York Times* of June 2, 1925:

It was learned yesterday that a big New York bootlegging ring has given orders to a shipyard in the metropolitian district for construction of a fleet of armored rumrunners as fast as the famous Cigarette. As soon as these boats are finished, it is predicted, they will go off and give the Coast Guard a battle. They will carry machine guns.

Crews of rum-running ships are said to have refused to go out to sea since the blockade started unless they were afforded protection against Coast Guard fire. The Cigarette, which can do 42 knots, was seized for the third time yesterday in a dry dock in Staten Island, charged with violation of the navigation laws. She was taken to the Battery. Her name had been painted out and she had been repainted and refitted. She had bulletproof windows. Customs officials said it was a violation of the law to change the name of a ship without a permit.

The *Lynx II,* described by the Coast Guard as "one of the fastest operating in New York Harbor and one of the most troublesome to our patrols," offered another example of the new sophistication in inshore rum boats. At eight in the morning, about six months after publication of the

New York Times story, a telephone tipster informed the Coast Guard that *Lynx II* had passed through Hell Gate on its way to a marine garage at the foot of 132nd Street, Port Morris, New York. Boatswain L. Wiklund, in charge of the Coast Guard harbor tug *Wissahickon*, was dispatched up the East River to look for her.

He found her, exactly as described by the informer; she was having her batteries recharged, her engines were still warm, and no one was aboard. Wiklund discovered that the 55-foot boat, with a speed of at least 22 knots, had aboard more than 300 cases of liquor, principally champagne, worth about $80,000. He seized the vessel and towed it to the Barge Office, where it was examined.

The vessel was protected with armor sufficient to make it proof against machine-gun fire. It was painted Coast Guard gray and aboard were found two pieces of canvas of the same color on which the designator "CG-4" had been stenciled in the same manner and size as the letters and numbers on government patrol boats. The commander, New York Division, observed, "These were obviously to be used to give the vessel the appearance of a Coast Guard patrol boat by attaching them on each side of the bow of the hull of the vessel. In every way, it is evident that the vessel is especially equipped to run liquor."

In a similar case, Commander William H. Munter, destroyer force commander at New London, noted concerning the rumrunner *Charlotte,* a former subchaser,

She is rigged and so arranged, even as to ventilators and other deckhouse arrangements, to closely resemble one of our 75-footers. In the rigging, the yardarm, similarly placed to that of a patrol boat, bunting is carried which can easily be mistaken in the distance for a Coast Guard flag. It is beyond doubt why this similarity is attained. At night, and at a distance during daylight, the Charlotte will often be taken for a Coast Guard patrol boat.

On one occasion, the Charlotte also was discovered at night with tow-lights displayed, in order to deceive, since there was no tow attached to her at the time.

In June, 1926, Munter also had something to say about the *Marge,* which, about three weeks earlier, had been spotted in Block Island Sound and chased up the Sakonnet River, in Rhode Island, by *C.G. 187.* The patrol boat fired more than ninety shots from its one-pounder, but the *Marge* did not stop until she was intercepted by a second Coast Guard craft in the river. Munter observed, "Failure of this boat to stop caused an extraordinary expense to the government in ammunition. . . ." He was referring to the fact that fines for running without lights or refusing to halt on command — if no liquor was found aboard — were usually light, perhaps $500 or less, and in the present instance, it was likely that $500 worth of ammunition had been expended in order to bring the *Marge* to. So the government did no more than break even, and perhaps not that.

This rumrunner was a typical example of a craft built for the trade; there could be no doubt in the world as to what her business was. She was equipped with armor plating and shatterproof glass in the pilothouse, which was built to accommodate only the head and shoulders of the man at the wheel. The craft had three Liberty engines and no accommodations for crew, everything being devoted to the stowage of liquor in two large compartments, one forward and one aft of the engine space.

The *Marge* showed up again, and soon. On December 9, 1926, at 1:20 in the afternoon, Lieutenant Commander John S. Baylis, skipper of the destroyer *Paulding,* observed two speedboats standing south along the beach near Nauset gas buoy, off the east coast of Cape Cod. The *Paulding* increased speed and headed for them; they put about and started north for Peaked Hill buoy, in an obvious attempt to avoid being boarded. At Peaked Hill buoy, the *C.G. 242* attempted to stop and board one of the boats, then identified as the *Marge* — and fired at her, and chased her, but she refused to stop. The rumrunner, valued at $75,000, capable of developing 1,350 horsepower and of attaining a maximum speed of 45 miles an hour, roared across Massachusetts Bay in broad daylight.

The rumrunner, low in the water and obviously carrying a heavy load, turned on everything she had, set a zigzag course — anticipating that she would be fired on — and the spray kicked high into the air behind her. Baylis took up the chase; the *Paulding,* with black smoke pouring from her four stacks, entered the bay at a 30-knot clip.

Few such chases were so highly visible; most of them were after dark or offshore, or both. When the destroyer's forward gun began to boom, it attracted considerable attention on the shore. *Paulding* fired six three-inch shells, all of which "dropped close by" the *Marge,* but still she did not stop. A contemporary account reported that "the sight of the destroyer lying back on the horizon, smoke streaming behind her and the shots splashing perilously close to the speedboat ahead was one that thrilled the spectators. Straight up the bay the chase led. . . ."

Paulding chased the *Marge* for one hour and fifty minutes, and Baylis then began to be concerned about increasingly shoal water. At about that time, Surfman Harry M. Bailey, lookout at the Brant Rock Coast Guard station, was observing the rumrunner as she passed; four men on her deck were jettisoning cargo over the starboard side. Brant Rock phoned the station at North Scituate, reported that a destroyer was in pursuit of a speedboat about five miles offshore, was firing at her, and that the craft being chased appeared to be heading for the North River.

In response, T. P. Stanley, boatswain's mate 1st class, skipper of the picket boat *2360,* started for the North River. He spotted the *Paulding* lying off the Scituate bell buoy and ran alongside. Baylis told him what had occurred, that the *Marge* refused to stop; he asked Stanley to search for the rumrunner, seize her, and put her crew under arrest.

The search was brief. The rum boat was tied up to the

wharf of a sand and gravel company. An official of the company said that she had arrived only a short time before, that six men had landed, one of whom told him that the motors were disabled and that the boat would not be able to proceed until repairs were made. He asked permission to leave the boat there for about two hours in order to obtain new parts from Plymouth.

However, Stanley discovered that the members of the crew had gone to Greenbush depot and boarded a train for Boston. When federal permission was granted to force the locks on the boat's hatches, no liquor was found aboard; no papers were found that would help to identify her owners. Such anonymity was not unusual.

The Coast Guard naturally watched the shipyards to discover who was building craft that would eventually become their adversaries. It was frequently difficult to discover who really owned and put up the money for construction of these boats, usually registered as yachts or fishing vessels, even though law-enforcement agencies had their suspicions. Inspection of such vessels prior to their launching at least gave the government an idea of what they were up against as the rumrunners strove increasingly to produce reasonably noiseless, uncatchable, and unsinkable craft for running the inshore blockade.

On November 8, 1929, for example, Boatswain's Mate W. W. Worcester, skipper of *C.G. 281,* "stood up Narragansett Bay, 11 a.m., made fast to dock at Crowninshield's shipyard to investigate new speedboat Mona Lola." This vessel was found to be equipped with two Sterling Dolphins, six-cylinder engines of 300 horsepower each, and a Fiat of 300 horsepower, totaling 900 horsepower. The port and midship engines were rigged to use the port exhaust, which was equipped with a No. 6 Maxim silencer, and the starboard exhaust took care of the remaining engine, with a No. 5 silencer.

Mona Lola had two compartments for carrying liquor; one included all the space abaft the engine room and the other was between the engine room and crew's quarters under the pilothouse. Together, they would hold more than 1,000 sacks. The inside of the pilothouse was armored with steel plates about three-eighths of an inch thick. The vessel hailed from Newport.

I interviewed a master boat builder who was employed by the Casey Boatbuilding Company of Fairhaven, Massachusetts, for twenty years and who very possibly participated in the construction of as many rum-running craft as anyone in the Northeast. It was inevitable that several of the boats on which he worked eventually made headlines. He started boatbuilding in 1927 and recalled:

What we built involved alteration of conventional design to get more speed. Most of the boats in this area were forty-five to sixty feet; a few were bigger, and the biggest was eighty feet, the Maybe. The speed of the round-bottom boats was 17-18 knots top; some of the V-bottoms would do 40-plus miles per hour. I helped build ten big ones, in the 45-foot and up class; these included the Madame X, El Sol, Old Lady, Tossup, Acme, Sea Gull, and Nola. Of them all, Nola was probably as fast as any in the whole fleet; she was designed by the famous naval architect William H. Hand Jr., and he was one of the best V-bottom designers in the business. I would say Nola could do 35 to 38 knots with 800 cases aboard, and 40 knots or better empty. Most of the fast boats had Detroit Aero or Liberty engines; some had two, some had three — Nola had three, each of 300 horsepower.

I also helped build some 30-footers, used for shore boats. They ran them onto the beach; their bottoms were flat, with a tunnel stern — the propeller was up inside the boat that way so it wouldn't get damaged. They could take 600–800 cases off the big boat and because they didn't draw more than a foot, foot-and-a-half of water, they could run right inshore.

The fast boat didn't really come into its own until 1925. It didn't have a head or anything. It was all deck and hold, with a capacity of 800–1,000 cases. It had no bulwarks and no rails, just a toe rail on the outside. It had a pilothouse forward, with just room enough for a man to steer. Sometimes, it carried a dory aft. Some had smokescreen devices; some had underwater exhaust, to muffle the sound, and some had armor plate.

Those fellows weren't all bad. They may have been thought of as criminals, but the majority of them were every-day guys and good-hearted fellows. They did have the money. Some of those boats were making two trips a week when the moon wasn't full and when you saw them come to the boatyard with their brand-new Cadillacs, Moons, Auburns and Pierce Arrows, you knew what they were up to.

We built at least a half-dozen rumrunners that were made to look like yachts; a couple of them were rigged as motor sailers. They were almost identical to the rumrunner hulls, but all dick-eyed up; they had cabins that were finished off in mahogany. They probably would carry 500–600 cases. Some of the vessels, like the Madame X., Tossup and Old Lady, looked like small draggers, although, often as not, they had no fishing gear.

I mentioned the fact that I had heard that Major Casey, who owned the boatyard — Major was his given name, not a title — never would allow the rumrunners to be christened at launching with anything stronger than ginger ale. The boatbuilder nodded. "He was a very religious man," he said. "He didn't believe in moving pictures, smoking or drinking, yet he knew what the boats were being used for. He knew who the fellows were, but it was business to him. He closed his eyes. He was in the business for money."

"How much money?" I asked.

"Well, we used to figure a hundred dollars per foot for construction."

The *Nola* he remembered especially, and with good reason; she was known as the "queen of the rum fleet." This craft was approximately 48 feet long, 12 feet in the beam, and she drew 5½ feet. Her pilothouse, hold, engine room, and stern were armor-plated and her port holes were of bulletproof glass. She was launched on August 18, 1931 ("She had to come back briefly," said the boatbuilder, "so we could beef her up under the pilothouse to support the weight of the armor plate.") and what happened to her made local history.

"The story I got from the rumrunners," said the boat-builder,

was that she was coming in with a load. Probably if they hadn't been so greedy that they not only filled her hold with liquor but stacked it on deck, too, what happened wouldn't have.

The people ashore wanted her skipper to go around Vineyard lightship and come into Buzzards Bay from the west to land the stuff. They had heard that three 75-footers and a four-stacker were waiting for him. But he was a daredevil; he said, "No, they never can catch me," so he chose to come through Vineyard Sound, which was shorter.

The liquor on deck was "Belgian" alcohol in five-gallon tins. It actually came from several places other than Belgium and was widely used as a base for making Scotch whisky. The deckload proved to be *Nola*'s undoing.

Five months to the day after her launching, December 18, 1931, *Nola* began the run through Vineyard Sound; there were, in fact, three patrol boats and a destroyer, whose skippers knew she was coming and who were determined to catch her if they could. The chase began about ten that night, when Chief Boatswain's Mate Cecil Mc-Leod, commanding the Coast Guard patrol boat *813,* sighted *Nola* running without lights off Gay Head. He signaled for her to halt and when she refused, the patrol boat opened fire with machine guns, in due course, aiming directly at her pilothouse and engine room. The bullets had no effect whatever against her armor plate.

McLeod then directed his guns at the cargo piled on *Nola*'s afterdeck. Almost immediately, the alcohol caught fire. Despite the blaze, the rumrunner continued to flee, with the *813* in pursuit. McLeod sent up flares, signaling for help, and two patrol boats, *C.G. 2297* and *C.G. 405,* responding at full speed, joined the chase. Ordinarily, *Nola* could have outrun them all, but the rapidly spreading fire and a couple of rounds from the *405*'s one-pounder brought her to a halt. The patrol boat drew alongside and five men leaped from the burning rumrunner to the Coast Guard craft.

Two crew members from the *813* then quickly boarded the *Nola* to obtain some liquor for evidence. They found a man lying behind the pilothouse with a bullet in his thigh. He said he had tried to get into the pilothouse, found the door was locked, and after the machine-gun fusillade began, he lay on the deck, where he was hit.

The *813* radioed for an ambulance to stand by at Vineyard Haven and proceeded there, to put the wounded man into the Marine Hospital on Martha's Vineyard. Crew members of the *2297* then boarded the still-burning *Nola* and secured a couple of cases of liquor. By this time, the Coast Guard destroyer *Wilkes* had arrived and put a line aboard the rumrunner, intending to tow her. However, within moments, a series of explosions shattered *Nola;* she burst into flames and sank.

There is more to the story. When the five men boarded the patrol boat, the master of the *Nola* gave his name as Arthur Folger. That was not his name. The *Nola*'s skipper was Frank Butler — and on the following day, Coast Guard officials announced that he had been "long sought for liquor-carrying activities." The other item of interest, a touch of irony, was that the patrol boat *813,* which brought about *Nola*'s downfall, was one of more than 450 former rumrunners seized by the Coast Guard and converted to government use — principally because of their speed — over a ten-year period. As a rumrunner, the *813*'s name was *Tramp* — and Frank Butler had been her skipper.

Nola was by no means the only rumrunner that ever carried more liquor than was practical for the moment. On December 4, 1932, the 45-foot rumrunner *Liberty* was coming in with a load at the western end of Long Island

Sound. She was carrying 1,397 cases of liquor valued at $42 a case (shore delivery price) or a total of $57,674. The vessel itself was worth $25,000.

She was so heavily loaded that she had almost no freeboard; her decks were nearly awash. Spotted by a patrol boat, she was overhauled within a few minutes because she was so deep in the water that she could make no speed; overloading thwarted the hull design that made these boats fast and it did not take many extra sacks beyond the designed capacity to slow them down considerably.

Her four-man crew was arrested and a Coast Guard prize crew was put aboard to take *Liberty* into port. However, between the time of seizure, about 2:40 A.M., and 5:50 A.M., increasing wind kicked up a sea and *Liberty*'s pumps were unable to keep ahead of the water that came aboard. The Coast Guard crew had to abandon her and she went to the bottom, representing a total loss to rumrunning interests of $82,674.

On occasion, when the rumrunner found that he was going to be caught and there was no opportunity to throw his cargo overboard, he sacrificed *both* boat and cargo, and some of the smuggling craft were so equipped as to make this an easy and rapid procedure.

The smuggler *Hither* was bound in, south of Muskeget Channel — between Martha's Vineyard and Nantucket — about 9:30 one night loaded with sacked liquor and kegs of Islay. McLeod, aboard *C.G. 813,* was anchored off Cape Poge Light and picked up her dark outline through the glasses, even as the sound of her engines was heard. He buoyed his anchor, got under way, and turned his searchlight on her; the deckload was plainly visible. When he fired a burst of machine-gun bullets over her after she refused to heave to as ordered, *Hither* picked up speed and laid down a smokescreen. McLeod then hauled to windward and opened fire into her engine room; about 10 P.M., she slowed down and the patrol boat went alongside.

There was a heavy southwesterly swell running and the

C.G. 813 was pounding badly against *Hither,* but McLeod got her crew off and sent a boarding party to inspect the rumrunner. Her forecastle was half-full of water and the Coast Guardsmen could hear it rushing in from the port side. There was already too much water aboard to find out how it was coming in. The engine room was still dry, the port motor was running, but *Hither* was settling by the head. She was awash by 11:30 P.M.; she sank at midnight in ten fathoms, southeast of Cape Poge. It was discovered that *Hither*'s owners had recently had two six-inch sea-cocks installed in her and McLeod concluded "some member of the crew opened the seacocks."

Similarly, the *Albertina* was stopped four miles west of Vineyard Sound Light Vessel by Boatswain S. N. Prentiss, in charge of *C.G. 235,* shortly after midnight. Prentiss said,

We boarded the vessel and found her to have about 200 sacks of contraband on deck. Three men were standing on deck back of the wheelhouse and as none made any attempt to take our line, I went forward on Albertina to secure it. While I was doing so, the three men came forward and they jumped aboard the patrol boat.

I turned around and saw a man come out of the Albertina's engine compartment and at the same time, flames were flaring up in the engine room. I grabbed a fire extinguisher and tried to put the fire out. I looked in the engine room; a gas line was disconnected and flooding the space with gasoline.

Despite Coast Guard efforts to contain the blaze, it was out of control by 12:50 A.M. *Albertina* went to the bottom between one and two in the morning, a flaming load of booze suddenly snuffed out in the chilly waters.

This last-ditch device of destroying the vessel is an illustration of the degree to which liquor and equipment were expendable because the rum-running interests were well bank-rolled and making a lot of money. Usually, it did not keep the rumrunners out of court. In the instances of the *Albertina* and *Hither* — and in many other similar cases — the smuggling craft remained afloat long enough for the Coast Guard to obtain liquor for evidence and the rumrunners were arrested anyway. But scuttling the craft did, of course, insure that the fast boats would not be seized by the government and added to its fleet of patrol vessels.

Incidentally, about four years before *Albertina* came to her fiery end, she was the subject of some very private Coast Guard concern, although her master at that time — whoever he was — probably was never aware of it.

The *Albertina,* a former subchaser, had been seized off New York. In a conversation with an investigator of the Department of Justice, her skipper said that he had been boarded at sea off Fire Island Lightship on November 17, 1926, by the officer in charge of a patrol boat, whose number he gave. The rumrunner said that he had arranged with the Coast Guardsman "not to be arrested", by promising to pay him some money. The *Albertina*'s master repeated this statement when questioned by Coast Guard officials to whom the Department of Justice report was given.

This kind of statement by smugglers was not uncommon; because it was not, the Coast Guard tended not to take seriously whatever rumrunners said when they were caught. However, investigation revealed that a patrol boat *was* alongside the *Albertina* at the time in question, that a petty officer *did* board her from the patrol boat, and that although the patrol boat radioed a report to the cutter *Seminole* during this period, it did not state that she was alongside or boarding the rumrunner.

The matter was further complicated by the fact that the Coast Guard had recently been advised that the petty officer in question had been paid $2,500 in Jersey City, New Jersey, by people "known to be in the rum-running business." An officer in the New York District concluded, "It is not believed the Albertina procured her cargo of liquor *after* she was boarded [by the petty officer] but that the liquor was on board *at the time* [he] went on board of her.

. . . If this is actually the case [that the petty officer was paid $2,500], it would tend to show that he is dishonest and unworthy of holding a position in the U.S. Coast Guard. It is recommended that an officer be directed to investigate the matter."

However it came out, payment for immunity from arrest off Fire Island Lightship — if such payment actually was made — obviously did *Albertina* no good off Vineyard Sound Lightship.

A final word on the rumrunner's effort to reduce his inshore risks must necessarily concern his choice of landing places. These tended to fall into patterns for the obvious reasons that what was used were those places and times that worked with the least fuss. Summer residences at or near the shore, including docks — vacant from Labor Day until June — were handy. Isolated sandy beaches were fine if local sea conditions generally permitted dories to ferry the liquor ashore and if trucks could get close to pick up the load. Commercial docks were useful in smaller ports if they were removed from residential areas, especially if their owners could be paid to shut an eye. In some places, bagged liquor was floated ashore. In others, it was dropped into shoal water and recovered later, often because either daylight or pursuers were pressing the smugglers. A friend of mine wrote, concerning the Gloucester area, "Some used the trick of sinking bottles of liquor in a sack with a buoy encased in salt, which sank to the bottom of the marsh or beach water, but the salt melted in several days, releasing the buoy to the surface of the water where land-based rumrunners could spot it and pick up the hooch."

His use of the word *hooch,* although it was not uncommon in Prohibition days, is as interesting as the salt device, principally because of its derivation. The word comes from *hoochinoo,* a variety of Hutenuwu, the name of a Tlingit Alaskan Indian tribe. It came to refer to a distilled liquor made by them, the result of a decoction of boiled fern sweetened and mixed with flour. I have a feeling —

based not on scholarly research, but the recollections of the late Captain George Fred Tilton, a bowhead chaser off Point Barrow in his prime — that the nineteenth-century American whaleman introduced the word in the United States.

On then, to consider the classes of rumrunners, an incident of civilian protest against Coast Guard effectiveness, a suggestion that the rumrunner had much in common with a guerrilla fighter, and the revelations of a veteran rumboat engineer.

CHAPTER IX

I N THE BEST TRADITION of smugglers and smuggling, the skippers of the inshore boats buttressed the exceptional abilities of their commands with a mixture of canniness, good seamanship, and intimate knowledge of their watery ways. For the most part, they could also count on the friendship, sympathy, or at least the silence of their neighbors near the beaches.

Sometimes this was paid for. A friend of mine related that his grandfather, who had little money, lived on a small farm that fronted on Buzzards Bay. One night in the early twenties, a man whom he did not know came to the door and said, "We want to use your beach and the road that goes down to it two-three times a week. We'll pay you good money for it. We'll be down there at night and gone by morning. Only thing we ask you is, don't tell anybody about this and don't come down to the beach to see what's going on."

The farmer agreed, and every Saturday morning thereafter there was a sealed white envelope in his mailbox stuffed with more bills than he made in a week of work. He never came face-to-face again with anyone involved in the operation, never knew the identities of any of them. Nights, lying in bed, he heard the big trucks roll by his house on the way to the main road, but, as he told his grandson, "I didn't so much as even peek under the curtain at them. They money was so good and I didn't want to spoil anything."

Thus, the rumrunner possessed those important advantages — including flexibility and informality of operation — that guerrillas have in their conflict with government forces. They were completely at home in their environment; they could make even the weather work for them; they were free to choose their times and places from a fairly wide selection; they could use decoys to draw off the government units, and they could change their minds without notice. In these post-Vietnam years, we know much more about the difficulties of trying to control or wipe out such loosely organized lawlessness that thrives on knowledge of the countryside and empathy of the populace, but in the twenties, Washington had had no such experience. The early reaction of federal officials was an assumption that rumrunning could be halted without great difficulty, or at least confined to such levels as to be discouraging to its principals, given adequate government money, men, and vessels.

On August 24, 1924, Captain Peter J. Sullivan, the officer in charge of the customs marine patrol, reviewed its five-month record; the patrol was "holding the rum front" until congressional appropriations for increased Coast Guard capability bore fruit. Sullivan said that the unit, designed as a stopgap measure had captured 300 rum boats,

154

seized cargoes worth $2,000,000, and brought about fines and penalties of more than $100,000 in the 50 percent of its cases that had come to trial.

The patrol guarded the coastlines of Connecticut, New York, Long Island, and New Jersey. Sullivan said that when it was initiated, liquor was entering Jones Inlet "in a steady stream" and at Montauk, "which was as bad as Atlantic Highlands, conditions were so easy that bootleggers would land, drive the natives off the beach, and then land their contraband in peace. It was a cinch for them."

But he said that when his patrol was given new boats that would go faster than 25 miles an hour, it began to "bottle up" the landing places and reduce the fleet of speedboats carrying booze. Machine guns were issued, with orders to use them, and the patrol used them, he added. "The rumrunners always keep a step ahead of the government in boats," Sullivan said; "don't worry about that. But we're always a step ahead of them with our machine guns; don't forget that, either.

"We will match our men against any unit in the country. They know the game, know what to do, and it's not eight hours with them. They eat on the boats, sleep on the boats; in fact, we can hardly keep 'em off the boats." The result of this vigilance, he suggested, was that the liquor traffic was greatly reduced; at Jones Inlet, he quoted "the bootleggers themselves" as saying that it was about a twentieth of what it had been.

Sullivan noted that the patrol's intimate experience with the "bohees" had taught it some of their rules. A runner usually never lands at the same place twice in a row. He tends to have four or five "drops" and rotates his landings and may even develop a new set after having used them all. A runner never goes out without having decided what drop he will make coming in. Confederates on shore signal whether the coast is clear. Once, flares and bonfires were used; later, flashlights of various colors were introduced and the signals were often in code, Morse or something homemade.

The customs officer divided rumrunners into two classes, fishermen and gangsters. "The fishermen do not put up a fight, but rely on speed to get away. They are good sports and when overhauled, take it with a smile, and say, 'Well, we're caught.' The city men, on the other hand, are hard.

"The axiom of honor among thieves does not hold among the illicit liquor fraternity. A bootlegger's faith and trust in another bootlegger is only as far as he can throw him. Hijacking is on the increase, revealing the instincts of men in the bootleg game to prey upon each other."

Everyone would not have agreed with Captain Sullivan's appraisal of enforcement effectiveness. About three months later, Wallace E. J. Collins, former U.S. attorney in Brooklyn, who was then living in Huntington, Long Island, protested, "I am reliably informed that they are trucking liquor through Long Island as much as they ever did. The other day, 10,000 cases were landed here in Huntington, I am informed, and nothing was done about it. That liquor has now gone on. . . ."

Still, it wasn't always easy. Early in May of 1925, a New Yorker, who chose to remain unidentified, although his account was published, was invited by friends to make a trip to Rum Row for a load of liquor. They ran out to the Row on a foggy night, took aboard 110 cases, and then ran in for the Jersey shore, planning on making it shortly after daybreak. But as it became light, they were spotted by "two gray government boats on the horizon," which, although miles away, started for them.

"Now it's going to cost us exactly $5,000 to get out of this hole," one of the rumrunners remarked.

"The meaning of his words became immediately apparent," the New Yorker wrote,

as the crew started to dump the cargo overboard. Three by three, the cases of modern pirate loot splashed into the water. The

156

speedboat was as innocent as a baby buggy and dancing as light as an egg before the government craft had diminished by one-half the distance between their position at dawn and ours. The curious effect of this maneuver was to bring the government boats down to slow speed and finally to send them off in a wide circle which carried them into the invisible distances beyond the horizon.

The eldest runner explained, "They had their glasses on us. They know exactly what we've done. It would be useless to chase us now."

The effect of the blockade, unless continued until all the runners have been starved into other avenues of earning endeavor, will be not to suppress liquor, but to send its price skyward. Try now to buy your case of Scotch from your Manhattan purveyor for last week's price of $48 per case.

My rumrunner hosts said, "We are neutrals selling ammunition to combatants. We break no law which we recognize. How can we be classed with the hijackers who hold us up on the high seas and, taking cowardly advantage of the fact that we can never complain, sink our ships with all aboard or blackmail us into paying over 50 percent of our profit? Or with the bootleggers who, after they have bought from us, perpetrate all sorts of clandestine crimes such as forgery, bribery, and adulteration of pure products, in the course of their tradings?

"No sir, we are decent American citizens with a taste for high adventure, risking our honest American dollars and our American skins in a peculiarly daring form of commerce."

When we landed, empty-handed, from our expedition, I was led by two glum hosts back to the charming suburban villa in which, ten hours before, we had taken leave of the rumrunner's evening-gowned wife and a flock of nightgowned children in charge of a governess.

The most interesting aspect of this account is that it introduces another kind of rumrunner: the affluent, probably college-educated, professional person who became a skilled boat handler through years of yachting experience and familiar with the coast because of a lifetime of summers spent there. Such runners were much in the minority, especially as the chances of being shot at increased because they could, after all, afford to pay somebody else to take the risk. But they got into the business, not only because they were accustomed to drinking socially, but because of the likelihood of quick and large return on investment and, as the gentleman rumrunner observed, "a taste for high adventure."

On many occasions, even when the smuggler got his liquor to the beach, guided by the shore signals to which Captain Sullivan alluded, he was not home free. On a bleak January night, the commanding officer of the Southampton, Long Island, Coast Guard station was checking a report of a boat close to shore, bound west; it was a few minutes after midnight.

He mustered a crew and started east along the shore, taking pains to keep close to the beach bank so that they would not be seen. Four miles east of the station, they came upon four teams of horses, some trucks, three automobiles, and eighteen men. On the beach, there was a red light in a box; its rays could be seen only from offshore. The armed Coast Guardsmen came out of the darkness quickly; they ordered the eighteen to line up for questioning. Before responding, one of them put out the red light; the Coast Guard skipper made him relight it, and placed a guard over it to make sure that it stayed lighted.

It was one o'clock in the morning. The Coast Guard officer wanted to know what they were doing on the beach at that hour with their vehicles. Looking for wood, they said. He ordered several of his crew to guard them and then waited to see who or what would respond to the red light.

Thirty minutes later, there was the sound of a boat engine; it gradually became louder, and when the craft was approximately in line with the red light and fairly close to shore, its motor was shut off. There were some noises out in the dark, eventually the sounds of oars against tholepins, and in a few minutes, a dory with one man in it nosed up on the beach. In the dory were twelve cases of champagne. The Coast Guard skipper added the doryman to the eighteen under guard, emptied the dory, and rowed off-shore to see where it had come from.

Not far off, he found the motor launch *Del Ray II,* out of Montauk; she had three hundred cases of champagne aboard. The Coast Guardsman arrested her two-man crew and seized the liquor and the boat.

Captain Sullivan, in his appraisal of the customs patrol effort, suggested that because of it "this flourishing traffic was driven elsewhere." It certainly was true that the runners, reacting to beefed-up picket-boat and shore patrols, did not always land their cargoes on the beaches nearest to their markets. In a memorandum to the assistant commissioner of the Bureau of Prohibition, Charles S. Root, chief intelligence officer of the Coast Guard, outlined the pattern of the rum-running operation in and about Providence, Newport, and Tiverton. After naming several boats in the ship-to-shore operation and identifying key figures, he observed,

[They] also sell liquor to New York runners, who go to Providence or Newport and buy their liquor for approximately $40 per case. They are using oil trucks, that is to say, trucks with tanks resembling those used by the Standard Oil Company, for making deliveries in bulk. About one month ago, this office received information to the effect that the British schooner Alpaca was expected to make a landing [in this vicinity], the liquor to be run to New York in furniture moving vans.

Still, most of the boatmen, for obvious reasons, stayed in the areas they knew best and where they were, therefore, best known. The inevitable visibility of the inshore rum fleet by day — and of the rumrunners themselves, often busy about their boats at the dock or in the harbor — was, in a certain sense, incongruous. A Coast Guard officer once equated this situation to that of a hunter who observes a flock of geese within range the day before the gunning season opens — and twenty-four hours later, they are nowhere to be found. The rumrunner, even though known, was pursuable and arrestable only within very strictly defined limits — and he made the duration of these circumstances as brief as possible. So there were no mystery men, no mystery boats; instead, this was a transparent, one-sided game of tag, in which all the principals were known, and all the adversaries well acquainted. For example, on November 20, 1929, Boatswain William W. Worcester, officer in charge of *C.G. 281,* observed fourteen rum-running vessels in a four-hour observation cruise from East Greenwich, Rhode Island, to Fall River, Massachusetts. This was not an unusual day's report. And so well did the patrol boat crews know the characteristics and customary whereabouts of the craft they pursued that they could identify them by elimination, if not by sight.

C.G. 285 was outbound from South Dartmouth, Massachusetts, at four P.M. on New Year's Day, 1930, when a speedboat of the rumrunner type was sighted, headed south out of New Bedford. Boatswain M. D. MacLellan changed his course to intercept the speedboat and signaled the engine room for full speed; he stood off past Dumpling Rocks and sounded his klaxon horn, to which the other craft paid no attention.

In the next half-hour, MacLellan fired four blank warning shots — he was delayed in firing solid shot because the speedboat first got behind a tug with a barge in tow and next placed itself in range with Cuttyhunk Lighthouse — followed by four solid rounds, from his one-pounder. The rumrunner, initially about 1½ miles distant, gradually increased this lead to two miles; at one point, she put on her lights, but maintained course and speed. The patrol boat's first shot landed about a hundred yards ahead of the target and the other three rounds well astern, as the runner put more distance between them. The speedboat disappeared in the distance, headed southwest, and still unidentified by the *285.*

MacLellan returned to New Bedford to see which of the

rum vessels customarily berthed there was absent. He said, "I found the gas screw Good Luck of New Bedford missing. I feel certain this boat was the Good Luck. After talking to the master of the Good Luck the following night, I am certain there is no mistake. The master claims he heard no shots and saw no patrol boat."

In at least one instance — and probably more — Coast Guard interest in a boat adhering to a pattern that made it suspect provoked civilian protest and some high-level communication in Washington between a member of Congress and the Treasury Department. The rum-running interests not only had plenty of money to hire proficient attorneys; they had many friends in Congress who thought Prohibition was a mistake and who had voted against it.

In this specific case, the boat was the *Idle Hour,* ordinarily moored at East Greenwich, Rhode Island; the prelude to what happened to her involves a chase and an informant working for the government who probably was also aiding the rumrunners. The *Idle Hour* was registered out of New York.

Shortly after midnight on July 27, 1929, Boatswain Alexander C. Cornell, skipper of the patrol boat *C.G. 290,* observed the shadow of a boat coming slowly upriver north of Black Point, Sakonnet River, east of Narragansett Bay. The craft was hugging the shore and had no lights showing. The *290* stood down toward the other vessel, which then changed course abruptly and headed downriver. Cornell approached to within 100 yards of the boat, put his searchlight on her, recognized her as the *Idle Hour* and blew his whistle for her to heave to.

Idle Hour turned quickly, resumed her course upriver, put on a burst of speed, and threw out a smokescreen, beginning to zigzag. Cornell fired a blank one-pounder, followed by a machine-gun burst across the bow, as a warning. When the chase arrived at Almy's wharf, the rumrunner turned directly for it; the patrol boat cut in toward the wharf and fired another burst. *Idle Hour* made a sharp left turn and headed upriver — it seemed likely that she had been expected to unload at Almy's.

The smuggler was still roaring through the night at full speed. The *290* scored some direct machine-gun hits on the port side of the after cabin and then lost the quarry in the darkness, close to the west shore of the Sakonnet River. Cornell stood in close to shore, inspecting the beaches and docks on both sides of the river. He placed a guard on Almy's dock and sent a boat up several creeks to see if *Idle Hour* had ducked into one. He checked the docks in Tiverton and spoke with Rhode Island state police at Colburn's Wharf and found they had seen the boat passing up through the bridges.

Cornell concluded that, having been frustrated in her plan to unload at the dock, the rumrunner had headed for her home mooring at East Greenwich. He arrived there at quarter past four in the morning and found her there, tied up. The vessel showed every sign of having been left hurriedly; engines and exhaust pipes were very hot, oilskins and boots lying about were still warm, straw and lint from burlap sacking were strewn over the decks, and the tender was missing. There were two holes in the after cabin, made by machine-gun bullets, and numerous scars on the hull, from the same cause. Apparently the crew of *Idle Hour* had thrown their cargo of liquor overboard during the chase.

The *290* took *Idle Hour* in tow and picked up the crew member of the patrol boat who had been left at Almy's wharf. He said that two closed cars containing six men had remained in the vicinity of the wharf until the Coast Guard vessel stood upriver. They then flew a kite with a red and white lantern attached, and left.

The Coast Guard's firsthand knowledge of *Idle Hour*'s operations was buttressed by information provided by an informer in the southeastern Massachusetts area. This man, initially appointed for thirty-day intervals, primarily provided the names of rum vessels and the times and places of their movements. It is ironic that he is remembered by his contemporaries as having been of invaluable assistance in facilitating these movements; with the help of a private laboratory, he obtained a paint — apparently fluorescent — that responded only to a particular kind of light. With the light and the paint — aided by his own intimate knowledge of the coast — he established markers guiding rumrunners through shoal and rocky water to isolated landing places.

On October 20, 1929, this informer wrote to Captain W. J. Wheeler at Coast Guard headquarters in Washington: "I will do my best and be honest in all my dealing; you can put your trust in me. . . ." Having reported on several rum boats, he added, "The following night, or next night, the Hobo and the Idle Hour came in from offshore without a load, did not connect with the offshore vessel, came in by way of East Passage [of Narragansett Bay], with their running lights lighted, crossed over to West Passage between Conanicut and Prudence Island, and made their moorings at East Greenwich. These two boats came all the way in without being stopped by any patrol boat. The above information I have received from conversation with the suspect rumrunners."

Late in 1929, presumably as a result of the *C.G. 290*'s seizure of *Idle Hour,* the Providence attorney representing her owner wrote to Felix Hebert, U.S. senator for Rhode Island, to protest "the manner in which small boats are being taken away from their moorings and docks and being detained by the Coast Guard, and at great expense to their owners. It is certainly not conducive to orderly administration of law."

The lawyer went on to say that the master of the "gas yacht" *Idle Hour* had had difficulty of this nature, and that it stemmed from orders issued by F. A. Nichols, commander of the Coast Guard section base at Woods Hole.

"I dislike very much to await Mr. Nichols' arrival in this jurisdiction to take advantage of the Rhode Island statutes which would permit me to place him under arrest in an act of trespass," wrote the attorney, "but if those highhanded methods of seizure and detention and later release without any cause are not immediately dropped, I will . . . seek to bring the actions of these men before the federal tribunal."

Senator Hebert forwarded the complaint to the Treasury Department and Seymour Lowman, assistant secretary of the Treasury, responded to the senator. Mr. Lowman pointed out that it was the practice of the *Idle Hour* to go to sea in the afternoon and return in the early hours of the morning and that recently and previously, she had been intercepted and showed "very evident signs of having carried contraband liquor."

The assistant secretary added,

The Idle Hour is not fitted out as a yacht, the crew is not of the type of men usually found on a yacht; she is ill-kept, painted a dirty gray, with portholes covered so that no lights are visible from the outside. The quarters are rough and cramped and the only other compartment except the engine room consists of a large cargo space aft, which we believe is for the purpose of carrying contraband. A chart was found on November 6, 1929, in a locker, showing courses to a point at sea known to be the rendezvous of a rum vessel found on that day.

Mr. Lowman noted that the *Idle Hour* had been boarded several times, had never been detained "longer than necessary," that her owner never had been on the boat when it was boarded, unless he gave an assumed name, "which could be suspicious in itself," and that the boat gave little evidence of being used as a yacht. He concluded in his letter to the senator, "I have to suggest that you consider whether the owner's attorney should not be warned that he take no part in embarrassing the Government in the performance of its rightful duty."

The last chapter in this exchange concerning the "gas yacht" *Idle Hour* occurred on May 31, 1932, at nearly two in the morning. Patrol boat *C.G. 401* was patrolling the Western Passage and sighted flares from another Coast Guard vessel, indicating the need for assistance. Chief Quartermaster Arthur B. Gibbs stood around North Point, Conanicut Island, sighted a speedboat running without lights and pursued it. The speedboat's skipper, maneuvering in his own smokescreen, apparently became confused; he grounded on the island.

Gibbs reported: "At 2:15 A.M., seized the American gas screw yacht Idle Hour of New York, with a cargo of contraband liquor, prisoners having escaped as soon as the vessel grounded . . . she had 297 sacks, 25 cases, and 26 kegs of assorted foreign intoxicating liquors."

In August of 1928, Lieutenant Commander Charles S. Root, Coast Guard Intelligence officer, wrote two memoranda on the rumrunner *Eaglet,* which offer a broad outline of the offshore-inshore boat operation. After naming her owner and crew, Root commented,

This vessel has successfully operated for a year and uses a wharf in the Sakonnet River, just north of the Stone Bridge. This is the "drop" most frequently used. The owner buys his merchandise from a Providence man and "bulls" from the Good Luck, Lucky Strike, and Firelight. He has no storehouse, but sells his goods at the drop.

The Eaglet is capable of carrying 1,400 cases, but the owner usually runs about 800, in order not to hamper the speed of the boat. The Lucky Strike and Good Luck, believed to be owned by a Rhode Island man, have a carrying capacity of about 2,500 cases and have been very successful. They are double-enders and can turn so rapidly that they are easily able to elude destroyers when visibility is low. They usually take station off the coast and are believed to be in constant communication with Providence, where their owner maintains a station which was especially built for this purpose.

[These offshore vessels] also are unloaded by the speedboat C-4809 and another speedboat called the Tramp; with the Eaglet, it is said these boats can unload the seagoing vessels in three nights, if they can make contact before 10 p.m. This early contact is necessary because the offshore vessels owned by this person almost invariably hover east of the longitude of Nantucket."

A former engineer of inshore rum-running vessels, who worked in the area from eastern Rhode Island to Cape Cod, provided some interesting insights into the smuggler's view of the pattern. "The way it looked to me, the attitude of the Coast Guard was, 'If I see you, I'll take you in, but I hope I don't see you.' Nobody liked the law.

"One time the Star landed at Horseneck Beach [Westport, Massachusetts]. People took the crew in and when the Coast Guard and the Feds came around, people said they never saw anybody. Well, trucks had been loading the stuff on the beach and all the natives had some. The stuff was seized and on the way to the Customs House, the guys on the trucks got some. There were one hundred sacks missing by the time they got there. Then they decided to ship the seized liquor to Woods Hole [to Coast Guard Section Base 18] and there were another hundred cases missing by the time they got there. The whole affair ended up in court in Boston and by that time, it had all disappeared from Woods Hole.

"So they had a shakeup at Woods Hole. The new commander's name was Nichols [F. A. Nichols]. The rum-runners called him 'Half-a-Dime.' He came up to Peirce and Kilburn's [a Fairhaven, Massachusetts boatyard] and some of us were waiting there for weather reports. The old chiefs on the six-bitters were there and he said to them in a loud voice, 'Are these the guys we're after?' One of the chiefs said, 'I don't know, sir.' 'What are their names?' Nichols said. So one of the chiefs said, 'Well, that one is named Stuttering Charlie.' So Nichols came over to him and said, 'Is your name Stuttering Charlie?' And the fellow said, 'M-m-m-m-y n-n-n-ame's Ch-Ch-Ch-arlie, b-b-but I'm no g-g-g-goddam Ch-Ch-Chinaman.' Another fellow said his name was Popeye; he didn't like the name but that's what we called him and his eyes looked it. When Nichols came to me, I said my name was Charlie Noble. [Author's note: Charlie Noble is the sailor's term for the galley smokestack.] Nichols said to the chief, 'You believe that?' and the chief said, 'Oh sure, he's got a cousin on one of these boats named Collision Bulkhead.' So Nichols got disgusted finally and walked off.

"I was on the *Wanderer*. She had a beautiful engine and exhaust system. Even at twelve hundred revolutions, you could stand on the dock and never know that engine was running. She had a four-inch exhaust and a little silencer. One time a man came down from the factory that built the engine and listened to her and I said to him, 'How come it works so well, so quietly?' and he said, 'Everything, including the curves in the exhaust pipe, is just right.' She was so quiet that one night I went up the Sakonnet River and I saw a little light go on; it was a man in the pilothouse of a Coast Guard patrol boat lighting a cigarette, and he never heard us.

"One time we were almost unloaded and somebody yelled, 'The Feds!' I started the engine and went out so quietly that nobody on the beach even knew I was out there. I still had about a hundred fifty to two hundred cases of Double Eagle in tin cans and I dumped it in the rocks on the starboard hand; there's a reef there, and we went after it in small boats on the full of the moon. They never looked for us on the full of the moon; we sailed twelve days a month on the dark of the moon.

"This young fellow who hadn't been in the business very long came to me and he said, 'Those federal men are crazy. One of them was chasing me and firing a pistol and he was yelling, "Stop or I'll shoot you!" So I stopped and he came up to me and kicked me in the ass and said, "What did you stop running for?" So I ran again and he yelled, "Stop or I'll shoot!" What in hell is that all about?'

"So I said to him, 'If he caught you, you would go to

court. If you went to court, he would have to testify. His courtroom time is taken out of his annual leave time. He didn't want to lose leave time, so he didn't want to catch you.'

"We went into Horseneck one time and there was a schooner yacht there. They put a flashlight on us, so we yelled, 'Put out the damned light!' and they did. When we got in to the beach, I threw four cases into the dory and went alongside them. 'What do you want?' somebody aboard yelled, kind of scared. 'All we want you to do is be quiet,' I said. This fellow said, 'We put the light on you because we were afraid you'd run us down.' I said, 'We saw you long before you saw us.' I gave them the booze and said, 'Stay quiet. Don't put on any lights and don't drink the booze until we go. Then you can make as much noise as you want to.'

"The way we worked it was that if it was a thick night and you couldn't find the regular drop, you always had an emergency. One time we went into the Sakonnet River; we were late getting in and a man in a dory came out and said, 'The Feds are on the beach.' So we went back to the emergency drop and by the time we got the stuff off, it was five-thirty to six A.M., so the boss said to one of the fellows, 'Take my car and go up the road to where you see a mailbox.' He described it; it had a different kind of standard, and he said, 'That's where the chief of police lives. Tell him to get his men down here and get this stuff off the beach before the Coast Guards see it.'

"It was cold weather one time and I called P. and K. [the Peirce and Kilburn boatyard] to have them start the generator to get my batteries charged. They sent a kid from the machine shop and he found that the sea intake in the generator had iced up, so he got a blowtorch down in there to thaw it out. Well he had a fire going in that boat in no time and there were two six-hundred-eighty-gallon tanks full of gas in there. So the gang on the dock threw a dozen sealed balls of tet [carbon tetrachloride] down in there and smashed them and closed all the hatches and it put the fire out, but I couldn't use the boat that night.

"So the boss said, 'Go on the beach and work on the Cape.' There was an Italian fellow there with a string of cottages. We used to pay rent on the cottages for a whole winter. The gang would go down there in the afternoon and the lady there would serve us Italian food. That was the first time I ever had spaghetti and I cut it up with a knife and fork and she got mad.

"When it got to be six P.M., the boss said, 'Want to go for a ride?' So I said, 'Sure,' and we went down back roads and through the dunes and marsh and came to a farmhouse, and the boss knocked at the door. The farmer, his son, and his wife were eating dinner. The boss said, 'We want to use your barn tonight.' The farmer said, 'What for?' 'Never mind,' said the boss, 'we just want to use it.'

" 'You're a bunch of them damned rumrunners and bootleggers,' the farmer said, 'and you're not using my barn.'

"So the boss put a hundred-dollar bill on the kitchen table and said, 'We're using your barn.' And we walked out. I thought it was kind of high-handed.

"Well, about seven-thirty, the phone rang where we were and the operator told us the farmer had called the Coast Guard, the state cops, the local police, and the Feds. So about ten P.M., we got this kid to get his girlfriend and he drove with her right into the farm yard and there were all these police and they had pistols and made them get out with their hands up. 'What are you doing here?' they said. The kid said, 'I go to school with the fellow that lives here. I was almost out of gas and if I don't get my girl home by 11 o'clock, we'll both get killed, so I wanted to get some gas here.'

"The farmer came out; he had a pump in the barn and he said, 'It's O.K., I know this young fellow,' and he gave him a can of gas. So the young fellow came back to report to us and he said, 'Boy, they've got pistols and machine guns and shotguns and they're in the house, in the chicken coops, in the barn and under the barn; they're all over, and millions of them.'

"So we just had the big boat [the offshore vessel] come right in to the town dock, knowing that all the cops were on the farm, and we unloaded right there into the trucks, and off to Boston.

"One fellow in the business had a farm in Rhode Island. He had a couple living there to take care of the place and when he wanted to use it, they would go away for a little while. In back, he had a small place of his own that was beautiful; it was like an office, but it had a lounge, and a shower, and the whole works. He had a Doberman pinscher named Duchess and if a stranger came around, she bared her teeth and wouldn't leave him alone until her owner hollered 'O.K.'

"I was working on the beach because my boat was being worked on and when we finished there, I was hot and my mouth was full of burlap shavings, so I said to him, 'I'm going up to the house,' his place, that is. So I went up to the house; I walked right in and Duchess was on the divan. She bared her teeth, but I sat down quietly and started to read a book. Then, in a little, I went to take a shower. She let me get in the shower but then she stood in front of it and every time I tried to get out, she would come at me. I stood in that shower, naked, cold, and shivering — I put the hot water on every so often — and without cigarettes, for an hour and three-quarters until the boss came and got her to let me out.

"At the farm, they backed the trucks right up to the farmhouse. He had a special key and lock and the whole floor in the kitchen raised up about four feet on hydraulic jacks. Then we had dump trucks with chutes at the back and we would slide the stuff right down underneath the floor and there were guys down underneath there stacking it as fast as it came down. They would take it out of there in trucks when the moon was full; when the moon was full, they never stopped us.

" 'What's your profession?' some people would say to me sometimes and I said, 'Interior decorator.' One lawyer said that we could put rum-running right on our income tax. He said that anything you put on the return can't be used against you, but I figured that they would at least keep an eye on me if I put that, so I never did.

"Rum Row for us was about twenty miles out. Generally, the guy who owned our boat owned the outside boat, too — that was the *Elizabeth H.*, skippered by a fellow we called The Cowboy. It took us two hours to two and a half to load; the boats carried one thousand to three thousand cases — that is, burlap sacks, twelve bottles to a sack. They used to send the stuff in wood to St. Pierre Miquelon; there it was put in big warehouses and they had mountains of broken-up cases. Considering wages for the crew and what they paid for it, it cost them fourteen dollars a case to bring the stuff down.

"I never saw any money change hands out there. We handled the stuff sack by sack. In the beginning, they would smash up ten to fifteen cases every trip, tossing it aboard us, but after a while, they used to throw a square of air mattress down to us to put on the deck. Two boats worked our outside boat; one would get three trips and the other two, with the average load. The *Tossup* was a rough-weather boat. She was heavy, built like a fisherman, and if the weather was bad, she got all five trips. When the Coast Guard picket boats were called in because the weather was so bad, we'd go out.

"We took some hellish beatings, believe me. One time, we were lying alongside loading and she banged so that she split the deck and water was leaking down on the engine. I had to put canvas over the engine to keep it dry. If you had a diesel, you didn't have to do it, but with a gasoline engine if we were getting water down on it, we used to squirt pyrene fluid on the engine to keep it dry. One time, my skipper was below cleaning up some oil mess with a can of gasoline, and he had an epileptic attack. The gasoline got on the hot engine and we had a fire in a second. We always carried plenty of fire-extinguishing equipment and we got it out right away and I got a clothespin in his mouth and pretty soon he was all right.

"For pay, the skipper got a dollar a case. As engineer, I got thirty-five cents a case, plus thirty-five dollars a week. I was the only one paid a regular wage because it was my job to keep the boat in shape ready to go, tuned up and all that. We'd average three hundred to four hundred dollars a night. It took us a couple of hours to come in and it was then that you were on your toes the most.

"The boss was particular on two things and the first was, no guns aboard. The boss said, 'Don't put up any fuss. Just go along with them if you get caught.' The worst you got was a small fine and two years' probation. One guy got caught and was out at eleven o'clock in the morning; the next night, he got caught again and all they did was give him another year's probation. If a boat was caught, the government would auction it off and everybody went to the auction, having already decided on a price. When it got close to the price, if there was anybody from outside bidding on it, a rummy would step up to him and tell him not to bid on it. So the owner would get his boat back at a reasonable figure."

"The rummies scared off the outside bidders?" I asked. He nodded.

"The other thing the boss was particular about," he continued, "was don't bring anything else in but liquor. But one time we were alongside the outside boat and The Cowboy had some French perfume. It was about Christmas time and he wanted to send some to the boss's customers. So The Cowboy tossed a sack of perfume to us; the trouble was, it was rough out there — the sack hit a stay, shot down below, landed on the galley stove and broke. The skipper said, 'Well, they may not see us coming, but they can smell us.'

"We went in, unloaded the booze, and when we were going into the harbor, the picket boat came alongside and the Coast Guard chief said, 'I'll see you after I check a couple of other boats.' So we tied up and were down below, shaving and cleaning up and getting ready to go ashore, when he came aboard. The chief went into the forecastle, about up to his waist in the hatchway, then he smelled and stopped, and went back up. Then he waved his hanky and said in a soprano voice, 'Boys, where have you been?'

"Another time, it was getting to be Christmas and we were thinking about presents. The boss said, 'If you want a case to give away, just ask me, but don't leave any on the boat.' I had twelve bottles of Double Eagle on top of the engine under a piece of canvas. A Coast Guardsman came aboard and he put his hand right on the engine. My heart thumped a little, but he never found it.

"Some Coast Guardsmen had a hand out every time we went out. There was one fellow who was skipper of a picket boat and he'd come aboard and say to our skipper, 'What's the weather going to be tomorrow?' and our skipper would maybe say, 'The wind is going around to the east'ard and blow like hell.' So the Coast Gaurdsman would say, 'Then I'm going into Nantucket and lay up there a while.' Or maybe our skipper would say it would go into the nor'west and blow and the Coast Guardsman would say, 'Well, I'll go into Hyannis and get up under the lee.' That way, we could tell him where we didn't want him to be the next day, and then our skipper would mail him two hundred or three hundred dollars in an envelope. And the telephone operator got hers, too, the same way.

"One time we were coming in and I had been in the hold on my knees for a couple of hours and I was full of burlap shavings. I went to get a drink of water and somebody had forgotten to fill our water tank. Now I can't drink liquor; it makes me sick right away. So I opened a bottle out of the load, French champagne. I rinsed my mouth and spit it out. This other fellow said to me, 'They're paying fifty dollars a bottle for that ashore and you're using it for a mouthwash.' I said, 'You can have what's left in the bottle for five dollars.'

"Most of our landings were in the Sakonnet River, at Horseneck and down the Cape. If you got chased, the Old Stone Bridge operator [in the Sakonnet River] would open it in a hurry if you showed a light. Then he would close it and get out of there. The Coast Guard would come up and blow and blow and nothing would happen. Then they'd have to call him at his house and he would come down, looking all sleepy-eyed, and finally he would open it and we would be long gone by then, but one time he closed the bridge a little too quick and took a fellow's pilothouse off.

"At Horseneck, there was no dock but a bunch of six-teen-foot dories would come out; a dory can carry quite a lot and they would take it in to the beach and the trucks were right there. There were a couple of fellows who were hijackers; they had an open Cadillac touring car. Once in a while, they would tear down to the beach with their lights on; everybody on the beach would think it was the Feds and run. These fellows had taken the back seat out of their car; they would load the back full of booze and take off. Well, they came down one time and one of our people working on the beach had brought his rifle. When they yelled, 'You better give up!' instead of running, he shot both their headlights out and then he fired another shot at the front seat. We found out that third shot went right through one side and out the other and there was blood on the car seat. We figured that he had just nicked their behinds. They kind of laid off after that.

"Down on the Cape where we went, there was a huge estate. You went in a narrow opening coming in from the sea; there was always a little bar there that you hit, but you gun the engine and keeping going and the swell will lift you a little, and you can hop over it. Then there was a quick left turn and right there was a sea plane hangar. We went in there one night and I bet there were six thousand cases there from boats unloading. There were four boats and one of them was a big local one.

"The Coast Guard couldn't get in there because of the shoal water and there were trees between us and the ocean so you couldn't see anything going on. In winter, we could unload into the hangar; there was nobody there but the caretaker. All he did, if he heard trucks, was to roll over and go to sleep because he knew we wouldn't damage anything and he got a dollar a case. When the moon was full, they would get trucks and roll the stuff to Boston.

"One trip, we just couldn't go alongside [the offshore vessel] it was so rough. We headed for Provincetown and off Peaked Hill Bar, there was a four-stacker [Coast Guard destroyer] in a hurry. I don't know where he was going or why but he was deck under and diving into it, more like a submarine than a ship. He put his lights on us, but he didn't stop. We had no charts for Provincetown but we went in there from memory and the gale kept us in there for from four days to a week.

"One time, a four-stacker boarded us. I had been in Washington visiting my brother-in-law. Without thinking, I had put a pencil of his in my pocket. The four-piper lieutenant came over to us in a dory and on the way, he dropped his pencil overboard.

" 'What's your name?' he asked all of us. He had a seaman paw through the coal in the stove locker; he went through the clothes locker, the books. We had a new chart aboard and he held it up to the light to look for divider marks which might show whether the boat had been in a location known as a Rum Row contact point. But our skipper was one ahead of him; he had pricked it full of divider marks all over.

"Then I loaned the lieutenant my pencil to replace his

and just before he left us, he looked at it and saw that it was marked 'U.S. Navy Department,' because my brother-in-law was a chief naval architect for years. The lieutenant said to me, 'How come?' I shook my head quickly as if to indicate that mum's the word. He never said anything more and I assume he thought that I was a government undercover agent.

"When we didn't go into New Bedford, we often went into Newport. There was a duty-stricken [Coast Guard] chief there and he always went into the engine room and smelled and tasted the bilge water there. One time, I said, 'Why do you do that?' and he said, 'Well, there's always certain breakage when you load liquor and I can taste the liquor in the water.' I said, 'Well, I'm locked up here half the night running the engines and I piss in there.' He never tasted our bilge water again.

"Those engines were beautiful; they were aircraft engines, Liberty V-12s. We bought them brand-new from federal government surplus for one hundred dollars an engine, with the cosmolene on them and still in the crates. Gar Wood and Capitol used to convert them to marine use.

"There was a fellow in New Bedford who was a tool and die maker. He had a shop in his backyard as a hobby and he wouldn't bother with regular jobs, but he would take in one that was a real puzzler. He could turn stainless steel that you would swear was mirror-plated. So what we wanted was two engines driving to one gear box and a shaft from the gearbox to the propeller, so that you could run either engine singly or both together. We asked him if he could do it and he said, 'Come back and see me in a week.'

"When we went back, he had sketches on brown wrapping paper all over the place and he said, 'I think we can do it.' He made the cases and the whole works of stainless steel and they ran perfect. You figure four engines and two shafts, souped-up Liberties of seven hundred horsepower each, that's twenty-eight hundred horsepower in a fifty- or sixty-foot boat."

"Would she do thirty knots?" I asked.

He grinned. "Better than that. And I'll tell you something. In the early forties, I was piloting ships into Argentina [Newfoundland], where they had an Air Force and an Army base. There was a Coast Guard patrol boat there checking all the traffic and the fellow on the bridge remembered me from rum-running days and he hollered, 'Hey, is that you?' and I said, 'Sure is.' After I got in, I got a boat and went over to see him. We talked some and he said, 'You know those gear boxes? [Author's note: They were installed on the rumrunner *Maybe,* which evidently was seized by the government at some point.] We took them all apart and the government tried for three-four years to duplicate them, but they have never yet made one work.' "

At one point during the interview, the former rum-runner was discussing an especially competent skipper in the inshore rum fleet who got into trouble through mischance. He said, "He went out and the Coast Guard started chasing him. His regular engineer wasn't aboard and the new engineer got scared and was laying between the two engines because he was afraid of getting shot. So when the skipper rang for stop, in response to the Coast Guard order, nothing happened and the Coast Guard thought they were trying to get away and opened fire on them. After that time, they always put a shutdown on the bridge of the rum boats so you could control it from topside."

He was not able to identify the boat involved but it seems very likely that it was the *Lassgehen,* out of New Bedford, whose seizure in that instance not only provided drama and tragedy, but resulted in a singular court case.

At midnight on September 4, 1931, the fifty-one-foot *Lassgehen,* with a load of liquor aboard, was running without lights east of Kettle Island, outside Gloucester, Massachusetts.

Chief Boatswain's Mate Roy Fitzgerald, skipper of the patrol boat *C.G. 2394,* heard *Lassgehen*'s engines and stood southeast to intercept her. Six minutes later, he sighted her, turned his searchlight on her and saw sacks of liquor piled on her decks. Fitzgerald said, "I turned the searchlight on the Coast Guard ensign and blew the horn continuously. There was no one visible on deck.

"She turned to port, increased speed, began zigzagging and threw out a heavy screen of smoke. After chasing her for five minutes with searchlight on and horn going, I fired two single shots, well clear, from the Thompson machine gun. I then shifted over to automatic firing and let go five bursts of about three shots each, well clear. Then I fired two bursts at her stern and while I was firing at the stern in order to disable the steering gear, she suddenly swung around to starboard. We being on her starboard quarter at the time, owing to the heavy smoke screen which the speedboat was throwing, we couldn't see her in time and a burst raked her broadside. She then stopped and we came alongside."

The crew of *Lassgehen* lifted a man out of the engine room and one of them said, "He's shot." The wounded man, who eventually died of his injuries, was taken aboard the patrol boat; Fitzgerald put a prize crew aboard *Lassgehen* and the two craft started for Gloucester in company. Aboard the rumrunner, Boatswain's Mate 1st Class William P. Kelley recalled,

We were proceeding at full speed to Base 7, being closely followed by C.G. 2394. I was standing just abaft the pilothouse and was armed with a machine gun. The prisoners were ordered to remain on the Lassgehen's after deck.

They huddled in consultation and then said that the engineer on watch below should be relieved. I told them the motors were running all right and to stay where they were. They very gradually moved forward and although I threatened them, they continued forward until three of them obscured the entrance to the engine room. Under the cover of these three men, a fourth, unseen by me, dropped into the engine room and set fire to that compartment. This man immediately came on deck and almost immediately, a sheet of flame shot from the engine room hatch.

I signaled the C.G. 2394, which came alongside and took off the prisoners. Two of us put over the Lassgehen's dory and, from the deck load, placed several sacks of liquor in it for evidence. We then let the dory drop astern on a long painter.

We shot all available fire-extinguishing liquid into her engine room through a hole which we cut in the forward engine room deckhouse.

The master of the Lassgehen said that he did not know exactly how much liquor was aboard, but estimated the cargo to be five hundred or six hundred sacks. The deckload was piled helterskelter, excepting around the pilothouse, where a barricade for protection against machine-gun fire was carefully stacked. At the time of this writing, 0530, September 5, fire occasionally smolders in the engine room, although it has been well drenched. The boat is leaking considerably, necessitating constant pumping. . . . A thorough investigation will be made at the earliest opportunity, particularly into the nature of the smokescreen device and any possible chemicals. . . .

Three items in reports of the incident filed by F. W. Brown, commander of Section Base 7 at Gloucester, are of special interest. On September 5, Brown noted that the first name of the *Lassgehen*'s dead crew member was Joseph and that another crew member, whose name he was unsure of, "was, and is, at the time of this writing, still dead drunk."

On September 9, Brown reported to the U.S. district attorney in Boston, "The smokescreen which the master of the Lassgehen admits was used, caused William F. Kelly, boatswain's mate 1st class violent illness and necessitated his being rushed to the hospital, where oxygen treatment was resorted to in order to save his life. Another member of the crew of the C.G. 2394, Ralph O. McKie, boatswain's mate 2d class, was likewise affected to a lesser degree."

Compare Brown's statements of September 5 with this direct quotation from the recollections of the former rum-runner whom I interviewed: "The Coast Guard put aboard a prize crew and they started taking her in. The skipper [of the rum boat] said, 'You mind if I have a drink?' and they said no. So he took a drink out of a bottle and he said, 'Well, Joe, boy, here's a drink for you and a drink for me.' And he kept this up and was pretty high by the time they got to Gloucester.

"So they were marching him to the brig and they turned left and he turned right or failed to make a turn and found himself out on the street. There was a Coast Guardsman there, so he asked him for a match and the Coast Guardsman said, 'Get out of here, you drunken bum.' So he did.

"Now if he had been sober, he would have gotten on a bus, but because he wasn't, he kept wandering around the streets until he found himself back at the Coast Guard base and they said, 'We've been looking for you' and locked him up."

Brown's report of September 9 was the first step in proceedings that, in November, 1932, resulted in a U.S. District Court judge's finding the engineer of the *Lassgehen* guilty of "interference with Coast Guards by means of a smokescreen." The Associated Press reported that the case was believed to be the first of its kind ever tried in the United States. In his finding, Judge James M. Lowell said,

The appellant appears to have been the engineer of the Lassgehen and to have put in action her apparatus for making the smoke screen.

It is argued in his behalf that the statute covers only forcible interference and that the smoke screen, which was only an obscuring device, did not amount to "forcible interference." The court found that if the smoke screen had no effect except to obscure the Lassgehen, no crime was being committed by it. According to the government's evidence, however, the effect of the smoke screen, when breathed, was to make the helmsman of the cutter sufficiently ill to incapacitate him from performing his duties.

We have no doubt that this was a violation of the statute, without regard as to whether that result was or was not intended. Force may be chemical, as well as physical. Poison gas may be as deadly as a bullet.

The defendant contended that Kelly's illness was a mere pretense, a smoke screen to divert attention from the unfortunate killing of the man on the Lassgehen. The trial judge took no such view of the evidence. He submitted the point to the jury with a strong intimation of his opinion about it. They were, however, clearly and strongly cautioned not to accept his views about facts unless they agreed with him. If he thought the defendant's contentions plainly unmeritorious, he was certainly within his right and probably within his duty to say so. . . . It is perfectly clear that the defendant knew his boat was being chased and that he used the smoke-making apparatus in an effort to help her escape. . . . The judgment of the district court is affirmed.

CHAPTER X

THE RUMRUNNERS had better and faster boats than their government pursuers, in many instances, but one advantage that the Coast Guard did have was the ability to intercept and decode the smugglers' radio transmissions. This radio traffic was very important to the rum vessel, its shore contacts, and the inshore craft that unloaded it; by this means, offshore contact points were established, times of rendezvous agreed upon, identities of customers, agents, and supercargoes confirmed, orders placed, warnings transmitted, and deals consummated.

Mostly, the rumrunner codes were relatively simple, of necessity, because the unskilled had to be able to handle them. But even the more difficult systems eventually were broken by Coast Guard Intelligence, which thus played a major role in keeping government units informed of the smugglers' plans and movements. Both Intelligence personnel and government agents monitored the traffic.

For example, in January, 1925, Agent 2002 advised that "the I'm Alone was located on Stellwagen Bank yesterday. This is about fifteen miles due north of Provincetown, on the tip end of Cape Cod. It looks as though the Copeman got rid of 20,000 cases on her first arrival, but so far has failed to sell the 7,000 with which she arrived at Halifax a few days ago. If you are able to tap St. Pierre, you may get something good."

The same agent on January 3, 1926, informed that he was "in receipt of advices that between 6 and 7 P.M., almost daily radio orders are broadcast to smugglers in the Long Island Sound vicinity. That at 8 P.M., December 27, the following radio message in Morse [sharp on 455 meters] was heard: 'Three boats will land at Fishers Island, one boat will land four miles east of Eastern Point.'

"At 9 P.M., the following radio phone was heard: 'WIBA calling MLO.' The source of the information in this memorandum is a reliable man at New London, where this message was intercepted. He also pointed out that Station WIBA is at Madison, Wisconsin, indicating bootleg use of that call letter."

I daresay that until this moment, neither the Coast Guard nor the customs agents were aware that one of the rumrunners' shore-based operators with whom they had to contend was a fourteen-year-old boy. He is now in his sixties and consented to be interviewed on the subject for the first time in his life; during all the intervening years he had remained silent because, he says, "We always had a code. Nothing said. And I'm not going to give you any names, because there are people still around."

"How did you happen to get into the business at fourteen?" I asked him.

"Well, my family was poor, but ever since I was a kid, I was interested in electricity and electronics. One time they had a big fire at the telephone company and they threw a lot of stuff into the city dump. I went there and picked up dry cells and bulbs and some other stuff and I used to fool around with it. I knew some ham station operators and I used to play around with this business.

"My brother was a mason. He used to go to Nantucket winters when things on the mainland got slack and do chimneys and plastering. When I was fourteen, my mother asked him to take me down there to see if I couldn't get a job, too. I went to the cranberry bogs on a Sunday; he wanted me to work there, but I didn't want to. He said, 'If you don't find a job in a few days, you'll have to go home.' I said, 'I'll get by somehow!'

"I got a job washing dishes in a tearoom, for my meals. The natives used to come in there for coffee. This day, they had a midget radio going and there was interference from code. There was a state trooper who was friendly with the girl whose father ran the place; he was there, and they were talking about the station interference. Somebody said it was probably the Coast Guard and maybe there was a boat in trouble. There weren't many stations operating in those days, so it almost had to be the Coast Guard. I was sitting there, taking down the code, just for the fun of it, and I said to them, 'It's the Nantucket Coast Guard all right, but they're talking to Boston headquarters about what provisions they want.'

"The state cop, the girl, and a couple of other guys who were in the place just looked at me. Nobody said anything. But a little later, the girl says, 'My father wants to see you.' I went to see him and he asked me if I knew anything about riding horses. Well, I used to go to a farm on the mainland and help take care of the horses and I took a few out riding, so I said yes. So I was set up in a little building, and her father said to me, 'You'll get your meals and you don't have to do any more dishes.'

"Pretty soon after that, they took me to a place where there was a barn; it had a room in it, full of radio equipment, and it was good equipment. They said, 'We'll protect you. Nobody needs to know.' It was about a twelve-by-ten room that had been used originally for storing ice; it was all insulated and shielded. Sets then were not shielded by crystal control; it was raw AC. Those few that had receivers on the island — mostly home battery jobs — my interference raised hell with. Everybody needs a frequency now but then, there wasn't much of that. If you heard anything, the number one chance was that it would be the Coast Guard or a steamer.

"I'd go in there each day from five P.M. to six P.M. I'd call the mother ship and everything would come back in a prefix of R, meaning Roger, O.K. We had to be notified by ten each night in order to get clear by daylight. Unless things got hot in a certain section, they'd go along with the mother ship's positions. If any changes were made at either end, I was there. The mother ship would send me the location.

"Every night at ten, the fog rolled in; whichever way the wind was blowing determined the location of the landing. If things got hot ashore or if the wind was wrong for the mother ship — you could always tell her signal — we'd change locations. They made landings every night if conditions were right; always on the south side, because the prevailing wind was southwest and would bring the stuff in. I never saw a landing, but I understood they threaded the stuff on a line, floated it, lashed together, and hauled it in.

"The guys took good care of me. My bosses were off-islanders, from Boston. If you didn't blab and behaved yourself, if they took you under their wing, they'd protect you. I sent so much money home — twice a week, I sent money orders home — that my mother got worried. She wrote, 'You must be doing something wrong.' My brother wrote to my mother about me; he said, 'I don't know what he's doing, but he's making a lot more money than I am.'

"I had a good life, the best of everything and worked

only one hour a day. The three guys who took care of me had their tommy guns with them all the time; they were floating with money. They used to travel in a limousine and at Tom Nevers Head, they had a two-motor airplane. Their girlfriends flew in from out of town.

"Daytimes, I used to go to the Siasconset dump. There was a lot of good stuff there. Summer people even used to run their cars into the dump and leave them there when they went home for the winter. There was a Moon car, from Oregon, that had been left in the dump. The spotlight worked and the engine would run. A friend of mine on the mainland wanted the tires, so I went to the dump, and I was sitting in the car. The fellow who ran the dump came out of his building and chased me away.

"The three guys who took care of me found out about it and they took me back to the dump. The place was fenced in with wire. They put tin cans on the fence posts and then they took out their tommy guns and filled those cans full of holes. The dump guy came out of his building. There were some thirty-gallon copper water boilers there; they were valuable and I suppose the poor dump guy was saving them for somebody. They shot those boilers full of holes. Then they said to the dump guy, 'This boy can come here anytime he wants to. You get back in your shack or we'll drill you.' And he said, 'Yessir, sure, O.K.' He didn't dare complain to the police. I took the tires off the Moon and it cost me so much to ship them to the mainland that it almost wasn't worth it.

"I came to fear those three guys. I stayed clear of them. They'd say, 'You want to take a ride?' three fellows and three girls, and I wouldn't bother with them. I'd walk off. I said to myself, 'I've gotten into this thing, I don't know how to get out.' One night, they asked me if I wanted to take a ride. My only fear was that I would get in trouble. They took me to the beach at Siasconset about ten at night and it was loaded with people. Some were nude. Nantucket was three to four years ahead in styles. They had rich people and movie actresses there. On the island was the first time I ever saw a woman without stockings.

"The three guys had to get rid of the people because they wanted to land liquor there that night. They ran around the beach, knocking over umbrellas, hollering, and swearing. I said afterward, 'That was quite a thing you did,' and one of them said, 'We didn't want to use any guns.'

"The officials knew both sides of it, what we were doing and what our competitors were doing; they kept their noses clean. An outfit from New Bedford was competing with us, trying to get into Nantucket. My people hijacked the other people's liquor; they said, 'We'll do a job on them.' Shortly after, one of our people said to me, 'We've had some trouble. We're going to a spot where some stuff is hidden. A hundred thousand dollars' worth of stuff that's been hijacked.' So we went by it and I didn't really see anything.

"A little later, I went into a store and ordered a milk shake. I noticed the guy behind the counter, who ordinarily was friendly, was very cold to me. There was a swinging curtain at the back and suddenly, I saw two heads behind it, half sticking out. I left in a hurry, because I was scared.

"I went to the tearoom and told the girl. She said, 'I'll get my father,' and when he came, he said to me, 'Stay out of sight,' because somebody had started a rumor that I was the only person who knew where the stuff was. My people said to me, 'Take off on the next steamer; go to the mainland and stay there. You'll get a check every week until it cools off.' For six months after I left, I was drawing a salary."

In response to the question of how much money he was paid, he just smiled. "I was down there for two years and it was big money for that time," he said.

"Four-five months later, I was standing at a bank, waiting for a streetcar. A fellow went by and I recognized him. He came back, headed for me, and shook my hand.

187

He said, 'The fellows want to thank you. Even though you were on the opposite side, you didn't blab. Anytime you want a job on the island, there is one.'

"I found out afterward they sent him to the mainland to shake my hand and straighten things out. He said to me, 'We found out you had nothing to do with it.' When he sees me now, he shakes my hand and says something about the 'good old days.' There is a code of ethics. You know; the skippers of the boat know you, but you never say anything. Not even now, you don't, after all this time."

The fact that the rumrunners occasionally changed their codes suggests that they gave some thought to the possibility that the Coast Guard might be monitoring their radio traffic and might eventually succeed in reading it. But considering how important radio was to them, they were remarkably careless or naïve about this threat to their operation and even about the likelihood that the government eventually would locate their shore stations if they did not move them from time to time.

In retrospect, it appears that the smugglers were unaware of the priority that Coast Guard Intelligence placed upon this aspect of rum-running, did not know with what vigilance the radio messages were monitored, and greatly underestimated the government's ability to decode them. At one point, the Boston office of the Bureau of Prohibition forwarded to the Coast Guard for analysis copies of intercepted traffic between illegal shore stations and offshore liquor carriers.

The government cryptanalyst recognized and categorized the material immediately; the Coast Guard had been monitoring and reading transmissions from the same sources for months. Stations FKS and GNE were in the vicinity of Boston, and they worked with the Canadian rumrunners *Bambi* and *South Wind,* which generally operated off Cape Cod. Its code was private, arbitrary, and elementary; the traffic was principally times and places for making contact with shore boats, reporting weather conditions and the activities of Coast Guard vessels.

Station ZA was located on the New Jersey coast, near Red Bank, and it operated with the offshore vessels *Temiscouda* and *Upsalowitch*. A three-letter code, easily breakable, was used.

Group ABC consisted of two shore stations, both in the neighborhood of Boston, and three deep-water boats, *Bambi, Madalyne Webb,* alias *Shogomoc,* and the *Mudathalapadu.* The cryptanalyst added, "Until comparatively recently, the traffic of this group was being read with facility, but within the past few weeks, a new three-letter code has been introduced and solution of this code of necessity must await an accumulation of sufficient traffic."

The following are fragments of intercepted rumrunner radio traffic during the last nine days of December, 1930:

I am being picketed by a 125-footer and I cannot get clear.

Be ready tomorrow 40 miles south from Montauk lighthouse to meet Josephine K. to take his load. Will meet you at 7 a.m. Further instructions later.

List off Josephine K. gin 908, second-grade scotch 908; 907 extra special scotch, 7 brandy, 81 champagne, 702 pints or tens of rye, 231 pints of rye, 907 rye.

Well OM can't make it this time. We have new station and have to see ABT it. Can't leave here until it's finished. Carpenters aren't finished yet and can't leave new OPR HR WEN IM AWAY. Was asking other night ABT it. Was asking him ABT U coming HR. BT HE says OK except he doesn't want YR wife. He doesn't trust women much, for that reason he wouldn't have U HR. When you see him talk to him ABT it ANIWA. Don't tell him what I SED. If he SES anything ABT UR wife tell him U WD put her in apartment and she WUDNT HV to NO what was taking place at all.

The value to the Coast Guard of being able to decipher the rumrunner traffic not only allowed them to anticipate the smugglers' movements, but on occasion revealed a new method of getting liquor ashore.

Late in December, 1930, Lieutenant (JG) Charles L. Duke reported to his superiors from Cape May, New Jersey, "Just thought you might possibly be interested in some information I picked up last night from a Prohibition special agent. He claims that the president of the —— Oil Company called him up and told him that some of his coastwise tankers were running liquor.

"The system is that the boat leaves Marcus Hook, Pennsylvania and gets its liquor offshore and then proceeds to Bridgeport, Connecticut, and repeats operations there in inverse order, returning. We will keep a good lookout here."

Initially, Coast Guard officials — less interested in possible smuggling by coastwise steamers than they were in the operations of offshore foreign rumrunners and their American contact boats — did not respond enthusiastically to Duke's letter. But an intercepted radio message decoded at about the same time buttressed the report with fact:

Go to 10 miles SE by E from North End lightship to meet a tanker that will be under way with full running lights. Will meet you at 2 A.M. Polarine type with bow submerged. When you come alongside be very careful not to run on top of him. When you meet tanker tell George that Jack will meet him at Jackknife Bridge, Newark Bay, with money and take off load. Ask George what time Sunday he can be at Jackknife Bridge. Don't load him until he answers this question and we OK it.

If you load tanker, make arrangements with your captain, tell Ed to give him all fuel and lube oil you can spare and at 11 A.M., Gerry to give him balance of your load.

As Lieutenant Commander F. J. Gorman, Intelligence officer, observed in a reply to Duke, "You will note that the rendezvous of the tanker with the rum ship was ten miles SE by E from Northeast End lightship, which links up with the procedure given in your letter."

On several occasions, the Coast Guard, using either patrol boats or a radio-equipped truck for monitoring, located illegal radio stations. The question then was to balance the value to the government of two courses of action: raiding the station, knowing that the liquor interests would establish another somewhere else, and it would have to be located and a new code broken, or allowing it to continue to operate, and keeping it monitored and under surveillance.

Sometimes the government raided.

Early in 1931, authorities were monitoring traffic from a rumrunner station in Newark that had been located about a month before. It was a major operation, a $100,000 investment that occupied the entire top floor of a "sumptuously furnished" fourteen-room house. This unit was operated on 500 watts and was described by government officials as "powerful enough to be heard around the world and of the size and equipment of the ordinary broadcasting plant." Carlos N. Bernstein of the Department of Justice said that the station "flashed its directions at night on a 5,000-mile radius."

The rum-running ring that owned the station operated with seven or eight Canadian vessels of about 125 feet, each capable of carrying from 4,000 to 6,000 cases of liquor per trip and all operating on a regular schedule between St. Pierre and the Long Island–New Jersey area. These boats included the *Lomargain, Good Luck, Ada M., Audrey B., Eleanor Joan, Winona R.,* and *Selma K.* According to government information, this fleet-radio station setup had been "taking its dictation from New York interests since February, 1930."

When the prospect of raiding the station arose, Lieutenant Frank M. Meals, Coast Guard Intelligence Unit, weighed the question carefully. "I was in somewhat of a quandary as to what to do," he said. "I hated to concur with the other departments as to pulling the raid, inasmuch as it would kill off our source of radio information and would not particularly benefit the Coast Guard. The

Department of Justice and the Department of Commerce people were quite willing to be governed by my decision in the matter. . . .

"We were letting them operate until such time as we could break down sufficient of their code to determine their affiliations. Recently, however, we had copied conversations concerning a new station [so] there was the imminent probability of the station moving to a new location. There was likewise the ever-present probability of a change in code. Taking all of these things into consideration, I decided we had much to gain and little to lose by knocking it off. . . ."

At nine in the morning of January 20, the raid took place; fourteen agents of the Department of Justice made the actual seizure, and it might have been much more complicated had the station operators been more security-conscious and not been taken completely by surprise. Meals, who accompanied the Justice raiders, related, "No difficulty was encountered, although a formidable system of bolts and bars applied to doors leading to the radio room. Fortunately, but one door was actually locked and this occasioned us only slight delay. Two code books, two ciphers, and miscellaneous messages were seized."

Two men and a woman were arrested, the latter when she went to a cabinet in which was found a .37 caliber automatic pistol.

About four o'clock that afternoon, another shore station belonging to the same gang started up and sent code messages to two vessels offshore, directing them to return to St. Pierre and await orders. The boats were further instructed to take no more orders from "this or any other station," indicating that the shore operators were fearful their new station might also be raided and that the government would use it — or the Newark installation — to send decoy messages to the rum ships.

Sometimes, once a code was broken, it was far better for

the government to leave the shore station alone and reap the rewards of knowing in advance what the rumrunners were going to do. An outstanding instance of this procedure involved the British-registered motor ship *Amacitia,* which the offshore patrols had been watching for some time. On October 27, 1932, the destroyer *George E. Badger* intercepted *Amacitia* thirty miles south of Nomansland buoy and began to trail her; the Coast Guard had been reading *Amacitia*'s coded radio messages for some time. The object of the *Badger*'s trailing was to keep the black "stirred up," so that the rum skipper would remain in doubt as to whether he could report to his shore station that he was free for a contact on the night of the twenty-ninth. *Amacitia*'s master decided that he was not free on that date.

Sometime between the twenty-ninth and November 1, *C.G. 214,* commanded by Lieutenant (JG) P. F. Colmer, with the assistance of Radio Electrician R. W. O'Donnell, intercepted radio traffic from *Amacitia* reporting that she would land liquor in Buzzards Bay. On the night of November 1, the Coast Guard was waiting and watching for her. By that time, the government knew exactly where in Buzzards Bay the landing was to take place.

At about 8:10 P.M., *C.G. 833,* skippered by Lieutenant (JG) R. M. Ross, was notified by the Woods Hole base that the British vessel was in the vicinity of the bay and was scheduled to unload her liquor on West Island. While steaming across the bay from Quicks Hole, bound for the landing site, Ross was contacted at least twice more by his base, which continued to monitor *Amacitia*'s transmissions. He knew precisely when the smuggler was standing up the bay and later, when she was in position, waiting for her shore party at Puppy Rocks, in Naskatucket Bay.

In the darkness, *C.G. 833* stood into Naskatucket Bay at slow speed; it was 10 P.M.

About a half-hour later, Boatswain's Mate 1st Class

Stanley Zylinski sighted a small boat without lights approaching the stern of the patrol boat. As it drew closer, someone in it flashed a red light on the water. Ross yelled, "Come alongside!" and there was an affirmative answer from the smaller craft, whose occupants, maneuvering in the blackness of the night, obviously still were not aware that they were approaching a Coast Guard craft, rather than the *Amacitia,* for which they were looking. The small boat came alongside; her crew quickly realized their error, but it was too late — the Coast Guardsmen made her fast and commanded her crew of eleven to come aboard the *833.* They did so without resistance, but they resisted questioning.

"Who is the master of this boat?" they were asked. "Who is the owner?" "Who is in charge?" There were no answers forthcoming. Ross put the eleven men down in the after hold; he anchored the rum vessel and then proceeded cautiously "on various courses about the bay," searching in the sometimes shoal and rocky waters of Naskatucket for *Amacitia,* somewhere there in the deep night in the shadow.

Boatswain C. R. Grenager, taking a tip from the rum-runners, rigged a strip of red cloth over the end of a flashlight and showed this around the horizon. Ross thought he saw an answering red flash from the direction of Puppy Rocks, and at 10:45 P.M., the Coast Guardsmen sighted a second unlighted small craft approaching. As it came close, a man in it shouted, "Hey, Bill!" and Ross responded by telling him to come alongside. The small boat made as if to do so but then started to turn away, someone in it having recognized the patrol boat. Zylinksi fired his .45 into the water as a warning and at the bark of the pistol, the small boat hauled around and came alongside. The four men in it were also placed in the patrol boat's after hold.

Meanwhile, the *C.G. 813* had arrived and took up the

search for the *Amacitia*. Rupert H. Germaine, fireman 1st class, said,

We proceeded into the head of the bay and saw a long, low, dark object. I thought it was a large rock at first, but then as we came closer, I saw it was a boat without any lights showing.

As soon as we got alongside, Chief Boatswain's Mate Alfred E. Phalen, Boatswain's Mate 1st class Daniel Dorey and I jumped aboard. Phalen and I were to take the forward part and Dorey the after part of the boat.

Phalen knocked on the door of the pilothouse and ordered the men out. They did not come out, so we went in. We saw one man at the wheel. I saw a bullseye flashlight on the port side of the house, on a shelf with some maps. The lens of the flashlight was covered with a red cloth. Phalen took the man at the wheel out on deck and ordered me to see if there was anyone else in the house back of the pilothouse.

On the after starboard side of the captain's quarters was a door, which I opened quickly. It opened into a room which had two bunks on the starboard side, a radio sending set, and a cabinet. One man was sitting down with one hand on the key, working it. I ordered him to stand up and move away from the radio set. As he did, he reached toward the set and I told him, "Stop, and stand up!" and I made him put his back toward the wall. I kicked open a door on the port side of the radio room. There were three men in the room. I ordered them to come out.

The radio operator, described by Germaine as a "rather heavy-set, light-complected man, with his hair a little longer than most men wear it," was faithful to his task to the last. The message he was tapping out when apprehended — the last transmission from the *Amacitia* — was "The Coast Guard is here" and as the Intelligence monitors picked it up, they knew the drama that had begun six days before south of Nomansland buoy had ended successfully for the government.

What it amounted to — because the Coast Guard had been successful in breaking the code used by the *Amacitia* and her shore station — was that the patrol boats had taken into custody twenty-six men and seized 3,500 sacks of liquor, valued at $160,000, a motorship worth $100,000, and two motorboats worth $10,000. Moreover, there was no indication that the ring operating *Amacitia* knew that their code had been compromised; presumably they attributed the seizure to plain bad luck. This meant that the government could continue to read their traffic — an advantage that almost was placed in jeopardy in the government's effort to prosecute the *Amacitia* defendants.

Captain W. R. Trenholm of Halifax, master of the rumrunner, said he had run into a heavy storm offshore, that he could make no headway steaming into it, and that he had headed for the coast, seeking shelter. He acknowledged that he had seen shore lights, presumably those of New Bedford, but that he did not know where he was, so he had continued, finally anchoring where his vessel was seized. In so doing, Trenholm stated, he was taking advantage of the international treaty that allowed ships, no matter what their cargo, to take safe haven in stormy weather.

Because of the size and location of the seizure, its international aspects, and the number of defendants, the *Amacitia* incident attracted considerable public attention. The government wanted very much to win the case, knew privately that it had every right to win it, but found itself in the position of not wanting to present in court the very evidence that would insure conviction.

On November 14, 1932, Lieutenant Meals wrote to Miss Ellen L. Buckley, assistant U.S. attorney in Boston:

I am enclosing clear text copies of the messages intercepted between the Amacitia and her shore radio station on the occasion of her seizure and just prior thereto.

It is my understanding that you desire these messages for the purpose of having before you the details incidental to the seizure of this vessel and that you will not use them in such manner that their existence becomes known to the rumrunners or the public. This last is very essential, inasmuch as the smuggling organization operating the Amacitia has continued to use the code employed at the time of the seizure and there is great possibility of more seizures being made, providing no immediate change in code occurs.

Should it become known that the government is in possession of their code, they would undoubtedly change same, to our subsequent disadvantage.

The case for the prosecution then had to be based on a refutation of Captain Trenholm's claim that his vessel was in distress because of bad weather. The Coast Guard noted carefully that the steamer had ample quantities of oil, water, and coal; food enough for several weeks; that her main engines and all auxiliaries were in good running condition, and that there was no evidence of leaking.

Chief Phalen added, "There was no evidence that the vessel had been rolling or pitching recently. The sea, as we came across the bay, was moderate and all the gear in the Amacitia's cabins, such as books, magazines lying on the settees, were undisturbed. A medicine cabinet contained a number of bottles and boxes upright, undisturbed, and in order. The pilothouse decks and bulkheads were dry. The brass work was bright, with no signs of salt water, and a barrel of apples on the forecastle deck by the hatch, although unsecured, was upright and undamaged."

The Amacitia's defense also was weakened, of course, because it was ridiculous: the government knew this, and so did the public. Trenholm's statement prompted the New Bedford Evening Standard's Cooper Gaw to comment on the editorial page:

A British skipper sailing along our coast discovered a harbor of refuge hitherto unknown as such to navigators and cartographers. Caught in a blow, he presumably left the ocean for the sound, and the sound for the bay, and then utterly ignoring New Bedford, whose harbor is a source of local pride and justly celebrated in history and romance, and kept going until he had penetrated the almost secret recesses of Naskatucket Bay.

The old adage, "Any port in a storm" was spurned by the captain of the Amacitia. Not any port for this gallant explorer, but one particular port, among harbors a veritable shrinking violet, half-hidden from the eye. One can imagine the tenseness of the moment when the ship dropped anchor in this peaceful haven. There has probably been nothing like it since DeSoto first saw the Mississippi or "stout Cortez" stood with all his men silent upon a peak in Darien and stared at the Pacific with a wild surmise.

Oh Naskatucket, oh Naskatucket, harbor of refuge, though you don't look it. But no, I have not the art to indite the ode that this discovery demands. Until this week, Naskatucket Bay had only neighborhood fame. Today, it is known the country over, yes, even across the seas, and it may figure in an international affair — for the time being, the most celebrated harbor of refuge on our coast.

In due course, the government was successful in obtaining a verdict against *Amacitia* — without using the radio messages as evidence — essentially because the motorship was anchored without lights, had proceeded to the anchorage under her own power, and was found to be in good seaworthy condition, with adequate supplies.

As a lighthearted footnote to the matter of rumrunner radio traffic, a message intercepted in late December, 1930, was in plain language, contrary to general practice — presumably extreme aggravation resulted in the lack of caution — yet the transmission remains as unexplained today as it was then: "P2 BE QRMFM that goddam bastard chinese whoor AGN."

CHAPTER XI

INEVITABLY, rumrunners died, Coast Guardsmen died —
and vessels died in the extraordinary patterns produced
alongshore by this unique thirteen-year "war."

One of the most mysterious instances of rumrunner
deaths in the whole Prohibition era concerns the matter of
the former pogy steamer *John Dwight*. At 7:25 on the
morning of April 6, 1923, a Friday, the *Dwight* was observed at the western entrance of Vineyard Sound, roughly
between the Coast Guard stations at Gay Head, on
Martha's Vineyard, and Cuttyhunk. At that time, the
vessel was seen by the Cuttyhunk station. The fog was exceptionally heavy that morning and before that hour,
neither station had been able to see the steamer; because

of the poor visibility, the lookout at Gay Head never did see her.

Through binoculars, the Cuttyhunk Coast Guard skipper observed what he thought was a distress signal flying from the *Dwight*'s single mast forward. About halfway up the spar, it looked like either a dark woolen blanket or a black oilskin coat. He decided immediately to go to the steamer to determine whether she was in trouble. He handed the glasses to his number one man and ordered the lifeboat launched. As he started down the stairs, number one called him back, shouting, "Captain, she's sinking!" A small cloud of steam was coming from the starboard side, and the stern of the *Dwight* was slowly settling.

Meanwhile, at Gay Head, the officer in charge heard a steamer's whistle out in the fog in the direction of Cuttyhunk. He described it afterward as "a long, drawn-out blast that slowly died away." It was no conventional distress signal but extraordinary enough so that he felt uneasy and he ordered a boat's crew to go out into the sound to investigate. The Coast Guard later concluded that the whistle blast did not come from the *Dwight*, but it remains to this hour as a possible element in the mystery.

Circumstances then intervened to delay both boats' crews in reaching the position where the steamer was last seen. The Cuttyhunk crew, unable to launch a boat at the nearer, and very treacherous, Canapitsit Channel, had to steam the length of Nashawena Island and enter Vineyard Sound through Quicks Hole. The Gay Head boat had been under way only a short time when it developed engine trouble and the crew was forced to row most of the distance. Had either crew made the trip in a shorter time, answers to some of the questions that still linger might have been available.

The Gay Head crew reached the scene first and concluded it had arrived because there were barrels floating, of which the Coast Guardsmen recovered eleven. Each barrel contained 120 half-pint bottles of Frontenac ale, produced in Montreal; each bottle was wrapped in straw. Island fishermen, some little distance away, also were recovering barrels of ale when the Cuttyhunk lifeboat arrived.

It was immediately obvious that there was something unusual about whatever had happened. By this time, the fog had lifted sufficiently so that a white lobster-pot buoy a mile away could be seen with the naked eye, yet, apart from the barrels of ale, there was nothing to indicate that a steamer had gone to the bottom in that area only a short time before. Neither Coast Guard crew saw one man, alive or dead, or any floating wreckage, or life preservers or small boats. For miles around, the sound was empty of any clue as to what had happened or, for that matter, as to the identity of the steamer, although that was clearly determined later. The Coast Guardsmen searched the waters of the area thoroughly and found nothing more.

Twenty-four hours later, at approximately 7:30 on the morning of April 7, all of the conventional signs of the tragedy began to appear; one would give a great deal to know where they had been in the meantime. Seven dead men in life preservers were found floating in the sound. The body of a man identified as Harry King came ashore in a small boat at Menemsha on the Vineyard; it came facedown in the bottom of the craft; the back of the skull was crushed. In the boat was a cheese knife. There is to this day a confusion as to the condition of the seven bodies in the life preservers.

Sheriff Walter H. Renear of Vineyard Haven was quoted as saying that "nearly all the bodies picked up in the sound bore evidence of a wicked, free-for-all fight. There was lacerations and bruises about their faces that came from contact with some solid, blunt instrument." Others were not so sure. My father, Joseph Chase Allen

— who covered the story for the Vineyard *Gazette* and the Associated Press — and persons to whom he talked who had seen the bodies, concluded that the damage to the dead could very well have been caused by sand fleas.

Other things began to show up. A large gray hatch cover and a deck cradle for a small boat were recovered from the sound. On Naushon Island, across the sound from the Vineyard, searchers found a lifeboat and two name boards, later discovered to have come from each side of the steamer's pilothouse, bearing the name "John Dwight." One other item of information may have been related to the sinking, although that was never established. The steamer *Dorchester* passed the *Dwight* in the sound about five minutes before she sank in approximately 100 feet of water. Members of the *Dorchester*'s crew observed a small boat in the immediate area; there were three men in it and the boat was about 150 yards from shore. Neither their identity nor their destination ever was determined, but they were the only living persons known to have been in the vicinity at the time the *Dwight* went down.

A team of federal and state officials, the latter led by Massachusetts Attorney General Jay R. Benton and Commissioner of Public Safety Alfred F. Foote — aided by a veteran commercial diver from the Vineyard — embarked upon the investigation. Some of the circumstances leading to the steamer's dramatic end began to emerge.

The *Dwight* had formerly performed some service for the federal government, and eventually had been sold to civilian interests. Five or six weeks before her last trip, she was overhauled and repaired at Newport, Rhode Island. She had left that port a few days before the sinking. Those responsible for her gave fictitious names and addresses to port officials, which made void all of the ship's papers.

It was concluded that the steamer had a crew of fifteen. Her skipper was Captain John King, although there were two persons aboard bearing the title of "Captain." The other one was Malcolm J. Carmichael, who probably served as navigator. Harry King, the only dead man identified, was from Brooklyn, and was the son of Captain King.

It was theorized that the *Dwight* had been acquired to carry a cargo of liquor from Rum Row to some port in the Northeast. A contemporary account suggests, "It is understood, although the fact has not been corroborated, that the Dwight was accompanied by another vessel working in the same deal; that the Dwight, being equipped with a hoisting boom, was to handle the barrels of ale, bigger and heavier than the cases of whisky, which, it is thought, were taken aboard by the second craft . . . and that both vessels visited the mother ship at apparently the same time." If there was a second vessel involved — sailing in company with the *Dwight,* but not observed by the Coast Guard lookouts because of the fog — it could have been her whistle which sounded the "long, drawn-out blast" heard at Gay Head.

In any event, the mother ship contact had been made, the liquor was taken aboard the *Dwight,* and the barrels of ale were stowed both below, in the hold, and on deck; it was the latter cargo that floated when she sank.

At some point during the investigation, authorities were informed that there was a large sum of money aboard the steamer; $225,000 was the amount most often referred to. Some of the informants said the cash had been pooled by the fifteen men aboard to swing a liquor deal involving Canadian and Boston rum-running interests. Others who knew something of the illegal liquor trade or who investigated the *Dwight* affair said that someone from the steamer, perhaps Carmichael, had made a business arrangement in New London, possibly involving the cargo of ale, for which he received $100,000. In Newport, Captain King was reported to have transacted some kind of a deal to deliver liquor, for which he was paid an additional $125,000. The obvious line of thought here was that if the *Dwight*'s load of booze had been sold twice, some might have found this upsetting and sufficient motive for doing in the steamer and some (or all?) of her crew. However this may have been, the only money ever known to have been recovered was fifty dollars in the pocket of one of the dead men.

There was also the matter of a phone call. Although authorities never made a public statement concerning it, newspapermen covering the *Dwight* story reported that one meager clue was "a telephone conversation between somebody in the area and somebody in Boston relative to a rum-running plan" at about the time of the sinking. It was understood that a telephone operator had reported the call to the investigators. If this was the case, presumably, officials never were successful in determining who called whom.

Initially, there were great hopes that a diver might be able to provide the inquiry with helpful information, but it did not work out that way. A diver, David J. Curney of Vineyard Haven, got down to the wreck, but the current in the area runs hard, the slack-water period is brief, and, as an observer wrote on May 13, 1923, "The water is deep and the pressure per square inch on the diver is something more than fifty pounds. In addition to this, and the sound waters, chilled by recent winds from the north and north-east, are at present, frigid, greatly hampering the diving work and materially lessening the length of time a diver can remain under water.

"Diver Curney's hands became so cold during the two 15-minute trips he made last Tuesday down to the Dwight that it was with difficulty, he later asserted, that he was able to pull on his signal line. All sense of feeling in his hands and fingers was numbed by the cold waters, he said."

About all that the diving established was that the hold was full of bottled ale that soon was rendered worthless by sea water. No bodies and no money were recovered. The engine room was a mass of wreckage, as if an explosion had taken place there. On the floor of the engine room was what one diver described as a sword or cutlass. It was not recovered. The identities of the "young and clean-shaven" men whose bodies were found in the life preservers never were established.

Two principal theories — piracy and mutiny — emerged, and persist to this day. Earle D. Wilson of the New Bedford *Standard-Times,* who spent considerable time on the Vineyard covering the investigation, wrote a thoughtful analysis a month and a half after the sinking. He observed,

Perhaps the theory more generally acceptable than any other is that of piracy. It is a logical theory and possibly answers more of the questions raised by the evidence than any other.

The purpose of the Dwight's trip could not have been secret. It must have been known to many men to whom $100,000 would be a sufficient sum to justify anything, even the cold-blooded murder of fifteen men.

Possibly the fifteen in the unlawful scheme realized this fact. Possibly that is why the two pilothouse name boards were found at Naushon. Assuming that there was a possibility of being boarded and robbed by those who knew that she carried so much money, what is more logical to believe than that her captain ordered the two name boards removed and left behind, perhaps with the lifeboat at Naushon? There was her name "John Dwight" in eight-inch letters of glaring white standing out on a black background on each board, almost an invitation to pirates who knew of the coin she carried.

Two facts strengthen this view. First, if, as some hold, the two boards were ripped from the pilothouse and thrown into the lifeboat as oars when the crew deserted the sinking ship, where are the men who used them as oars? They had committed no crime. Why strike for the little deserted island?

And second, the two boards, recently painted, show no evidence of hard usage. Their edges have not been scraped of paint where they would rub against the boat's gunwale as its occupants used them as oars. And most conclusive, they were not ripped from the pilothouse. They were taken off carefully. One of the eight screws that held them to the pilothouse is missing and on the remaining seven, there are no wood particles to indicate they were pulled forcibly from their holes. And if the boards had been ripped from the pilothouse at the last minute just before the boat was sinking, if two boards bearing the name of the ill-fated vessel were the best substitutes for oars desperate men could think of in such an emergency, they would be pried loose so quickly and energetically that they would bear some mark to show that haste, some gouged place where the instrument used as a lever would make at least a dent. But the boards are not marked. They are as smooth and clean and free from damage as when they left the paint shop not long ago.

The heavy fog offered the pirates a thick cloak for their crime that made their task comparatively easy, although it is more than likely they would have proceeded with their purpose even in sight of the Coast Guard stations, so sure were they of their ground and so rapidly did they work. The Dwight herself was not on lawful business. Her crew had reasons for not being anxious to bring the authorities to the scene.

As she was making her way slowly through the fog, the theory goes, the Dwight was joined by another vessel. The Dwight's lookout suddenly saw a huge shape loom up to starboard, on the Gay Head side. There were a few hurried commands, desperate efforts to avoid collision, perhaps, and the other vessel came up alongside. Then the boarding, and a terrible and bloody fight. The promoters of the enterprise were known to the boarders and were the marked men of the crew. One of them no doubt held the cash.

Captain King was a small man. His son, Harry, was a strapping big fellow, probably the biggest on the vessel. He rushed instinctively to the defense of his father. No ordinary blow felled him. He was struck from the rear. The back of his skull, crushed in, proves that. Another big bruise on his forehead shows that his head struck one of the thwarts in the small boat when he was thrown, or kicked into that.

The battle was brief. Once the boarders got the cash, their objective, they were ready to flee. The vessel was then scuttled, in true piratical style, and the boarders slipped away in the fog, to let the Dwight sink slowly in her grave. Three of them later put out in a small boat from the pirate ship for land, to telephone someone in Boston of their success. They were seen by the Dorchester, but never identified.

Another theory with many proponents is that of mutiny, of being scuttled by her own crew. In fact, nearly every theory admits that the Dwight was scuttled. There are too many arguments against accident, explosion of boilers, opening of seams or collision, to make any of these appear feasible.

Supposing several wealthy Bostonians and New Yorkers, together with some less rich, planned the deal. With too much money involved, each would want to be as close to the scene of action as possible. It is believed that almost every man who had any money invested in the scheme was aboard when the Dwight went down, if not every man. No man trusted another. Say that eight of the fifteen, desirous of reaping the lion's share of the harvest of goldbacks, schemed to rob the other seven.

The heavy fog was made to order for them. They had waited patiently for it. Each man picked his own opponent and, at a given signal, the mutiny was on. The fight would be no less bloody than that against the pirates. Gold was the prize; down into the cabin, up into the pilothouse, that little package of money was the goal. Possibly, in anticipation of the intensity of the struggle, the attackers had taken the precaution to equip themselves with life preservers. Perhaps they scuttled the vessel first and then attacked while the others were rushing for the lifeboats. If the fight was as fierce as indications show it was, then it is possible that the three men the Dorchester saw in the boat off the shore a little later were the sole survivors of the bloody strife — they and the money.

Maybe the whole crew was in mutiny against the two captains. Maybe a part of the crew was in league with the pirates and double-crossed the others in their own vessel. Maybe the two captains were in league with the pirates and disappeared with them and really are in Cuba today, as has been rumored. Maybe one of the two captains was in league with the pirates and he alone escaped. The "maybes" are limitless, as any one of the official investigators will freely admit. If they could answer certain questions, they could answer the main ones.

What was the cheese knife doing in the boat with the body of Harry King? Had he used it to defend his father? Or was he in on the mutiny and used it in the attack? Or did he attempt to escape and took the knife with him to cut the small boat loose from the larger vessel? Why were there no oars either in his boat or in the boat picked up on Naushon?

If the strap found on the gunwale and believed to have been used as a rowlock for the piece of wood ripped from the boat's floor was from a life belt, where is the belt? It would float. Did lifeboat and King's boat float off the steamer's deck when she sank or were they launched previously?

How did the name boards from the Dwight get into the lifeboat? Is all the evidence found so far merely a "plant," from the floating bodies to the name boards, intended to throw investigators off the trail? If so, who's doing the planting, and why?

Question marks, question marks, question marks. The officials are surrounded by them, buried beneath them. And today [May 12, 1923], nearly six weeks after the disaster, one more big final question is slowly forcing its way into the consciousness of those most familiar with the meager details of the mystery: Will the riddle of the sinking of the John Dwight ever be satisfactorily solved and settled for all time?

Ten days after Mr. Wilson posed that question, Massachusetts Attorney General Benton announced that the conditions under which the rum-running steamer *John Dwight* was sunk, with a loss of at least eight lives, remained "as much a mystery as ever." He said he had heard reports from officials of his own department and from the commissioner of public safety on investigations pursued by a diver and detectives in recent weeks, adding that, as far as the state "is concerned, the inquiry is complete, without having developed sufficient evidence to warrant any criminal proceedings."

Federal agents exploded four TNT bombs in the *Dwight*'s hull in July, 1923 and then ceased watch over the spot, satisfied that nothing was left to be salvaged by liquor-seekers. The "riddle of the sinking of the *John Dwight*" remains as unsolved today as it was on that day in May more than a half-century ago when Mr. Wilson struggled to discover the truth within the grim and muddied record of her passing.

Rumrunners died, and so did Coast Guardsmen. One of the worst losses of life sustained by the Coast Guard service during the Prohibition era occurred on Sunday, February 20, 1927. That day was marked in the area of Cape Cod and eastward by a gale that was described as "one of the wildest northeasters that has scourged the Cape in nearly thirty years." It was sufficiently severe so that the Cunard liner *Caronia* was twenty-four hours overdue at Boston because she hove to off Nantucket to ride out the storm. For smaller craft, it was worse; the fishing schooner *Natalie S.* of New Bedford, Captain Dan Mullins, was bound in from Georges Bank when a huge wave hove her down, washed one man overboard, tore off her pilothouse and part of her rail, and sluiced her dories over the side.

But it was the Coast Guard patrol boat *238,* off Cape Cod's outer shore and near the tip, which tragedy struck the hardest. Her skipper was Boatswain Jesse K. Rivenback; he had received his latest promotion and assignment to command the patrol boat on the previous Monday. It was his first command, and he had taken the *238* out for his first rum patrol on the following Wednesday. His motor machinist, Cornelius Shea, had had two years of service in the Coast Guard, having enlisted after receiving his discharge from the Navy. Shea was thirty-seven, his enlistment was to expire in the next month, and he planned to retire. There were eight men aboard; the ninth, Edward S. Cronin, was ill in Chelsea Marine Hospital and had been unable to join his boat when she sailed.

It was five o'clock on Saturday afternoon, February 19, when the patrol boat was first sighted through the murk of a blizzard by a Coast Guard lookout ashore. A flashing blinker light from the *238* told the watchers in the tower that the craft's engines had gone dead and its radio was not operating. Rivenback realized his peril; his message for help was urgent, and it was relayed immediately to the Coast Guard base at East Boston. Four vessels from that base, including the destroyer *Paulding,* under forced draft, steamed to the patrol boat's relief. At that hour, the *238* was three miles offshore, with two anchors overboard, and a tremendous sea running. Those ashore took some comfort in knowing that the $41,000 vessel had been commissioned less than a year before and that her hull was in good shape.

Soon the whirling snow and darkness closed in, but the lights of the patrol boat could still be seen. The appearance of a large steamer only a short distance offshore gave momentary hope to the anxious watchers on the beach. They signaled frantically, but the ship held to its course and quickly disappeared into the night.

Meanwhile, the *Paulding,* having butted out of the North Channel at about half-past seven, steamed into the gale; she was taking seas green and solid right over the bow and was forced to reduce her speed from 18 to 12 knots. The run from Boston Lighthouse to the Cape was somewhat easier because her skipper, Lieutenant Commander John S. Baylis, was able to set a course that allowed the destroyer to ride and roll in the troughs, but the problem was that both wind and sea were increasing. By the time *Paulding* was within ten miles of the Cape, Baylis had to reduce speed again; his ship was being pounded savagely. It was an hour of critical decision and he concluded that to pursue the effort to aid the patrol boat would be impractical and foolhardy; his first responsibility now was to save his own ship and her crew, if this could be done.

Paulding, hammered by wind and sea that in subsequent days were generally compared in intensity to the gale of November 27, 1898, in which the steamer *City of Portland* went down off Cape Cod with the loss of all on board, headed into the storm and began a long and painful effort to work offshore.

On the beach at about this time, crews from three Coast Guard stations, armed with Lyle guns and breeches buoy gear, set up their equipment, hoping for an opportunity to help those aboard the *238* if she came in close enough. As the night wore on, the wind velocity increased; by early Sunday, it was blowing 75 miles an hour, pitiless sleet stung the dogged beach patrol, the shore was coated with a treacherous sheet of lumpy white ice, and giant combers broke over the outer bars toward which the patrol boat, pounded and buffeted, was being blown.

Realizing that it would be high tide at 3 A.M., Coast Guardsmen ashore signaled to the patrol craft about 2:30 A.M. to weigh anchor, the hope being that the relatively light boat would be swept over the bars and up onto the beach. Meanwhile, four separate attempts were made to launch a boat from the shore, but the mountainous seas and heavy surf tossed the boat back onto the storm-pounded beach every time before the straining oarsmen could pull out beyond the line of breakers.

Had the *238* been washed over the bars, her crew might, in fact, have been saved; instead, she hung up on them, and lay there helpless, the ugly, thundering seas slamming into her endlessly. At 4:30 on Sunday morning, the lights aboard the vessel went out; the helpless watchers ashore concluded it was at that moment that the *238*'s pilothouse was ripped off and washed over the side. At 5:15 the crews ashore made a last attempt to help; they succeeded in shooting a line for the breeches buoy over the patrol boat, but no one on board appeared to take the line. If they still lived, they were too exhausted to help themselves or perhaps trapped in the wreck and unable to get up on deck.

At 7 A.M., the patrol boat rolled over. Two bodies washed up in the surf were those of Raymond H. Clark and Charles A. Freeburn, believed to have gone forward on the *238* four and a half hours earlier to get up the anchors.

The tragedy of the *238* was over, but the ordeal of the destroyer *Paulding,* which had left a safe harbor in an effort to aid her, had many more hours to go. In *Rum War at Sea,* the official Coast Guard history of the Prohibition era, Commander Malcolm F. Willoughby, USCGR (T), has recorded something of what the destroyer went through:

Green seas rolling over bow and fantail simultaneously shook her and pounded her into what seemed to be a stone wall. First, the dory lashed on deck was carried away, piece by piece. All the next day [Sunday], the seas wreaked havoc; they roared over the decks and spray froze as it hit. Getting about the decks was extremely hazardous. Water worked into the ship and everything and everybody became soaked. No cooking could be done. Seasickness was general.

Gasoline drums on the deck aft broke loose and went overboard. The anchor davit was bent flat to the deck; the jackstaff and stanchions were broken; tops of several ventilators were carried away. The sounding machine was smashed; the wherry cradles and the wherry were broken, and the motor dory was torn from its cradle and stove in, and the after steering wheel was badly bent.

This all had to have a fitting climax. During the dark hours of the second night, the starboard guy of the No. 1 stack carried away and with every roll to port, the stack went farther and farther toward the port rail. Frantic efforts were made to get a tackle on the guy to save the stack. The vessel was put on the port tack to get her rolling deeper to starboard and thus give the men working in darkness and spray and on slippery decks a better chance of success. Then the port guy went and the stack fell over to starboard, breaking the motor sailer davit and sending the motor sailer overboard.

Live steam now endangered the men; water coming on board struck the hot boiler, raising clouds of steam and threatening a boiler explosion. One man was washed or slipped overboard, but fortunately was rescued. The stack hole was finally secured by a tarpaulin. A fore stay had to be rigged to stack No. 2, as the other stacks were beginning to work badly. Meanwhile, the fallen stack was being cut away, and went overboard.

Just before midnight of the second night, Baylis deemed it unsafe to head into the gale any longer; Paulding was by this time 100 miles east of Boston lightship. He waited for water sufficiently tranquil in which to turn about. His chance came, and Paulding proceeded at full speed with helm hard over. The run back to Boston before the gale at 18 knots was a welcome relief from the pounding of the preceding 24 hours.

After reaching Boston, Baylis said *Paulding* had taken the hardest beating he had ever seen a vessel go through.

Two further items regarding the loss of the *238* are worthy of mention because of their poignancy. Freeburn, whose body washed ashore, had been scheduled to go on furlough that weekend; apparently the patrol boat had been due to come back into port either on the Saturday on which she got into trouble or early on the Sunday on which she was lost. Freeburn's mother, Mrs. George Freeburn of Philadelphia, was expecting him to come home; on the night of Sunday, February 20, she answered a knock at the door, thinking that he had arrived. Instead, it was a messenger, informing her of his death that morning.

Boatswain Rivenback was a native of Wilmington, North Carolina. Several weeks earlier, he and other crew members of the patrol boat *C.G. 237* had been rescued when the craft foundered after an accident. By coincidence, they were saved by the tug *Jupiter,* Captain Thomas Pateman, out of Norfolk, a vessel on which Rivenback had been second mate prior to entering the Coast Guard.

Whether because of this accident or for another reason, Rivenback, thirty-nine years old, had had a premonition of disaster. He said to a close friend on the Monday of his promotion — only six days before his death — "You know, I don't feel right. If anything should happen, have my body sent to Wilmington." This comment seems unlikely to have been made because of apprehension over his new responsibilities; his colleagues at Base 18, Woods Hole, described him as "a very conscientious and able man in his duties."

Men died, and vessels died.

On April 23, 1927, at seven in the morning, Lieutenant (JG) R. L. Raney, the officer in charge of Base 18, received a phone call from the keeper of the Gay Head Coast Guard station on the Vineyard that a fishing schooner was ashore, about three miles northeast of Squibnocket Point.

She was reported resting easily on a sandy bottom and working herself free, with a flood tide running, about two hours short of high water. Raney, aboard the *C.G. 282*, proceeded to the grounded vessel.

She proved to be the *Etta M. Burns* of Boston, loaded with what apparently was a cargo of fish. No members of the crew were aboard the sixty-foot vessel, and water in her hold was about two feet deep. Pumps were started to get her dry.

Two men who said they were crew members came from the shore. They told the Coast Guardsmen that the *Burns,* skippered by Captain Frank Rice, was on her way to Fulton Market in New York when she grounded in thick fog at 3:30 that morning. They added that there was no use pumping because they had tried it for a couple of hours without result, and they said that the master and other crew members had gone to the Chilmark post office to phone for a tug from New Bedford.

Raney went to the post office to ask Rice whether he wanted Coast Guard assistance. He did not find the schooner's captain, but two other crew members urged the lieutenant not to pull on the schooner as they were afraid she would sink as soon as she was hauled into deeper water. The Coast Guard officer suggested dumping the cargo of fish and attempting to float her, but the two men said they did not think this would work.

Raney found their reluctance to accept aid puzzling. He said, "I returned to the vessel and began a careful search of her. No papers could be found. The hold was apparently full of fish, but due to the unwillingness of the crew to dump the cargo, my suspicions were aroused and I began digging under the ice. About eighteen inches below the surface, a piece of canvas was found. Beneath this was a cargo of liquor."

The hatch was nailed down, a guard was placed on the vessel, and Raney and Boatswain C. B. Morse went ashore, located the *Burns*'s master and crew and arrested them.

By that evening, the Coast Guard cutter *Morrill* and the patrol boat *Petrel* had an eight-inch hawser aboard the schooner and were prepared to start pulling on her at high water early the next morning. However, weather conditions began to deteriorate; the moderate northwest breeze stiffened considerably and in a short time, seas were breaking over the *Burns*'s deck. Soon after, the four Coast Guardsmen on the schooner signaled that they were in danger of being washed overboard; they were taken off in a dory, all of them already soaked to the skin.

The breeze remained fresh; a heavy ground swell was building, and the schooner in the swash began to get a thumping. Something on her must have let go, because several cases of her liquor were observed afloat shortly after midnight and recovered by a surfboat. *Petrel* and *Morrill* pulled on the grounded vessel until they parted a hawser; they moved her seven feet, by which time the tide was ebbing.

Much of the next day, they pulled on the *Burns* without further result. The weather was getting worse; the sea was choppy, making it difficult to get alongside the schooner, the surf remained heavy, and twenty more cases of liquor washed out of her. As evening came on, surfmen from Gay Head were assigned to patrol the beach and at intervals during the night, the *Morrill* played her searchlight on the *Burns*.

The searchlight and the beach patrol were necessary because Vineyarders — quickly aware that a rumrunner was aground and that booze was floating out of her — gathered on the shore. Most of them were there to see whether they could pick up a few bottles — but not all were; even in this relatively minor incident, the sharp division of American opinion on the matter of rum was readily apparent. "Chester Poole patrolled the beach that night," my father recalled, "and for several nights, and smashed every bottle of liquor that he could find.

"Ben Abbot borrowed my hip boots to fish himself some

liquor from her and, on his return, gave me a pinch-bottle of something with a Scotch label on it. I opened it eventually and I would say that the contents were a rather poor variety of tea; there was not even a smell of alcohol."

Nevertheless, it was a night and a scene not easily forgotten: the clean salt smell on the freshening wind, the great black rolls of sea, trembling with white lace, thundering in on the sand; the dark shapes of the anonymous salvagers coming and going, bending and rising; the stricken schooner, hove down like a wounded bird, her masts already askew, and over all ("Turn that goddam thing off!" yelled some nameless oilskins in the shadows), the piercing light from the cutter, a mute warning that the genesis of the situation was lawless and that the law was at hand.

Two days later, the surf was still heavy and long swells were working in on the beach, making it difficult to get at the schooner's cargo. Her hull had been seriously damaged; her hatches had been smashed, and there obviously was no further use in trying to haul her off — the effort now was to salvage or destroy the liquor aboard. Storm warnings issued at Nantucket lent an imperative note to this task; clearly, time was limited.

Raney and his crew succeeded in getting aboard the *Burns*. "After placing four men and a boatswain on deck," he said,

I removed my clothes and went into the hold and, in water up to my waist, moved all the cargo I could reach up to the hatchway, where it was taken on deck and destroyed.

Sand had drifted in through a hole in the starboard side of the vessel and it was impossible to move a few cases which had been covered by it. During the afternoon, it became so rough that the men were ordered in from the schooner and all further attempts to destroy the liquor were abandoned. It is believed that the original cargo was not over 250 or 300 cases and that approximately 200 cases were accounted for. While there is no doubt that small quantities did wash ashore into the hands of civilians, the amount destroyed was undoubtedly most of the cargo.

At 7:45 P.M. on April 27, the weather was overcast, with rain, and J. F. Brady, master of the cutter *Morrill*, marking the increase in the force of the northwest wind, added, "Observed both masts and upper works of schooner carry away." On the following day, the cutter's work party cleared away and beached the masts and wreckage to prevent them from drifting away and becoming a menace to navigation.

By 2:35 P.M. on April 28, Brady noted,

All men withdrawn from the wreck. The schooner is breaking up. All cargo has been destroyed or confiscated and the wreck, in its present site, is in no way dangerous to navigation. Therefore, the schooner was abandoned.

The work on the Burns was very arduous and thrilling. It was necessary to land upon the beach through a very heavy surf both day and night, and invariably, this meant that the clothing of the men would become wet before they commenced to work and sometimes it was hours before opportunity presented itself to allow them time to shift to dry clothing.

These operations also involved hard manual labor and many physical dangers. Throughout the time the Morrill was salvaging and working about the schooner, the officers and crew were called upon to work hours and hours without sleep. This was done without complaint and Coast Guard spirit and loyalty were manifested in each and every one. And in clearing the schooner of the masts and wreckage, the crew was obliged to work in the surf in order to clear the shrouds, which were fouled and under water at all times.

I must add a personal note. Some time later, but probably prior to 1932, the wreck of the *Burns* was set afire and I was somewhat involved. We were a boys' Sunday School class, a dozen or so, from the Baptist Church in Vineyard Haven and were on a weekend outing at a South Beach cottage. We walked to the wreck and I remember to this day how massive, how lonely, how starkly tragic the vessel's remains were, the only work of man — and a shattered work at that — rising above the empty miles of sand. Not much of it was left, a chunk of one side, yet in the curve of the weather-silvered plank, there was still a hint of the grace that had made her go, once upon a time. The piece of wreckage, poised aloft like a half-cupped hand, was higher than our heads by far; its inner and outer planking, with heavy ribs between, was a natural chimney.

I cannot remember who gathered the kindling of driftwood, who placed it, jammed in a jagged hole at the base of the hulk, or who lighted the match. It is probably gentle irony that two of those present eventually became fire chiefs. But I can remember the beautiful and somewhat frightening dance of the first flames in the bright sunlight. The old schooner did not burn easily or quickly in the beginning, but suddenly what we had done was out of control. As if something within her, sensing the end of the end, had taken a great and terrible last breath, the draft roared up between hull and sheathing; fire, in fierce and writhing sheets, twisted like gold dancing out of the top of the wreck. Within moments, a column of black smoke — scar against the fair sky — began to wind a quarter-mile high.

We formed a useless bucket brigade, running back and forth to the sea with rusty tin cans found in the dunes, until we were breathless, and that is the way the town fire department, alerted by the smoke, found us when it came to do what we could not. Entirely apart from the fact — as the fire chief pointed out to us in a very low-keyed way — that we had done something that was neither safe nor sensible, I have wished ever since that we had not done it. Obviously, it did not make any difference to anyone whether what was left of the old schooner went up in flames, yet she had died hard and cruelly and deserved the right to return in peace to the earth from which her bones came. I suspect that I regard what we did as desecration of a grave, and if that makes no sense, I still cannot help it.

CHAPTER XII

W HEN THE REPEAL of Prohibition was near, a rumrunner operating out of the Buzzards Bay–Narragansett Bay area remarked to a reporter for the New
Bedford *Evening Standard*, "We threw overboard more
liquor than the Coast Guard and the Customs agents ever
seized and we landed a hell of a lot more than we threw
overboard." There is no way of determining the accuracy
of this statement but over a period of several years there
certainly was a large quantity of liquor dumped off the
Northeast coat.

Principally, the booze found afloat was jettisoned when
boats were hard pressed by the pursuing Coast Guard.
Sometimes, engine failure or deteriorating weather made it
necessary to lighten or empty a smuggler by throwing the

cargo over the side. But a lot of bagged liquor in the water was dumped into shallow areas near the coast because the runners feared capture or detection, especially if they were late getting in with a load and daylight was at hand. They returned to salvage their liquor as quickly as was practical — usually the first dark night, unless their boats or crews were under government surveillance. Sometimes heavy storm seas broke up these dumps, and the loose bottles floated away; sometimes, amphibious hijackers — always alert to such situations — attempted to raid them.

I know of a place where wind-stunted pines come down close to the beach and within recent years, property owners there have pried flattened lead slugs out of the bark of these trees with pen knives. Once, just offshore, there was a substantial liquor dump; it was the scene of at least one night battle between the liquor's owners ashore and the raiders afloat, in which shots were fired. I asked a former rumrunner who owned three boats and who I knew never had allowed the people who worked for him to carry firearms what he did about hijackers who tried to steal from his underwater dumps. He said, "We never had trouble but twice. First time, they caught us flat-footed. They were from out of state. We had quite a lot of stuff down there and the weather had been so rotten for several days that we figured we couldn't get it up very well, so nobody else could, either. Well, that's where we were wrong; we didn't even have anybody keeping an eye on it, and they came in there one night with must be two-three boats of some size and cleaned things up in good shape. When we went down there the next night, there was damned little left for us.

"Now, the way things worked, you could usually find out who pulled a stunt like that unless it was a couple amateurs working alone. We figured it had to be professional because they got a lot of stuff out of there in a hurry, and with no fuss. Had to be a gang. Well, we guessed who it was even before we found out for sure. And we found out for sure because we found out where they hauled the stuff to and stowed it. We didn't make a move to let them know that we knew, figuring that they'd come back again when we had some more stuff in the dump.

"They did, and we were waiting for them that time. We waited until they had their dragging gear overboard and couldn't get out in a hurry. Then we boarded them, from both sides at the same time — pitch dark — and there were more of us than there were of them, and besides, there were two of our people who used to do some professional boxing. We tied them up and whaled hell out of them with rubber hoses. We took turns at it. They never came back."

The stuff was everywhere, discoverable by amateurs and professionals alike. In the latter part of August, 1924, a New York newspaper reported that

Long Beach, Long Island residents who make a practice of night surf bathing have had the pleasant experience during the last week of snaring floating cases of White Horse whisky from the ocean. Although authentic figures are not available, it is estimated that about twenty cases have found their way to shore.

One party of young men, entertaining friends from New York City, swam through a covey of six cases on Wednesday night. Three of these were kept at the cottage which they occupy and their guests took the other three back to the city.

From the condition of the cases, it was believed that they had been in the water for some time. The wood was water-logged and the lead foil caps on the bottles had turned dull black. The straw stockings were pulpy and dropped from the bottles when they were removed from the cases. There were no marks on the cases other than the trademark of the manufacturer to indicate the source of the free liquor, which was reported to be of good quality.

The Coast Guard found a lot of it. Two patrol boats out of the East Boston base were steaming about fourteen miles northwest of Peaked Hill buoy and came upon 72 cases and cans of alcohol afloat. The flotsam was in a streak of oil about four miles in length; the conclusion was that a rumrunner had gone to the bottom. *C.G. 150,* proceeding from Provincetown by way of Billingsgate buoy, sighted a number of cases of liquor close to the beach at East Dennis and salvaged 185 of them. Three patrol craft recovered 183 cases from Boston Harbor in the vicinity of Nix's Mate and the following morning, a fishing vessel in the same vicinity picked up a drifting dory containing 37 cases of alcohol, Scotch, and cognac.

The Coast Guard was, of course, aware of the widespread use of inshore drops and at least once openly competed with civilians in recovering liquor from one of them. William W. Worcester, the boatswain in charge of *C.G. 281*, stood into the Sakonnet River and spotted a 33-foot former Navy steamer, the *G-975*, which the Coast Guard identified as a "well-known rumrunner." The people in the boat were talking with five men on the dock.

Worcester looked over the steamer, theoretically a fisherman, although she carried no fishing equipment and made no pretense of being engaged in fishing. He observed "six poles about fourteen feet long, with a unique combination of corkscrew and hook on one end," and he concluded, "I felt that these poles were designed for the retrieving of jettisoned sacks of liquor."

He kept a watchful eye on the *G-975*, which left her dockside berth shortly before seven on a mid-January morning. Worcester wanted to give her a couple of hours' lead, assuming that she was not going far and would, if given the chance, tip off the location of the drop. Once she had left, he went ashore to talk to a local resident. Yes, said the fellow, a friend of his, a caretaker of an estate, had told him just that day that on the previous night, boats without lights had been observed in a particular area, working close to the beach.

Accordingly, at nine A.M., the *C.G. 281* proceeded around Warren Point, "close to the beach, behind several rocks," and found the *G-975* at anchor. Worcester said, "Several remarks were made by the master of the G-975 which indicated that he knew about 200 sacks of liquor remained in the vicinity and that he had the intention of dragging for them."

The boatswain added, "I signified my intention of trying the fishing." He anchored his patrol boat alongside the steamer, improvised some grappling gear, and dropped it overboard. He hooked onto sacks immediately and brought two to the surface. Each sack contained eleven one-quart bottles of Indian Hill bourbon "in a new-type bottle with a patented seal and a screw cap."

Commenting on this incident, F. A. Nichols, commander of Section Base 18 at Woods Hole, said, "It is thought that this method of concealing the contraband is very often used when the shore is closely watched. A number of rumors have been received for a long time regarding the vicinity of Westport, Massachusetts, and it is thought this may be the answer."

The shore, including that of Westport, was often "closely watched," because rumrunners tended to use repeatedly those landing areas where conditions of land and sea worked well for them. A dramatic episode at Westport's Horseneck Beach involved the *Star,* formerly the Canadian vessel *Ammeg,* lost on her first rum venture under American registry, an incident to which the engineer of the *Wanderer* alluded in an earlier chapter. "We lost two brand-new trucks that night," he said ruefully. *Star,* caught in an unusual pincers between sea and shore government forces, was the victim of a tipster.

I first heard the story from the late William J. Fitzgerald, who was then a customs inspector in New Bedford. A word concerning Mr. Fitzgerald may be in order. In terms of historic appropriateness, if "Bill" Fitzgerald, a stocky former Secret Service agent in World War I, had not been a customs inspector during the Prohibition era — and had not been assigned to an area in which the rum traffic was heavy — it would have been a circumstantial tragedy. A contemporary remarked, "Can you imagine San Juan Hill without Teddy?" and that is about the way it was.

Fitzgerald pursued rumrunners with zeal and enthusiasm; at any hour, in any weather, he was on the docks, the beaches, and down on his hands and knees in the bilge of a captured vessel, looking for evidence. It was more than simple devotion to duty; he enjoyed it. He was commended by the Coast Guard. A rumrunner with whom I discussed him said, "I don't think the man ever went to bed. He was forever popping up in the wrong place and he was a damned nuisance." I suspect Mr. Fitzgerald would have appreciated that comment as much as he did the commendation.

What Fitzgerald called "the battle of a lifetime" occurred on the night of December 2, 1931. "We had advance knowledge that there was to be an attempted landing," Fitzgerald said, "and we went to Horseneck about nine o'clock. We sneaked around and lay in hiding there near a cottage until shortly after midnight.

"At that time, we saw two trucks, one of them a large van, approach, and a little bit later, about fourteen pleasure cars and five more trucks. It looked like a good-sized operation. These fellows, who were going to haul the liquor overland, were waiting for a signal to go down to the beach and get it.

"We left them alone for the time being and quietly moved down to the first cottage at Little Beach. We watched while a crew filled this cottage with liquor. They were entirely unaware that we were there and we trailed them to a second building that they were going to fill. We had already notified the Coast Guard at Woods Hole, and their patrol boats were on the way, coming across the bay at full speed. There must have been twenty men unloading liquor into dories from a rum vessel that was just offshore and carrying it up the beach to the second cottage. Two dories were bringing the stuff in. Two trucks by the house were partly loaded and there was a lot more liquor piled up beside them.

"It was a big gang altogether. We sent word for help

and the Westport chief of police and six of his men responded. When they got there and our man led them to where we were, we decided it was time to go after the rum-runners. We were very much outnumbered, but we jumped up and ran out of the darkness at them, yelling for them to halt where they were. They began running in all directions, toward the shore, along back of cottages, and everywhere they thought there was a way out.

"We fired at the forms running into the dark and then the rum-running vessel started its engines and began to back off and head to sea. We ran down to the edge of the shore and fired our revolvers at it. We managed to corral five of the men who were loading the trucks and after we had cornered those blocked from escaping from the house, I went looking into a shed nearby. I stumbled over another man hiding under a blanket.

"I got him up, turned him over to somebody, and ran down the beach again to see what was happening to the rum vessel that we had chased out to sea. It was a bright moonlight night, and it was something to see those two Coast Guard boats, roaring across the water to intercept the smuggler. We heard the gunfire begin, and the rum-runner appeared to keep going. . . ."

It was now three in the morning. *C.G. 813* first spotted the rumrunner, engines revved up and running without lights. The patrol boat put a searchlight on her, and identified her as the *Star* of New Bedford; there were about thirty sacks showing on the afterdeck. She refused to heave to on signal; the *813* fired a pan of machine-gun bullets with tracers ahead of her, and the *Star*'s reply was to set a course for Hen and Chickens Lightship, her throttle wide open. The *813* gave chase.

No one ever did explain what happened next. Up to that point, the *Star* had not been shot into, presumably no one aboard was injured by the shore gunfire, nor was there any indication that the craft was mechanically disabled. Yet abruptly, she swerved and turned toward the pursuing patrol craft; only by backing down at full speed did the *813* avoid a collision. It may have been that the rumrunner deliberately sought to ram her pursuer; in any event, the Coast Guard vessel then fired into the *Star*'s engine room, and that stopped her. The smuggler lay dead in the water, low, dark shape in the moonlight; the *813* closed the distance between them cautiously.

While a few feet of black water still separated the two craft, there was a shattering explosion aboard the *Star*, accompanied by a spectacular sheet of orange flame. Immediately, she was afire; apparently the machine-gun fire had ruptured a fuel line and hot engines had done the rest. The wind was strong from the northwest, the fire was spreading rapidly; its heat and the immediate danger of more explosions drove the rumrunner's crew of seven to the rail, tensely waiting for the *813* to close the distance and take them off.

In addition to the wind factor, there was a heavy sea running; it was a situation that called for both haste and caution — poor judgment or bad luck in maneuvering could very well result in injury or death as the seven were transferred from one craft to the other. The *813* lay alongside; trough and crest, trough and crest, the seas slid under the two vessels and when they rolled together, there was the protesting crunch of wood. The Coast Guardsmen picked their moments carefully — timing was of first importance — and one by one, they got their prisoners off the *Star;* two of them required immediate medical aid for second-degree burns on their faces and hands. The *813* then stood off at a distance; her crew watched the flames consume the *Star* — she was lower and lower in the water, and finally, there was steam, then less fire and no fire, and after, she sank and there was nothing in the night, now bright and quiet again, to mark where she had been.

Ashore, they had heard the shots, watched the flames rise against the dark, seen the patrol boat move alongside the smuggler. "It was some picture," said Fitzgerald. Then he added, "You know, there was so much liquor stored in one of those cottages that the floor broke under its weight. I hadn't seen so much liquor in a long time." The final score: a $6,000 rum-running vessel sunk by gunfire, twenty men arrested, and 1,100 cases of imported whisky and wine, valued at $100,000, seized.

From the law-enforcement view, this highly successful land-sea battle was exceptional in the degree to which patrol craft and beach forces were able to coordinate. I concluded from what Fitzgerald said that competitive rum-running operators tipped off the customs officials. Obviously, as the engineer of the *Wanderer* emphasized in recalling this incident, it was not the neighbors who informed the government — rather, they sheltered the rumrunners looking for a place to hide. This was not an uncommon reaction, especially in areas where the rumrunners were natives, and known, usually on a first-name basis.

Often, when a liquor landing was scheduled, someone would give the police a "tip," principally to mislead them. Selectman Walter Silveira of Fairhaven, Massachusetts, related that in those days when the chief of police was wanted, "the signal was to turn all the lights in town off and on three times and then he'd go to a telephone, call the station, and find out what was wanted. A favorite trick of the rumrunners was to call the station; they wouldn't give any names, of course, but they'd say something like 'There's a gang here in the North End and they're acting up, making a nuisance of themselves. Better send the chief here to break it up before somebody gets hurt.' So he'd go, because he didn't dare take a chance and not go. And he'd be miles away when they landed the booze on the shore." In some areas, the rumrunners made a practice of setting fire to isolated buildings of small value immediately prior to a landing. The buildings were always at some distance from the landing site; the fire demanded the attention of both police and firemen for long enough to get the liquor ashore and under cover.

A southeastern Massachusetts woman who still lives within sight and smell of salt water — and who described herself as a "lady rumrunner" — provided a refreshing firsthand account of inshore dragging operations at underwater liquor drops.

"In the beginning, my husband was quahogging in Priest's Cove and he dragged up liquor in his tongs. Some other fellows did, too, but the neighbors reported what was going on and the cops took the liquor away from them.

"But after a while, my husband got tips from crew members of rum boats where they had dumped when they were chased. After they got up what they could, he took what was left and they expected a cut, because they had put him onto where it was. There was always plenty left even after the boat's crew got up what they could. He used to get thirty-five dollars a case, twelve bottles to a case, for Benedictine and champagne, and thirty dollars for whisky, gin, and all the others. The stuff was in straw containers and burlap bags; the bags had what we called 'ears' to lift them by.

"Mostly, it was in fairly shallow water. There was some dumped off Penikese but the liquor was no good because there was too much undertow, and water got into the bottles.

"There was a load dumped off Kettle Cove. My husband was told to drag it up. He only dragged on dark nights and his drag was three feet long, a piece of iron pipe with eight halibut hooks fastened to it, four on a side. So my husband took his crew — four men worked with him — and when he got there, a boat from Martha's Vineyard was dragging for the liquor. The man on the Vineyard boat didn't want my husband to get the stuff; he shot at my husband's boat several times with a rifle. The bullets came pretty close and one of my husband's crew was shot right through the hair. If he hadn't had a lot of hair, it would have gone through his head.

"Some days later, they got up a couple of cases, but the

Vineyarder shot at them again and wouldn't let them drag. We knew a lot of the fellows in the business and a rum-runner from Nantucket used to come to see us. We told him about getting shot at by the Vineyarder; he knew the fellow and he said, 'That man is bad medicine. He'd just as soon shoot you as not.' "

I asked her how she had happened to go with her husband on his expeditions. It was unusual for women to participate in any aspect of the business, beyond covering for their husbands or lovers (although I know of one who rode shotgun on the booze trucks that rolled from the New Bedford area to Boston), but it was especially uncommon for them to be dragging at the drops — this was hard, uncomfortable work and often in cold weather.

"There was one time when my husband found out about a boat that got chased in at low tide," she said, "and it got caught on the rocks, and they threw the load overboard. They had dumped it, but they hadn't come back to get any of it up. I think maybe the Feds were watching the man who owned it, waiting for him to go after it. They knew who owned it, and we knew, too. There was maybe three hundred to four hundred cases and it was down about thirty to forty feet.

"It was probably about the middle of December of either nineteen twenty-nine or nineteen thirty when my husband and his crew started looking for this drop. They looked for a month and didn't find it. Finally, I said, 'I'll go with you for luck.' We got out there in the boat and I pointed to a spot twenty-thirty feet away from where we were, and that was it. The first thing they brought up was Benedictine, then some rum, and then two cases of Old Tom gin.

"We hired a big catboat to go after it, and first my husband brought it back by boat and then by car. When they were using the car, they worked two men to a skiff and daytimes, they kept the skiffs in the woods, covered with tree branches.

"My husband and his crew worked that place for about three months. Some nights, I'd get an apprehension and he'd say that I was crazy because I didn't think he ought to go that night. So then he and I and our two married friends would go down there in a car and pretend we were lovers, just so we could sit and watch. And pretty soon, a cop would come along and say, 'No lovers allowed around here,' and when he was gone, I'd say to my husband, 'Didn't I tell you there would be cops or Feds here to-night?' Somehow, I could just feel it.

"One night, he had some of the stuff on the beach covered with seaweed and the Feds came there and never saw it. Another time, they were working the drop and when the Coast Guard came into the cove, they laid down on a little island in the dark and nobody saw them there. And once, he had two flat tires bringing the stuff home — it all came to our house — but he kept on coming with his load anyway. He could take fifteen to twenty cases in his Model T touring car with the back seat out, but that was one bumpy ride.

"They'd been dragging at the drop one night and went below for a little sleep. A terrible storm came up, the anchor dragged, the line chafed, and the catboat punched a hole in her side from the rocks, and went aground. They got ashore and my husband phoned me to take him what they'd need to patch the hole — red lead, paint, tacks, canvas, and so on — so they could get the boat home and hauled out on the ways.

"I got all the gear together and went down there. And I discovered I couldn't get down to the beach without going through somebody's property. So I put on a bold front and went to the house where the fellow lived that owned the liquor my husband and his crew were dragging up, because that was the easiest way to get there. I told him there was a boat ashore down on the beach and I was taking them what they needed to fix the damage, so they could get to a boatyard.

"He said nobody was allowed to go through his land. I said it was an emergency, the men on the boat needed help, and I thought it was an unwritten law that you could go through anybody's land if men on a boat needed help and you wanted to get to them. He got mad as the devil and he said, 'You can't go through this land.' So I went through somebody else's property and my husband and his crew plugged the hole and got the boat back home."

I asked her why the man who owned the liquor in the drop didn't see or hear the hijackers when they were working. "They were careful," she said. "Never worked in the moonlight. And they had their oars muffled with flannel cloth. I ripped up an old blanket and they wrapped it around their oars.

"But by the time my husband had gotten almost all of it, the gang in town found out what he was doing and they went there in all kinds of boats. They were all picked up by the Feds — except my husband, who wasn't there that night — and they all gave my husband's name as their own. This was in, say, early March, and my husband had gotten all of the stuff he wanted and didn't go there anymore. We sold the whole of what we got to two fellows who trucked it to Boston. But the man who owned the liquor got my husband's name from all those fellows who were arrested. He knew it wasn't their names, but he was trying to find out who the real one was, so he would know who got his liquor.

"One time after that, one of his men followed us. My husband and I had been to the Olympia Theater in New Bedford and we were walking home. One of this man's henchmen started following us, in a car. He stopped us on the bridge, the other side of the Crystal Ice works, where the Nye Oil Company used to be. He asked my husband to give him a hand with his car. Something was wrong with it, he said. My husband was tall and thin; he didn't get into the car, he just leaned in and looked.

"I was leaning back against the bridge rail. I figured

that if the fellow pulled a gun, I was ready to kick him. My husband said, 'There's nothing wrong with your car.' He pressed the starter down with his hand and it worked. 'Maybe there was a wire off,' the fellow said.

"Then he tried to pick us up again on the bridge, but we wouldn't ride with him, and he tried following us to find out where we lived, but we took different yards and streets, because we knew the town well, and he didn't find out."

The fear of bodily harm was justified. There are no complete statistics to indicate the number of deaths directly related to rumrunning and hijacking, and certainly none to reveal the number of assaults. But I asked her — even while sensing the incongruity of posing such a question to an amiable female senior citizen in blue shirt and white slacks, seated in her tidy living room — whether she had knowledge of people having been killed in the business. She nodded.

"My husband's cousin was on a boat and he and two other fellows dropped to the deck when the Coast Guard that was chasing them opened fire. The fellow next to my husband's cousin jabbed the third man with his elbow and said, 'You all right?' There wasn't any answer because the man was dead.

"Another time, there was a boat from here that went out on a calm night. Well, they came back without one of the crew and they claimed he fell overboard, but the talk in the fleet was that he was pushed by somebody that didn't like him. That was what we were told. That's what we believed. One of the fellows in the boat with him went to tell his wife that he was gone. Nobody ever did anything about it.

"There was a house at the head of a wharf in town and the man and wife living there made friends with the rumrunners. They used to have drunken parties. We stood at the corner near that house one night and there was some slapping and commotion. The rumrunners were out in the yard and they were talking about somebody who had been murdered and put in a barrel of cement because he talked too much."

"Where did that occur?" I asked.

"Off Rhode Island," she said.

"There is no question in your mind as to what they said?"

"None whatever," she replied.

The structure of the rum-running operation, because of the widespread use of aliases, violation of boat registration procedures, deliberate concealment of boat owners' names, deceptions, including false destinations, sailing times, and purposes of voyages — and even failure of one spouse to level with the other — lent itself well to losing human beings without a trace.

As an example, just before daybreak on August 30, 1924, off Atlantic Highlands, New Jersey, a Coast Guard vessel came upon an inbound speedboat, which it pursued. The skipper of the cutter megaphoned, "Lay to, or we shoot to kill." The smaller craft inched up the throttle and took off; in the cutter's searchlight, her crew could be seen throwing liquor overboard. Aboard the cutter, the order to fire was given; as the gun burst struck the smuggler, three men were plainly visible in the cockpit. One slumped to the bottom of the boat and the other two collapsed and went overboard.

The rum boat halted, and when Coast Guardsmen boarded it, they found Earl Bennett of Atlantic Highlands lying there with a bullet in his chest and another in his hip. He would not disclose the names of his companions. "What does it matter?" he said. "They're overboard and dead. They won't tell." One hundred cases of whisky were aboard.

Kidnapping of hijackers was not common, but it occurred at least once. I interviewed the victim of a kidnapping, who got into the business of dragging for liquor, as did many, because work was scarce and one had to eat.

"I started salvaging at sixteen or seventeen," he said. "We didn't have no jobs. There was nothing else to do and you have to make a living. We used to go for clams and quahogs to start with, and then we salvaged some coal from a barge that was ashore near the lighthouse on West Island. I had a twenty-foot open powerboat with a gas engine.

"We got hot tips here and there. We went to Wild Harbor off Falmouth and got a lot of liquor that was dumped there and we hid it in the barge on West Island; the bow was sticking out of water. I had twenty-eight cases there one time. We bought a diving suit for five hundred dollars on Atlantic Avenue, Boston, and we took diving lessons just this side of the lighthouse on Palmer's Island in New Bedford Harbor.

"There was a fellow quahogging off Marion. He found some liquor on the beach, where it had washed up from a big cache just offshore. A storm had come up and broke open a lot of cases. So my friend Joe fixed this guy's car for him and took liquor instead of money and the guy told him where he found the liquor. We rigged up and worked nights; we used a three-pronged hook. We got hoggish after we got a few cases and sent a diver down. Fitzgerald from the Customs House and the Coast Guard came. We had liquor aboard, but my brother dumped it over, so they found no liquor on the boat.

"We got a real tip about stuff that somebody told us. A big load was dumped New Year's Eve inside Mishaum Point, near Barney's Joy (South Dartmouth, Massachusetts). This was nineteen thirty-three; it was cold, very cold. The stuff came off the *Maybe,* that was chased by the Coast Guard. There was something like three thousand cases. It was in twelve or fourteen feet of water and piled so high that you could see it in daylight, they told us.

"We went there after dark. I was in my boat and my friend John had his brother's thirty-six-foot Navy cutter with a Dodge engine. Well, other people were looking, too. We never had no lights, but there was this fellow in a speedboat and he was stranded, blinking his light. So we went over to him; there was three men in the speedboat. 'What's the trouble?' we said. He had a piston go right through his engine. They wanted us to tow them into Padanaram.

"So we said we wanted to know what they were doing there anyway and they asked us the same thing. They must have gotten some stuff because we could smell liquor. They must have broken some bottles. We said to them, 'How about a drink?' because they already had a few bottles. So they gave us a drink. And we said, 'Why should we tow you? We're after the same thing. Let's get together. We can give you a tow. You know where the stuff is.'

"We made a deal. I towed the speedboat in and went back and we filled up the two boats. We took it ashore to a little pier at Barney's Joy. We got fifty-one cases and they got fifty. [Author's note: There is historic appropriateness in landing liquor at Barney's Joy, especially clandestinely. Back in the days of the founding fathers, the place was known as Barnes, His Joy, because one Barnes used to go there, away from prying eyes, to drink in secret.]

"Well, remember, I was only eighteen. And the next night, we went back for more. We were greedy. I was on one side of Mishaum Point, in my boat, and towing a skiff. My brother and his friend John were in the other boat, on the other side of the point. The only thing was, the owners of the liquor were salvaging that night, too, and we didn't know that. There were two men in a varnished speedboat that started to chase me. One of them was shooting at me with a pistol. I didn't want to cut my rowboat loose, so I couldn't go very fast, but I opened her up as fast as she would go.

"The way I was steering, I was crouched down as low as I could get, reaching up to the tiller, so they wouldn't hit me in the head. I was steering from one side to the other because they were shooting at me. I tried to go to the other side of the point to meet the other boat with John and my brother, but the speedboat was too fast. They caught me. They had sawed-off shotguns and revolvers and one of them said, 'The big boss will fix you.' They towed me to Barney's Joy and ran the boat ashore.

"The place was full of marshes and there was a three-story garage. There was a man with a sawed-off shotgun. Three other fellows — the ones that we had helped the night before — were tied up to a big tree. They had been shining spotlights. The rumrunner gang made them take down their pants and they kicked them in the rear ends. The gang had a big Buick with no seats in the back to get the liquor in and they said, 'You bring the liquor back or you won't see your families no more.'

"I was lying like hell. They kept asking me questions and I said we didn't get any liquor. There was a guy watching me all the time. They got three hundred cases ashore from the boats and they were passing around hot coffee and sandwiches. I was shivering. The man that was guarding me kept asking me my name, where I live. Another guy with him said, 'You better tell the truth. Those other guys we got tied up are squealing on you. We know you got liquor.'

"How would I like to die? he says. 'You rather be shot or drowned?' I was shaking and I said, 'I rather be shot.' So he sent a guy to get a canvas bag and a mooring.

"They left me there alone. I was going to run into the marshes. Good thing I didn't. I found out there was a guy on the other side of the building and he had a gun in his hand. He talked to another fellow and then he said to me, 'It will be easier for you if you tell the truth.' So I told them where I have the liquor."

Of the 51 cases, only 14 were left; through the efforts of

a neighbor, he and his brother had sold the remainder for $40 a case. The 14 cases were at his sister's home in New Bedford.

"They made me sign a note to my sister: 'Give these men the liquor back or you won't see me anymore,'" he continued. "I wrote it the way they said. They took me from there to a farm where they stored all the liquor. Two guys had hold of me.

"At my sister's house, we had seven cases of liquor hidden down cellar and I had a big wardrobe with seven more cases in it, behind the clothes."

The rumrunners went to the homes of his sister and of his brother; the procedure was the same in each instance: they presented the note, demanded the return of any liquor that had been recovered off Mishaum Point, and said that failure to comply would result in the death of the hostage. One of the rumrunners had a pistol in his hand while the conversations were going on.

"People in the street near my sister's house saw these guys with guns," he resumed, "so they called the New Bedford Police Department. The Liquor Squad went to my sister's house and the rumrunners ran away. The police got the seven sacks down cellar but when they got to the wardrobe, my sister said, 'He keeps his clothes in that; it's locked.' So they didn't get the stuff in there, but they took my diving suit."

At this point, police throughout the area were given a description of the missing youth. It seemed very likely, since the rumrunners had been unable to recover their liquor, that his life was in danger.

"So they still had me on this farm," he said, "Fitzgerald, the customs man, and the chief of police in Dartmouth got into the act. Somebody said to the rumrunners about the death penalty for kidnapping. This was just after the Lindbergh case. I think they got scared then. They released me around Reed Road, in Dartmouth. They gave me three streetcar tokens and I took the Kempton Street trolley into New Bedford. After I got off, I was walking home and a cop on a motorcycle picked me up. They took my fingerprints and my picture.

"The next day, there was a big war at the liquor drop off Mishaum Point. They went down with machine guns and a boat. It was between rumrunners from Massachusetts and a gang from Rhode Island that was both rumrunners and hijackers. There was a fight on the beach. They came in big draggers. There was a big fleet and a lot of people there. There were ten or twelve skiffs working for the owners of the rum.

"I did not do any more liquor salvaging after I was kidnapped."

The references to a "big war" and a "fight on the beach" are historically interesting because they emphasize a phenomenon of this era: there were, in fact, crimes of significance that were ill reported or not reported at all, for a variety of reasons.

There is no reason to doubt the accuracy of the kidnap victim's recollection and knowledge. He did, after all, know to whom the liquor belonged that he was salvaging; he knew the employer of his kidnappers; he knew the leaders of the two gangs that fought for the liquor — and I know them — but these individuals and factors never were linked to the incident, either through newspaper stories or court action. As a matter of fact, on January 12, 1933, the New Bedford *Standard-Times* reported, concerning the kidnapping, "The abductors have not been found." Nor were they ever, although a number of people knew who possessed the answers to the obvious questions.

If, at this distance in time, it seems strange that an armed conflict involving a number of people could take place in a relatively small community without producing reported casualties and resultant publicity, the "Battle of Bergeron Farm," in Dartmouth, Massachusetts, on January 7, 1927 — which also was a confrontation between rumrunners and rumrunnner-hijackers — might be cited as somewhat parallel. This "battle" did result in extensive newspaper coverage, but consider these aspects of it:

— The Bergeron Farm incident was described by public officials and the press as a "gun battle between rumrunners, hijackers, and the police." Actually, the four policemen present were, in the words of one of them, outnumbered "ten to one" and they were forced to take cover after being caught in the crossfire between the combatants.

— The district attorney, in making the preliminary opening of a resultant court case, stated that as the car bearing the policemen reached the farm and stopped, "a gun appeared in the doorway of the automobile and was pointed directly at Officer [Albert] Choquette; that the officer grabbed the gun and pointed it away from his body and the gun was discharged into the ground; that Choquette fired his own gun into the ground; that the shot was evidently a signal for a general shooting, and that shooting took place, and lasted twenty minutes or more. . . ."

— The only known and publicly reported casualty of the battle was a cook at the farm, who was hospitalized with a bullet wound in the head, from which he recovered.

— In a related raid a few hours later, police rounded up a dozen men and, according to contemporary accounts, "several rifles, repeating shotguns, and automatic pistols were seized."

— Defense counsel, in outlining his case in the court proceedings that followed, described the situation in which his clients found themselves at the Bergeron farmhouse: "Suddenly, the door of the house where they were assembled was broken in and a gang of desperate men came hurtling into the house. Every one of them was armed. . . . The leader told the men who were sitting around there to hold up their hands, and they held them up."

— The district attorney, in his opening, said that at a particular time after the arrival of the "desperate men," a person associated with the farm was discovered to have left. The district attorney said to the jury, "One of those present [among the hijackers] said to [the man who was shot in the head], 'If he has gone to the police and the police come back with him, you'll be the first one to go, even if I have to lose my life.' " The absent person had, in fact, gone to the police and they did return to the farm with him.

The question is then, even granting limited visibility in the area of a country farmhouse in a generally unlighted section "after supper," how could approximately forty armed men shoot at each other for "twenty minutes or more" and do no worse than wound one person?

At least one eyewitness said there were more casualties. My uncle, the late Oliver S. Ashton, was one of the four Dartmouth policemen present at the battle. When the shooting began, Officer Ashton took cover beneath an automobile. He always maintained that "a lot of them were hit," that he saw "one fellow put into a car," and that "people came running out of the house to help some who had been hit." He said that he saw "fellows dragging people who had been hit and putting them into cars."

Understandable fear, both on the part of the public and of many small-town officials, played a part in concealing many things. "Everybody just pulled down the curtains when it got dark," a resident of the Dartmouth-Westport area recalled. "But sometimes, we'd peek around the edge of the curtain and somebody would say, 'They're going into So-and-so's barn,' and we'd see them with trucks and automobiles, carrying the stuff in and stowing it in the haymow. They stored the stuff in a million old barns.

"They meant business. We knew what the trucks were doing when they went by, but if anybody asked me to get out in the road and stop one of them — even if I was a policeman — I wouldn't do it. They had guys sitting next to the driver with sawed-off shotguns, the barrels maybe twenty-two, twenty-three inches long. Christ, that stuff would fan out fifteen feet wide if they ever fired at you. I wouldn't get out and try to stop them. I wouldn't blame anybody who didn't."

Sometimes, in attempting to get the booze out of the beach areas, they considered subterfuge rather than shotguns. "I was driving a bakery route then, house to house," a southeastern Massachusetts resident told me. "There was a lady lived on a farm near the water. I never could sell her. Then one day, I got a message, 'Mrs. Smith wants to see you.' I had heard that the federal men were looking in that section for stuff.

"I went to the farmhouse and her husband was there and he said, 'Where do you finish your bakery route?' So I told him and he said, 'Can't you change your route so that you can finish here? You can make some money.' He wanted me to wind up at his place with an empty truck and then I'd load it up with liquor and nobody would think twice about it because they would see my bakery truck making that route regularly. 'At the end of the route,' he said, 'you got a lot of room in that truck.' I let him talk.

"Then I said, 'I carry bread and cake. This truck has leaf springs like a baby carriage. You put any weight in there and it will show so that everybody in the world will know something's going on.' He said, 'There's a good dollar in it.' I said no.

"When I left the farmhouse, his wife said, 'Better leave a card.' Those days, you used to put up a card in the front window if you wanted the bakery truck to stop, and you weren't a regular customer. But usually, when they say 'Better leave a card,' that means good-bye, they don't want to see you anymore.

"That's what she meant."

CHAPTER XIII

THE PUBLIC QUESTION as to whether the federal government was justified in shooting rumrunners remained unanswered throughout the Prohibition era. If a law-enforcement official killed a gangster, that was one thing, but most rumrunnners were not gangsters, and most had never even broken the law before. Further, in some instances, what the public thought about the shooting down of smugglers afloat was influenced by inaccurate news reporting and the result compounded by government secrecy.

As an example, early on the morning of August 22, 1924, a Coast Guard picket boat in lower New York Bay pursued a deeply loaded motorboat proceeding at high speed. The motorboat proved to be the *Lynx II,* with several hundred cases of liquor aboard; she was captured, after some gunfire.

The Associated Press reported: "The Coast Guard fought with machine guns and revolvers, while the crew of the Lynx returned their fire with revolvers. None of the Guards was injured, although bullet after bullet found its way into the government boat."

In this instance, whether or not the rumrunners fired on the Coast Guardsmen is of importance in terms of public opinion, because the master of the *Lynx* was killed by Coast Guard gunfire. There is nothing in the official report of the matter by M. W. Rasmussen, superintendent of the Fifth Coast Guard District, to suggest that the Coast Guard craft was fired upon, that it was damaged by bullets, or that weapons were seized when the *Lynx* and her crew were captured.

The rumrunner *did* resort to aggressive tactics, resulting in the death of her skipper. Rasmussen said, "The crew aboard the picket boat had continued to fire into the [*Lynx*'s] hull, in an attempt to hit some vital part of the machinery. When it became evident that it was the intention of the rumrunner to run the Coast Guard launch down, the officer in charge instructed men handling rifles and revolvers to fire into the pilothouse." But it was not a gun battle.

Sometimes, publicity aroused sympathy for the rumrunners. The cutter *Seneca,* cruising near Rum Row, observed a motorboat leaving the side of a schooner and starting for shore. During a short chase, the cutter megaphoned the skipper of the motorboat to halt. The command was disregarded, and the three men aboard the inbound craft began throwing overboard packages, which sank. The *Seneca* fired on the motorboat with a machine gun, killing one of the three men. No liquor was on the boat when it was captured.

Within the following two or three days, several newspapers published an International Newsreel photo of two appealing youngsters — a girl holding a doll and a boy with a ball — sitting on a doorstep. The caption read: "Orphaned by Rum Row Tragedy. Ignorant of the death of their father, T—— J——, alleged rumrunnner, killed by Coast Guard officers Saturday, little Margie and her brother Tommy play in their Brooklyn home. Mrs. J—— denies her husband was smuggling liquor and claims his fishing boat was fired upon without warning."

Some judges were sharply critical of this kind of situation, in which the Coast Guard opened fire without having been fired upon. One such incident involved the motorboat *Herreshoff*, which was seized near the Edgewood, Rhode Island, Yacht Club. At the time of the capture, according to the New London *Day,* Coast Guardsmen claimed it had been preceded by a running battle, during which the armored craft was riddled by government fire.

But during a hearing in federal court before Judge James M. Morton, a Coast Guardsman, under questioning, acknowledged that the rumrunners on the *Herreshoff* had not fired at the pursuing government craft. Judge Morton then stated that "promiscuous firing by government men on boats that are being chased cannot be tolerated by the government unless the government men first are attacked." He concluded, "Had the shooting incident in connection with the Herreshoff occurred in Massachusetts waters under similar circumstances, and any of the occupants had been killed, then the government officers would be charged with murder."

This brings us to the *Black Duck* incident, which, in terms of history, deserves to be dealt with in some detail, first of all, because it never has been publicly. For many years, the related documents were classified material and not available; they now are. In addition, the *Black Duck* shootings probably were the most publicized and debated events of the rumrunning era; they stirred much of the nation, including the Congress, and they provoked wide-spread controversy and some bitterness. Finally, government documents on the *Black Duck* affair raise some question as to what really happened.

Even today, among people who were familiar with the principals, mention of the *Black Duck* stirs vivid memories.

The builder of rum-running vessels whom I interviewed recalled, "I was up on this boat working and Charlie and a young fellow came by. We had got to know each other pretty well, so I said to Charlie, 'What are you doing tonight?' 'We'll see,' he said, 'it all depends on how things are, what the weather looks like, and so on.' It was that night that he got peppered."

"Charlie" was Charles Travers, aged twenty-four, of Fairhaven, Massachusetts. He had "come by" to see how work was progressing at the Casey Boatbuilding Company on his new 60-foot dragger, which was to be equipped with two 100-horsepower engines. Travers had served a brief enlistment in the Coast Guard as a surfman; he was stationed on Cuttyhunk during his period in the service and his enlistment had expired in the spring of 1924. He had done some commercial fishing and he was a boatman of outstanding competence. His contemporaries, including some of the rumrunners with whom I have talked, agreed, as one of them put it, that he knew "all the water around here the way you know the back of your hand. He could find anything, day or night, clear or thick."

The boat builder revealed another side of Travers. "You have to remember those were hard times," he said. "If it hadn't been for some good-hearted guys who were making money off rum, a lot more people would have been destitute. Charlie was one of those. He helped people; truckloads of groceries or coal, they'd get it and never know where it came from. Many a family that he kept in food and heat would be surprised to know who did it. They never knew. If Travers had the money he gave away to charity, he would never have to worry. He was so generous that he could be taken for almost anything anybody wanted; even if the guy didn't need it, he could get it. All you had to say was, 'I'm in a pickle, I need a hundred dollars.' Mostly, that was the last Charlie ever saw of them. That's my opinion, through knowing him."

Charlie Travers was one of the principals in this incident. So was the "young fellow" who was with him at the boatyard. John Goulart, twenty-seven, a popular high-school football player in 1919 and 1920 and, for several years, Travers's partner in lobster fishing.

Another principal was Boatswain Alexander C. Cornell, skipper of the patrol boat *C.G. 290.* "He was one of the most outstanding skippers in the Rum War and a terror to the rummies," Coast Guard historian Willoughby commented, referring to Cornell. He also was an experienced officer. He held a chief mate's license in the U.S. Merchant Service, had resigned his commission as lieutenant, junior grade, in the Navy to join the Coast Guard as a boatswain, and his combined Navy and Coast Guard service totaled more than sixteen years.

A third principal was the *Black Duck,* numbered C-5677, a craft described in contemporary accounts as being a "50-foot speedboat capable of 30 knots, powered with marine aero engines valued at from $15,000 to $20,000, while the hull has a similar value." She was characteristic of the latter-day rum boats, fast, unencumbered by frills and of low profile, her silhouette broken only by a small pilot-house, a squat engine room trunk, and a dory on her after-deck.

The *Black Duck* incident occurred shortly after two o'clock on the morning of December 29, 1929, in Narragansett Bay. As related in news accounts published the next day, including statements from Coast Guard personnel, this is what happened.

According to the Coast Guard, the *Black Duck* was first sighted by the *C.G.-290* off the Dumplings, across from

Fort Wetherell, at the entrance to the bay. Fog was heavy at the time but the *Black Duck* was "making speed for Newport." When the patrol boat's searchlight picked out the craft in the murk, sacks of liquor were visible, stowed all over the deck.

It was reported that

Boatswain Cornell signaled for the Black Duck to heave to. Instead, the rumrunner kept speeding ahead. Cornell feared that with her superior speed, she would be quickly lost to sight and pursuit in the fog. Coast Guardsmen estimated the pursued craft was going 29 feet a second. A few minutes was bound to determine the success or failure of the Coast Guard effort. Boatswain Cornell quickly gave the order to fire to stop the rum boat.

As Cornell gave his order, the Black Duck veered out to sea. The maneuver raised waves which rocked the Coast Guardsman and upset the aim of her marksman. Shots intended to cut the tiller ropes or smash the rudder instead raked the pilothouse. Twenty rounds of ammunition were fired.

The bullets killed three men aboard the rumrunner: Jacob Weisman, thirty-five, of Providence; John Goulart, and Dudley Brandt, thirty-five, of Boston, and wounded the only other member of her crew, Charles Travers. The *C.G.-290* put into Fort Adams at Newport after the encounter, the bodies of the dead men were taken to the morgue, and Travers was removed to the hospital. The *Black Duck,* with 383 cases of liquor aboard, was taken to New London.

Historically, what is most interesting about this first published account is that it was attributed to the Coast Guard and it states that the deaths were caused because the *Black Duck* "veered out to sea," raising waves that "upset the aim" of the Coast Guard gunner.

Interviewed at New London, Cornell described how his patrol boat was lying in the eastern passage off Newport when the speedboat appeared.

We immediately identified her as the C-5677, which had eluded us for a year and for which we had been on search. We identified her because of her lines, and there was no mistaking the piles of liquor stored aft and along her port and starboard rails.

In accordance with Coast Guard regulations, we waved our searchlight so there would be no mistake on their part as to our identity. We then sounded the signal for them to heave to. Instead of stopping, they gave both of their engines the gun and fled. Realizing that the rum boat had twice the speed of our craft and was sure to escape in the fog unless she could be made to lie to, we started firing the machine gun across her stern and hull. We knew that the cargo in the stern protected the crew. We saw no one except the man at the wheel and he was protected by the piled cases.

In his desperate effort to escape, the pilot yelled instructions to the helmsman to sheer off and head out to sea. As the other boat sheered, she turned diagonally broadside to our fire. The machine gun, which was aimed across her stern, thus raked her port side and penetrated the pilothouse, killing the three men there instantly. As the men dropped dead, their boat stopped. We ran alongside and boarded her, and found the dead men and the wounded helmsman.

We are very sorry that this happened. We'd have given anything not to have had these deaths occur.

There are three items of particular importance in this statement. First, Cornell did not attribute the deaths to the fact that his gunner's aim was upset by waves as the *Black Duck* veered out to sea. Second, he said the three men were killed because and *after* the rumrunner sheered, intending to head out to sea, and that the machine-gun fire, "thus raked her *port* side."

In the hospital at Newport, Travers offered his own version of what happened. A bullet had struck his thumb, pierced the palm of his hand, and emerged through the wrist. He had lost some blood, he was under guard, and he was bitter. He claimed the Coast Guard gave them no warning and just started to "blaze away."

"We just came through the fog and up against them," Travers said.

The Coast Guard boat loomed up like a big mountain. We didn't know it was a Coast Guard boat but I knew it was another ship and there was danger of collision and I swung her over.

Then they commenced firing. The three of them were hit at the same instant and I guess they died instantly for they didn't even speak after they were shot. When the bullet hit me, I lost my hold on the wheel and the boat spun around sharp and then the engines stopped — Brandt had been watching them and of course he was dead. Pretty soon a boat came alongside from the Coast Guard and they took the others in and we went back to the "CG" and they told me I was under arrest.

We turned and went to the fort and the CG hollered up to the guard that he was the Coast Guard and had a wounded man and wanted a doctor and that he had three others he guessed were dead, and the doctor came down and looked them over and said yes, they were dead. And he put a bandage on me and told the CG to take me to Newport because this was an Army post and couldn't take in patients unless they belonged there or in emergency and he thought my wounds couldn't be called emergency.

Them three fellows were damn fine boys. I'm just sorry for them, that's all. They didn't give us a chance, not a chance, and they were right on us.

There are three items of special interest in this statement. Travers said of his course change that he "swung her over" to avoid a possible collision but did not state that he made a radical shift in direction such as heading out to sea would entail. Perhaps under the circumstances he would not have admitted an effort to escape anyway. But he did say the boat "spun around sharp" *after* the firing.

Additionally, he raised the issue as to whether the Coast Guard vessel identified itself and gave proper warning (in what the government later defined as a nineteen-second interval) before firing. He also indicated, as did Cornell, that after the shooting, the *290* went alongside the *Black Duck*. Sworn testimony indicated that the reverse occurred — the *Black Duck* eventually went alongside the *290*.

The testimony was given to a Coast Guard board of investigation convened by Lieutenant Commander Carl C.

von Paulsen on December 30, the day after the encounter. The record compiled by this board, including exhibits, undoubtedly constitutes the best available information as to what happened.

In this proceeding, it was first established that the *290* arrived at Dumplings Bell Buoy No. 1 about nine o'clock on the evening of the twenty-eighth and, being unable to anchor "on account of the depth of water," made fast to the buoy by the stern, her bow heading to sea. The patrol boat showed no lights, "as properly ordered by the base commander and Mr. Cornell. . . ."

In addition to Cornell, the crew of the patrol boat consisted of Chief Motor Machinist's Mate Louis Johnson, Boatswain's Mate 1st Class Lewis W. Gavitt, Motor Machinist's Mate 1st Class Risden Bennett, Motor Machinist's Mate 2d Class Andrew Rhude, Seaman 1st Class Lewis R. Pearson, Ship's Cook 2d Class Arthur E. Dye, and Seaman 2d Class Frank W. Jakubec.

Cornell told of hearing "the sound of powerful motors slightly on the port bow and coming from sea." As the rapidly moving, unlighted speedboat crossed the bow of the *290,* the numbers C-5677 — painted white in characters three inches high on a dark background — could be read.

"I waved the searchlight up and down," Cornell testified,

showing it on the Coast Guard flag at the starboard yardarm, kept tooting the whistle, and hailed this boat to heave to. When this happened, the boat increased her speed and cut over to our starboard side and tried to pass between us and the shore. After she got somewhat abaft of our starboard beam, the machine gun was ordered fired. The man at the machine gun [Pearson] has instructions to fire astern of the boat and, if necessary, to try to hit the boat some place where the crew would not be in danger.

When the firing commenced, the boat swerved sharply to the left, presenting the stern of the boat towards the C.G. 290. The gunner immediately stopped firing and the boat headed off at right angles to the patrol boat; then she turned right and the boat was lost in the mist. I was preparing to follow them when they reappeared, heading across my stern. There was then a man in sight on deck. I hailed him, holding a riot gun in my hand, and told him to come alongside, which he did.

He said, "The rest of them are down and all shot up. Get us in somewhere, will you, as soon as you can." I stepped over on the boat and found one man on deck, lying down, and two crumpled up in the pilothouse. I immediately got under way and headed into Fort Adams.

In this testimony, Cornell did not suggest that the *Black Duck* changed course abruptly in an effort to escape by heading to sea, although both Cornell and the initial Coast Guard statement to the press had said this previously. Moreover, his statement, "When the firing commenced, the boat swerved sharply to the left, presenting the stern of the boat towards the C.G. 290. The gunner immediately stopped firing . . . ," seems at variance with his earlier comment on this. When interviewed, he said, "As the other boat sheered, she turned diagonally broadside to our fire. The machine gun, which was aimed across her stern, thus raked her port side. . . ."

Since in turning left, the *Black Duck* would have had to present her stern before exposing her port side diagonally to the gunfire — and if the gunner "immediately stopped firing" when her stern was exposed, the question is raised as to whether her port side, not yet exposed as she swerved, could have been "raked."

What is further interesting is that, earlier, Cornell stated that after the shooting, "We ran alongside and boarded her," and on this occasion, he said the *Black Duck* came alongside the *290*.

Dye's testimony supported this version. "When I went on deck," he said,

the C-5677 was on our starboard quarter or a little astern, perhaps fifty feet away. There was a man standing on deck. The captain called for him to come alongside. He said, "I can't." He was standing beside the pilothouse. The captain called to him again and said, "You had better come alongside." He made a couple of attempts and finally bumped us on the starboard side.

Then the man whom I found out afterwards was Travers came aboard. He was shot in the right hand and his hand was bleeding. There was a man lying down underneath the wheel. The captain said, "Pick him up." We picked him up and laid him on the engine room hatch. I heard Travers say, "For God sakes, do something for those men."

Pearson's testimony seems to support Cornell's concerning the *Black Duck*'s movements. Pearson said,

I first heard the klaxon and then saw our searchlight. Mr. Cornell called me and said, "Man the machine gun." I ran to the forecastle and took the machine gun. I saw a speedboat coming up on our starboard bow. I would say it was between two and four of our boat lengths away from us, although this is a very rough guess, as I couldn't tell accurately at all and it was heading in toward our stern.

When it was well past my beam, Mr. Cornell said, "Let them have it." The standing orders which I have received from Mr. Cornell are to fire so as to give warning, either over the stern or bow of the boat. I aimed in the direction of the stern and fired a burst. I afterwards found out about 21 shots. When the smoke cleared, he was heading directly away from us.

The machine gun was jammed and I was trying to clear it. When he came alongside, I helped to tie up.

Here, Pearson is agreeing with Cornell's second statement in saying "he was heading *directly* away from us." He makes no mention of the *Black Duck*'s port side being exposed to his line of sight. Pearson did not say that waves produced by the *Black Duck*'s veering out to sea had upset his aim, as did the original Coast Guard statement to the media.

Bennett's testimony added some details relating to Coast Guard warnings and identification and supported statements that the *Black Duck* had "turned into" the gunfire, although he did not say which side of her was nearest the *290* when this happened.

"Mr. Cornell was standing and looking out of the starboard window of the pilothouse," he said.

Mr. Cornell said, "Here she comes." With that, I hopped off the chart board and looked for myself.

Mr. Cornell put the searchlight on our yardarm for a signal, also playing the searchlight up and down and blowing off the klaxon for a signal, then putting the searchlight on direct line with the course of the boat. After this, he gave orders to the seaman on the port side of the pilothouse to man the machine gun and commence firing, which he did. At this time, the Black Duck was off the side of us, coming around, about 300 feet away.

The seaman was firing at the stern of the Black Duck for a signal. The Black Duck turned directly into the firing of the machine gun, which swept her completely from stern forward. At the time of the jamming of the machine gun, the Black Duck was just in sight. Then she disappeared. Then her lights went on and she turned to come alongside.

Bennett was asked by the investigating officer whether any other signal was given to the *Black Duck* besides the klaxon horn and waving the searchlight. "Yes, sir. Mr. Cornell personally called from the pilothouse and told them to heave to," he replied.

Although there is nothing in the official transcript to indicate why the questions were asked, an excerpt from Pearson's testimony is interesting; he is being questioned by the investigating officer:

Q. Did you, in the period you had been on this patrol boat ever hear any person on the patrol boat threaten to shoot up the Black Duck or any other speedboat?

A. No, sir.

Q. You are sure you never heard anyone on the C.G. 290 threaten to shoot up the boat?

A. Yes, sir.

Pearson further stated that when he fired on the *Black Duck* he did not intend to hit the pilothouse and would not have "if the boat had not changed her course suddenly."

As a final comment on the board of investigation testimony, it is noteworthy that Mr. Cornell was asked whether Travers had made any complaint to him or others of the *290*'s crew. The following exchange then took place between Cornell and the investigating officer:

A. Not that I know of. I said to Travers, "I guess this will learn us all a lesson." He said, "Yes, it's learned me a lesson."

Q. You have testified that you said to Travers after he was shot, "I guess this will learn us a lesson." Just what did you mean by that?

A. I meant that the conditions that existed that night were bound to happen at some time, the way that these boats have been operating in the past and failing to stop when signalled by vessels of the Coast Guard.

Q. Did you mean by this statement that you had not given the Black Duck adequate warning and that you proposed to do so in the future?

A. No, sir. I meant that I was sorry that in carrying out of my orders that men had been killed on the Black Duck. I called the attention of Travers to the fact that it ought to teach him a lesson and that vessels should stop when hailed by the Coast Guard.

The Coast Guard investigation proceedings lasted six days. The board of investigation came to the following conclusions:

— [Cornell] swung his searchlight alternately upon the Coast Guard ensign on his starboard yardarm and on the C-5677, sounding at the same time, the klaxon horn. C-5677 increased speed decidedly and passed on the starboard side of the C.G. 290, between the vessel and the shore. No one was visible on deck at the time.

— The C-5677 passed the bow of the 290 at a distance of about the length of one patrol boat, that is, 75 feet. As she passed, in addition to the signals already given, Mr. Cornell hailed her, ordering her to stop. At this time, she was going at a speed of about 25 miles per hour, or 41 feet per second, approximately. She failed to stop or attempt to stop.

— The shooting took place between 2:10 A.M. and 2:15 A.M. by the pilothouse clock of the 290. As she was drawing away, Mr. Cornell gave the order to Seaman Pearson at the machine gun, "Let her have it." Pearson had been previously instructed to fire his first shots astern of any craft and he understood these instructions. . . . Pearson opened fire, and in accordance with these instructions, his gun being trained well abaft the beam of the C.G. 290, as he thought, at the stern of the C-5677. About the instant he opened fire, the C-5677 swerved sharply to the left.

— Twenty-one shots from the Lewis machine gun were fired. This took about three seconds. The C-5677 was observed by Mr. Cornell through the starboard pilothouse wind, abaft of the door during the firing. There was no intent by either Mr. Cornell or Pearson to fire into the C-5677.

— The C-5677 went out of sight toward the shore. A short time afterward, she reappeared between the quarter and beam of the C.G. 290, heading toward that vessel. After being thus sighted by the 290, the sidelights of the C-5677 were turned on. At this time, none of the crew of the 290 thought the C-5677 had been hit.

— Gavitt was awakened from sleep in the completely darkened forecastle of the 290 by the klaxon horn; found and put on his shoes in the dark, and reached the ladder leading to the pilothouse when the machine gun opened fire. Jakubec was awakened from sleep in the dark forecastle by the sound of the klaxon, put on a sweater and pants and was putting on his socks when the machine gun opened fire.

— [After the C-5677 was secured alongside], Mr. Cornell took immediate steps to proceed to Fort Adams, the nearest place where medical assistance could be obtained. Distance, about 1,460 yards. At this time it was foggy. The 290 arrived at Fort Adams at 2:45 A.M., or thirty minutes after the firing, and medical assistance was immediately requested. Under the circumstances, this was the shortest time in which this could be done.

— The C-5677 is of the speedboat type, lightly but strongly

built, painted gray, of low visibility, engined with two nearly new 300 horsepower engines, Detroit Aero Marines. Each engine is heavily muffled, with Maxim silencers. In addition, the exhaust pipes were hinged and were submerged when the C-5677 was fired on. The C-5677 was fitted with a device to produce a smokescreen. When unloaded in New London [her] cargo consisted of approximately 383 sacks of assorted liquors.

— Three men . . . came to their death in the pilothouse of the 5677. Death was instantaneous in two cases and nearly so in the third. One of these men was directly facing the 290 when shot and two turned toward her, probably crouched in the port side of the pilothouse of the C-5677.

— Dictates of humanity were fully complied with by the crew of the 290 and medical aid was obtained in the shortest possible time, and first aid was offered to Travers, who was the only man who could benefit by it. The C-5677 was duly warned before fire was opened. The marks of bullets striking the C-5677 are shown on Exhibit 2 attached. The C-5677 had ample opportunity to stop before being fired on and after being warned, if the master thereof desired to do so.

— Assuming Boatswain Cornell first heard the motors of the C-5677 one-quarter of a mile or 1,500 feet away, which may be considered a maximum and that the C-5677 proceeded at a constant speed of 15 knots, which is the minimum, probably 60 seconds would elapse before the C-5677 was abeam of the 290. The C-5677, however, increased speed materially and probably attained a speed of 25 knots or higher, when passing the 290, so the elapsed time was decidedly less than 60 seconds. Had the C-5677 maintained her course and speed, she would have been out of sight astern of the 290 in about 200 yards, or 15 seconds. It is the opinion of the board that Boatswain Cornell gave fully adequate warning to the C-5677 and further, that the crew of the C-5677 were fully aware of such warnings and the source thereof and that Pearson is not at fault and that Cornell acted entirely within the provisions [of the federal acts] and is not culpable.

— The board, from the testimony and his own experience in similar situations, believes that a speedboat, under the conditions being considered, cannot be stopped except by such machine-gun fire as will endanger life. It is the opinion of the board that the C-5677 was first actually sighted 450 feet off the bow of the 290 and that the shooting took place about as indicated on Exhibit 1, and that the elapsed time between these two acts was 19 seconds, that three men came to their deaths on the C-5677 and one was shot in the hand consequent on deliberate efforts of the person or persons controlling the movements of this vessel to escape from lawful examination mandatory on the officer-in-charge of the 290. Recommendation: that no further action be taken.

In 1964, given the perspective of time and availability of government records, including the board of investigation's findings, Commander Willoughby, the Coast Guard historian on the Prohibition era, corroborated Cornell's account of what happened as the *290*'s skipper — presumably with details fresh in mind — gave it in the New London interview on the very day of the shooting. Willoughby concluded,

As [the Black Duck] was drawing away, Cornell ordered the seaman [Pearson] who was alert at the machine gun to "let her have it." He opened fire, aiming astern of the craft in accordance with his previous orders and his burst consisted of 21 shots in about three seconds. At the same time, the Black Duck swerved sharply to the left, with the result that, instead of going astern, the shots raked the *port* side of the craft and penetrated the pilothouse. There was no intent to fire into the vessel, but that is what happened.

The principal question that arises derives from Exhibits I and II to which the board's report refers. Exhibit I is labeled "Sketch of Probable Action in Seizure of C-5677." The board concluded that "the shooting took place about as indicated on Exhibit I. . . ."

This reconstruction of the relative positions of the two craft suggests that while the *Black Duck* was within the limiting angles of machine-gun fire from the *290*, she first presented her starboard side, then her stern, as she swung left, and then the port side diagonally, as she continued moving harder to the left. This is in accordance with what Cornell said and Willoughby wrote and seems to bear out what Bennett was describing when he said, "The Black Duck turned directly into the firing of the machine gun, which swept her completely from stern forward," even though Bennett did not state specifically that it was her port side which was hit.

However, Exhibit II, to which the board of investigation also referred ("The marks of bullets striking the C-5677 are shown on Exhibit II attached.") shows bullet holes, bullet scores, bullets lodged, and probable path of bullets. According to this diagram of the *Black Duck*'s hull, no bullet struck her at a relative angle greater than 175 degrees — which is to say that no bullet struck her *port* side.

All of the bullets indicated on this exhibit traveled across the hull from starboard to port; their relative angles of entry vary from 159 degrees to 175 degrees. Eight bullet holes are indicated in a separate drawing labeled "Pilothouse looking forward." The exhibit shows the relative angles at which bullets striking the pilothouse (where, the board concluded, "three men came to their death") crossed the *Black Duck*'s hull ranged from 159 degrees to 170 degrees — that is, they were moving from starboard to port.

What is not clear from these reconstructions is whether the rumrunner veered sharply *before* being fired upon (as Cornell and Willoughby have said) or *after* being fired upon (as Travers said). However, all witnesses agreed that the *Black Duck* turned to the left; Exhibit II, showing no hits on the port side, suggests that her turning to the left was taking her *away from,* not *into,* the gunfire and that by the time she presented her port side diagonally, the firing had ceased.

Even two or three shots that struck her stern-on, perhaps as she started to swing left, were at relative angles of 172 degrees and struck the *starboard* half of her transom and the *starboard* side of the dory carried on her after deck.

A point of interest is whether Cornell hung on the Dumplings bell buoy for five hours waiting expressly for the *Black Duck*. It is established that the Coast Guard knew she was coming in with a load. In his account of the incident, Willoughby has written that "[she] was offshore taking on a cargo of liquor from the British oil screw Symor." Bennett testified that Cornell was looking out of the pilothouse window and said, "Here she comes." This may have meant that he had already recognized her or it may have been a general expression, meaning "some rumrunner is coming."

The rumrunners, of course, had their own interpretation of what had happened and undoubtedly assisted in spreading the report that the Coast Guard was "out to get" the *Black Duck* or Travers. It may have been knowledge of this rumor that prompted the Coast Guard interrogating officer to ask Pearson twice whether he had ever heard anyone on the *C.G. 290* "threaten to shoot up this boat."

Fifty years after the fact, when I interviewed rumrunners in the area, they still felt strongly about the matter. The builder of rum boats at Casey's in Fairhaven, one of the last people to talk with Travers before he sailed and got "peppered," said, "You know, that never should have happened. We always understood that the fellow on the patrol boat was put there at the last minute and that somebody else should have been there. When Charlie came up for the buoy, he figured that he was all set —."

"You mean he had an arrangement with whoever was supposed to be there?" I asked.

"That was the idea," he said.

The engineer on the rumrunner *Wanderer*, who also was Travers's contemporary in the smuggling business, was more outspoken. "There was no need of that," he said of the *Black Duck* shooting. "It was out-and-out murder. The Coast Guard was breaking the law himself. He was tied up to a buoy in the fog. The *Black Duck* was making up to the sound of the bell to get his departure, and the minute he came up, the Coast Guard opened fire.

"We heard that a contract — an assignment to a hired killer — had been put out on the skipper of the Coast Guard boat by the big shots in New York. The word went around that this was so."

Since this is a history and in no sense is intended as an exposé, the questions raised here are not even implicitly critical in nature but are posed simply to point out apparent contradictions in the record. Had the *Black Duck* shootings constituted just another incident in the Prohibition era, such contradictions would make less difference to any documentation of it, but, as historian Willoughby has observed, "The . . . episode had some unpleasant repercussions."

CHAPTER XIV

ALTHOUGH THE NUMBER of deaths alone marked the *Black Duck* affair as extraordinary in the annals of the "rum war," the "repercussions" which followed it are best considered by regarding the incident as a symbol, rather than a specific. In that sense, reaction to it revealed the continuing dilemma of many Americans: Was the rumrunner villainous, and if so, how villainous?

As in any war, government's attitude historically is that the objective is to win and that there is no room for sentimentality in dealing with the enemy. Moreover, since law was involved here, the government *had* to take the position that the law must be enforced. The government *had* to support those people charged with enforcing it. A Coast Guard official pointed out that the *290*'s intention was to disable the *Black Duck* and that "at no time did they fire at any men.

"It was an unfortunate killing," he added, "but rumrunners and all others on the sea are under the law of the sea that requires them to heave to upon signal of a Coast Guard craft. In this respect, it is difficult to see where the rumrunners are any different from burglars or other violators of the law who attempt to escape."

But important elements of national opinion — and some man-in-the-street elements — were sharply divided over the issue of whether Americans ought to kill Americans over an illegal bottle of booze.

The "repercussions" were immediate, some personal, some public, and they encompassed far more than the simple fact of the shootings; they raised questions of government integrity, of Coast Guard competence, of civil rights, of the reasonableness of the Eighteenth Amendment, and of whether ultimate responsibility lies with the man who pulls a trigger or orders it pulled or rather with those at far higher levels who establish patterns and policies.

Cornell received a threatening letter which had been mailed January 1, 1930, P.M., in Pawtucket, Rhode Island. It said:

Mr. Cornell, the Hun: This is to notify you and all your crew not to come ashore at Newport or Prov. and, in fact, New London, as you and your crew are known and will meet instant death as we are waiting for you.

We are true Americans. We are going to put such a class of men as you out of the way. You are worse than savages, so beware, as we will get you if it takes a year to do it. From the Gang, and not Rumrunners either. Death is waiting for you and your crew.

Two days later, a resolution adopted by an audience which filled Faneuil Hall in Boston called upon President Hoover for an "impartial investigation" of the *Black Duck* shooting. The statement declared,

We believe that we have a right to respectfully demand that you, Sir, as President of the United States, order a thorough and searching investigation of the facts surrounding this deplorable incident by somebody not connected with the Coast Guard or the Treasury Department.

By the continuance of such governmental practices as the incident above described, we can see nothing but the destruction of the liberties for which our fathers fought, for which free men have bled since the time of the Great Charter. We are not asserting the guilt of the Coast Guard, but we believe the attitude of the government, as at present taken, will justly give the impression that an attempt is being made to suppress the facts and whitewash a criminal act of the worst kind, and all this for the enforcement of an unpopular, unnecessary and stupid law which has no proper place in the Constitution of our nation, and which all intelligent people know can never be enforced.

Conrad W. Crooker, general counsel for the Liberal Civic League — which had conducted an investigation into the shooting — was one of those who addressed the Boston gathering. He denied that the rumrunners had attempted to escape or that they were given warning by the patrol boat before it opened fire with a machine gun. Crooker said his investigation showed that the men were shot down from a point-blank range of fifteen feet as the *Black Duck* was proceeding at four miles an hour in a dense fog directly toward the *290*.

The *290*, he said, instead of being in pursuit, was tied by the stern to the Dumplings bell buoy at the time. He said Boatswain Cornell, skipper of the *290*, was afraid to board the *Black Duck* after Travers brought her alongside the Coast Guard craft. "Those men were left to welter and die in their own blood," he said, adding that it was the cook aboard the patrol boat who, finally, in response to Travers's pleas, went aboard the *Black Duck* to help him with the three dead or dying men.

Crooker claimed that when Cornell finally took his craft the half-mile through the fog to Fort Adams, two hours after the shooting, a naval surgeon there said that Jake Weisman, one of the three killed, was still alive and that he was not pronounced dead until half an hour after his arrival. Crooker asserted that if the Coast Guardsmen had taken the men to shore more quickly, Weisman's life might have been saved.

John F. Fitzgerald, former mayor of Boston, also spoke, and after sharp criticism of the shootings, announced his intention of being a Democratic candidate for governor in the next year, with repeal of the state's Prohibition enforcement act as a platform plank. This was a direct challenge to Massachusetts Governor Frank G. Allen, who, only the day before, had publicly defended the state law.

William H. Mitchell, chairman of the meeting, said that 1,100 men, women, and children had been killed in the enforcement of Prohibition. He declared, "Official murder is still murder. When murder stalks abroad in the name of law, in God's name, repeal that law."

Following the protest gathering, a crowd charged the Coast Guard recruiting poster on Boston Common, bowling over Chief Water Tender George Briggs, who was on recruiting duty. Briggs rescued the damaged sign. A new sign was put up on the Common, at which time, it was discovered that vandals had mutilated a second Coast Guard poster in Dewey Square, outside South Station. Then came the announcement that the Common sign was being withdrawn and that the one at South Station would not be replaced. International News Service reported on January 3 that "Coast Guard officials termed the demonstrations not worthy of comment by any intelligent citizens."

At about that time, Secretary of the Treasury Mellon made a public statement to the effect that the Coast Guard had done nothing that was not justified and authorized under the law in firing on the *Black Duck*. He said that as much as the shooting was regretted, reports he had received indicated that the Coast Guard was acting "entirely within their instructions and observing their duty in what they did. They gave warning; the boat was endeavoring to escape, and they could do no less than they did." The secretary said the Coast Guard "is authorized under the law to use force to stop boats." Mr. Mellon's statement was in line with those previously made by Rear Admiral Billard, the Coast Guard commandant, and Assistant Treasury Secretary Lowman, both of whom had defended the Coast Guard.

In an editorial on January 5, the Washington *Star* offered comment on the Faneuil Hall meeting:

Joseph Walker, former speaker of the Massachusetts House of Representatives, addressed [the Boston meeting] and he is reported to have said, "The Constitution commands our respect, but the 18th Amendment is inconsistent with the Constitution, and deserves no respect whatever." Mr. Walker is at best a loose talker. He knows, and the whole country knows, that the 18th Amendment to the Constitution is a part of the Constitution and is sacred as any other portion of that document, as long as it stands there unrepealed.

Mr. Walker knows that the 18th Amendment was adopted by the states in accordance with the method prescribed by the Constitution itself, by an overwhelming majority of the states, including his own state, yet Mr. Walker and other prominent citizens of Massachusetts advocate a "rum rebellion." This country has seen in the past rebellion against the federal government because of the desire of certain individuals to have their rum without paying an excise tax, but it is not of record that the rebellion succeeded or was an affair of which the country is particularly proud.

"We are not here to defend rumrunners," Representative John J. Douglass is reported to have told the crowd in Faneuil Hall. If Mr. Douglass believes that the mass meeting in Faneuil Hall will be interpreted in any way except as a defense of rum-running, he is mistaken.

And former Mayor John F. Fitzgerald asserted that the rumrunners knew, as they brought their cargo of illicit liquor along, that "it would be consumed by governors of states, mayors of cities, selectmen of towns, judges of the Supreme Court, judges of the Superior Court, judges of the Municipal Court, in fact, by public officials everywhere." A remarkable indictment of the officials of his own state, by one who is said to be a candidate for the senatorial nomination in Massachusetts this year.

Early on January 7, a mob bombarded with stones the houseboat of Boatswain Cornell, shattering windows on the boat and terrorizing Mrs. Cornell and her five children. Her husband was not at home at the time. Mrs. Cornell said that she was awakened at 2:30 A.M. when a shower of rocks struck the boat, which was moored at Shaw's Cove in the Thames River, near New London. She looked out the window and saw twenty men. Her screams, she said, were answered with derisive shouts. The New York *Herald Tribune* reported from New London on that date, "As a result, the houseboat, the Wild Goose, was towed to the State Pier here today and moored alongside a Coast Guard patrol boat. . . . Boatswain Cornell has been kept to the Coast Guard base since members of his crew on the C.G. 290 fired the machine-gun volley that killed three rumrunners on the Black Duck."

On the following day, it was announced that Mrs. Cornell and her children were staying at the Coast Guard base and that Boatswain Cornell, skippering the *290,* "put out to sea" for the first time since the shooting and returned to base "after a short scouting trip."

The U.S. House of Representatives on January 7 heard some extensive remarks on the *Black Duck* affair, precipitated by Representative Fiorello H. LaGuardia, a Wet, from New York. He began by charging that the Prohibition law "cannot be enforced," and he said the case of the *Black Duck* "is but another paragraph in the shameless annals of Prohibition. I will not refer to the bloody murder of the three members of her crew, lest some hardened Prohibitionist burst into applause and again stain the pages of the Congressional Record.

The Treasury Department rushes into print to justify the slaying of these men, yet the record is bare of any facts showing that the Black Duck had refused to heave to or was in actual flight. The Coast Guard officials and the crew of the cutter have been hailed and praised for having well performed their duty, yes, their duty as seen in the light of Prohibition. Part of the liquor seized from the Black Duck was, in turn, sold by members of the Coast Guard. Citizens of this country are prohibited by law to drink alcoholic beverages and yet on the same day that the Black Duck was captured, members of the Coast Guard were crazy drunk at New London, Connecticut. Thirty-nine members of the Coast Guard have been found purloining part of every seizure of liquor made by them.

(Author's note: Mr. LaGuardia was confused here, possibly in part by a media error. Shortly before midnight on December 28, 1929 — approximately twenty-four hours before the *Black Duck* incident — Coast Guardsmen on patrol found the loaded British rumrunner *Flor del Mar* of Halifax, Nova Scotia, abandoned and on fire at sea. It was later determined that her crew set her afire to prevent seizure and that they rowed twenty miles in dories to safety. Crew members of the cutter *Legare* fought the fire for four hours, then manned the pumps of the waterlogged *Flor del Mar* to keep her afloat, transferred some of the liquor to the cutter to lighten the rumrunner, and finally were able to tow the smuggler — "in constant danger of sinking" to New London. On January 3, the Washington *Herald* reported, "Stunned by the caustic challenge of New London city authorities to 'clean house,' Coast Guard officials began a sweeping inquiry within their own ranks today. Court-martial proceedings already have been started in the cases of six men accused of having partaken in a drunken orgy on confiscated liquor Monday. . . . Every nook and cranny of the base was searched, it was said, for some of the missing Golden Wedding label rye, which was part of the cargo of the seized rumrunner Flor del Mar. New London has been peculiarly flooded with this brand of rye ever since the seizure Sunday and the unloading of the vessel." The Associated Press reported two days later, "With the beginning today of the general court-martial of Coast Guardsmen charged with intoxication and theft of liquor from a seized rumrunner, it became known for the first time that 24 men were involved. Twenty-three are accused of being intoxicated; one man only is specifically accused of stealing some of the cargo of whisky taken from the liquor boat Flor del Mar." A news photo distributed by International at this time — a picture of a New London woman charged with keeping a disorderly house, as a result of the "drunken orgy" — was accompanied by an erroneous caption. This read, in part, "According to police, it was at a party at [the woman's] house that Coast Guards consumed liquor taken from the Black Duck after three rumrunners had been slain.")

These disgraceful happenings along the coast of New England [Mr. LaGuardia continued] and the case of the Black Duck are simply typical instances of the conditions brought about by Prohibition. The Coast Guard ten years ago was one of the finest branches of the government service. The honesty, the courage, the cleanliness of Coast Guard men was traditional and held up as an example to every other branch of the government.

As soon as that service came in contact with Prohibition, it became contaminated. Look at it now; what Prohibition has done to the Coast Guard it will do to the Department of Justice within a very short time after that department is cursed with the duty of Prohibition enforcement. The attorney general of the United States, now the chief law officer of the government, and legal adviser to the President, will be transformed into a national supersleuth.

Not only the Coast Guard, but also the Customs Service. It was just two years ago that I exposed the demoralizing conditions in our Customs Service. There, too, was a fine service unit, until it came in contact with Prohibition. Only yesterday, in Providence, Rhode Island, a shipment of liquor was in the care of Customs Service men. Instead of guarding this liquor they proceeded to drink it, and the peaceful citizens had to run for their lives to avoid being shot by these agents of the government acting in the capacity of peace officers.

What other law is there on the statute books of our country, or any other country, that requires the daily taking of human life, the constant use of armed vessels, revolvers, machine guns and cannon to enforce?

Representative Carroll L. Beedy of Maine, a Dry, then rose to respond to Mr. LaGuardia, and he began by noting that the latter had confused the two incidents of vessel seizures. Mr. Beedy said,

The gentleman said that we might as well face the facts as they are, and not as we would like to have them, and on that ground, I meet him. His reference to the Coast Guard in the open sale of liquor seized on the Black Duck by the members of the crew of the Coast Guard vessel and the drunken orgy in which they participated was the particular statement which spurred me and moved me to attempt this reply.

The Black Duck was seized on the seas, within the treaty limits, and towed into the harbor, and not a bottle of contraband goods in the way of liquor was taken from her by a member of the Coast Guard. She was immediately turned over to the Customs and no sale of any liquor was made by ordinary seamen in the Coast Guard ranks. It is a lamentable thing that that charge should have been seriously made upon the floor of the House.

Whenever the gentleman from New York takes the floor, the Wet press of the country headlines in many cases these false reports and drags down the morale, or tends to drag down the morale, of this splendid body of men. The gentleman from New York and I ought to be very careful when we are attempting to give information to this House, to state the facts as they occurred.

Here is what the gentleman has in mind. That very day, there was a ship at sea run down by this Coast Guard patrol — the Flor del Mar. She was laden with liquor. The Coast Guard sent for men in New London to remove the liquor because the boat was sinking, or about to sink, as she had been set afire. They did rescue the ship and towed her into the harbor, and later sent for 100 or more men of the base in New London to remove that liquor from the ship.

I understand the fact is that these men, gobs, as we call them, ordinary seamen, yet red-blooded American boys, stood in the water for hours on that cold December night unloading this liquor. In the explosions which had occurred on board the ship [Author's note: There were "several explosions" while the vessel was burning, according to the commanding officer of the *Legare*], some of the boxes had been broken open and some of the gobs, to relieve themselves from the cold and suffering, opened the bottle and drank something out of it.

An observer noted that at this point, "The speaker here was interrupted by a gale of laughter, which swept the floor and galleries [prompted by his] description of the reasons why Coast Guardsmen unloading the confiscated cargo of the rumrunner Flor del Mar near New London, Connecticut became intoxicated, converting the unloading party into a liquor party. He said that many persons who stood in cold water for hours late at night might take a drink under the circumstances."

When the laughter had subsided, Mr. Beedy continued, "You will never get together men in the Coast Guard who, under these circumstances, will not take a drink of liquor when it's open before them." Addressing himself to the actions of rumrunners on dark nights when they sought to elude the Coast Guard patrols, Mr. Beedy said, "It is much easier for the Coast Guard to say, 'We did not see these ships.' No doubt the rumrunners think that before long, these boys will be sick of being accused as murderers, and suspend their vigilance. What would you do? Admiral Billard, appealing to his men, says, 'I can send a telegram to those boys tomorrow, telling them not to fire on a motorboat under any circumstances.' This is the crux of the enforcement problem. What would you have them do?"

Wells Church, covering the debate for the New York *Herald Tribune*, wrote: "The applause that followed this statement was prolonged. With perhaps two hundred members on the floor, it was noticed that not more than twenty-five refrained from applauding in some manner."

Representative Charles L. Gifford, congressman from the Massachusetts district in which both Travers and

Goulart lived, asked to speak at this time. He said, "Among these men [crew members of the *Black Duck*] our people are particularly interested in two of our boys. One was especially a fine boy. The people in my district are in a terrible frame of mind. They think those men were induced to disobey the law on behalf of somebody higher up. Must we encourage the Coast Guard to shoot them?"

(Mr. Gifford may have had some advance knowledge of the course of a customs investigation into this matter, prompting his allusion to "somebody higher up." On January 23, Boston customs officials said the *Black Duck* "smuggling affair was promoted by a Boston liquor ring," adding their investigation had "netted the government sufficient evidence on which to proceed against the group of suspected liquor barons.")

In a response to Mr. Gifford's remarks, Mr. Beedy took the floor again and declared,

Let us be careful of what we say here. Let no man say, "Let the Coast Guard shoot them up." I represent the Dry constituency, and I vote Dry, and I believe the Prohibition officials and the Coast Guard of this country will be permitted to make an honest and conscientious attempt to enforce Prohibition.

If a rumboat defies the demand of a Coast Guard officer to stop and permit a search, and starts to escape, then it is time for the officer in charge of that boat to command that they fire on that boat and attempt to disable, without, if possible, injuring anybody. But if she attempts to escape or maneuvers herself into such a position, knowing that this is a United States Government boat, and having the authority of this government behind it, that she is within range of their guns, then the members of this House, sworn to uphold the Constitution and to defend it against its enemies, must make these boys know that if they do their duty, a majority of the members of Congress and the people of the United States are behind them to a man.

Mr. Church reported, "Again, the clapping of hands filled the chamber. . . ."

In his first public address in opposition to national Prohibition — delivered before a meeting of the Women's Committee for Repeal of the Eighteenth Amendment at the Ritz Carlton in New York, Edward E. Spafford, past national commander of the American Legion, called the shooting of the three men "in moral principle, almost an exact parallel of the sinking of the Lusitania."

Mr. Spafford, a former naval officer, praised the Coast Guard as a "fine body of men condemned to do the dirty work." He added,

I am neither a Wet nor a Dry. I don't care whether we have light wines and beer, or whether we have everything, or whether we abstain totally, but I want no compromise with the people who put this iniquitous amendment, foreign to every principle for which our forefathers fought, into the Constitution. I want absolute repeal, and the vast majority of the members of the American Legion, whom I know as well as the next man, agree with me.

The other day, I attended a newsreel picture. Scenes of Coast Guard activity were shown, and an officer of the Coast Guard tried to explain why his men had done what they did. The hissing was so loud that it drowned out his words. That to me, as a naval officer, was an infinitely pathetic thing, because I know the officers and men of the Coast Guard, and I admire them. I know that they were merely obeying orders, the sworn duty of a military man.

The Lusitania, carrying arms to the Allies, fled from the submarine. The Black Duck fled from the Coast Guard. The Germans in the submarine, like the Coast Guardsmen, had orders to shoot to kill and sink, if they could not otherwise capture. The men were not to blame in either case. In the case of the Lusitania, where the whole world was aghast, we held, not the men in the submarine, but the government superiors responsible. In the case of the Black Duck, where a whole nation is aghast, we should hold responsible the superiors of these men who dealt out death for something not intrinsically wrong.

This I say with all the force of my being. Those men who advocate killing should not be privileged to hire honorable people to commit murders, but should be required to do the actual killing themselves and take the consequences of public opinion.

A subscriber to the Seattle *Daily Times,* one George Spencer, objected to that newspaper's editorial position concerning the Coast Guard and wrote a letter to the editor:

Because less than forty men out of a body of more than 10,000, or less than four-tenths of one percent, are accused of taking a few bottles of whisky and committing a breach of discipline, the Times condemns the whole Coast Guard.

That fine body of men needs no defense from one who was never in any government service. Does the Times really believe that the mob of hoodlums, the waterfront riffraff who tore down a recruiting poster in Boston, represents the true public sentiment in this, our United States? As for those blackguardly demagogues of congressmen from some of the Wet states who are now busy on the floor slandering and vilifying the Coast Guard, we all know what they want. They rant about that ungodly lawbreaking crew of the Black Duck not being given proper warning, which is not true. The facts are that the same rum boat was permitted to get away after many warnings on several former occasions.

An editor's note responded to Mr. Spencer:

So far from "condemning the whole Coast Guard," the Times has centered criticism solely upon the score or more of the Guards' enlisted men involved in charges of stealing and drinking seized contraband liquor, ten of whom already have pleaded guilty. The Times has never condoned lawbreaking or defiance of the authority of the United States. Mr. Spencer should have read more carefully.

The *Times* concluded editorially,

It cannot be questioned that the Coast Guard has come upon evil days. The sudden expansion of personnel has made it necessary, or seemingly so, to accept such applications as may be made at recruiting offices. Lower-grade applicants press for admission. It is not the fault of the Guard as such, but of the country, which imposes a distasteful task upon it, that better men do not offer themselves.

The Buffalo (New York) *Evening News* suggested: "If the Prohibition act has required members of the service to do duty that often has put the Guard in a bad light, the fault lies with the system that has added to their responsibilities a special duty that does not properly belong to the men who serve humanity well when lives hang in the balance."

"Great questions of the course of the Coast Guardsmen in the recent shelling of a rum boat off the New England coast still remain unanswered," observed the New Orleans *Tribune*. "After that bloody incident . . . some overenthusiastic mob then staged a new sort of Tea Party in Boston, during which they tore down Coast Guard recruiting posters. . . . Prohibition has cost both local police and federal agencies great loss of respect in such episodes."

Important newspapers came down on opposite sides of the issue. "It may be that bloodshed is inevitable in the enforcement of a law that large sections of the country treat with contempt, but does this excuse the raking of an unarmed rumrunner with machine guns at close range?" asked the New York *Herald Tribune*.

In specific editorial rebuke to the *Herald Tribune,* the Washington *Post* replied, "Newspapers that should know the law are joining in the clamor against the Coast Guard. . . . For 100 years, the law has provided that boats shall stop when hailed by a revenue boat and that the law officers may fire upon those who refuse to halt." And the Los Angeles *Times,* commenting on the shooting, observed that "the Coast Guard talked the only language smugglers and pirates have ever understood. . . . [This] is a somewhat dramatic answer to the Senate politicians who have been demanding what has been done about Prohibition enforcement, but not expecting a reply."

And finally, the Washington *Star* reported on January 12:

Representative Warren, D-N.C. said yesterday that remarks by Secretary [of the Navy] Adams, now en route to the London arms conference, in a speech in Boston, were a "deliberate insult and slur" against the Coast Guard.

Warren read from a newspaper article in which Adams was quoted as saying that the officers who fired on the rumrunner Black Duck, killing three men and wounding one, were "not Navy men, but Coast Guardsmen."

The North Carolinian said that such an utterance was unworthy of a man holding the high office occupied by the Secretary of the Navy, and added that Secretary Adams had "exercised his usual propensity for saying the wrong thing at the wrong time." Warren paid tribute to the Coast Guard, saying that "no braver, truer or more honorable man than Admiral F. C. Billard, Coast Guard commandant, has ever worn the uniform of an American officer."

On January 17, 1930, a Rhode Island grand jury considering the *Black Duck* deaths heard seventeen witnesses, including members of the crew of the *290* and, after deliberating an hour, returned no bill against any of the Coast Guardsmen.

On January 30, Henry M. Boss, Jr., U.S. attorney in Providence, wrote to the Coast Guard commandant in Washington:

My dear Admiral Billard: Permit me to thank you for the kind expressions in your letter to me transmitted by the attorney general in the matter of the case of the crew of the C.G. 290 before the Grand Jury of the State of Rhode Island. The successful result could not have been attained without the aid of Captain H. H. Wolf, commander destroyer force; Commander [Clarence H.] Dench, and Lieutenant-Commander [Carl C.] von Paulsen at New London. With their aid, I was able to convince the assistant attorney general of the State of Rhode Island in charge of the Grand Jury that it was his duty under the circumstances to act as an investigator and not as a prosecutor, in presenting the case to the Grand Jury.

On March 4, a federal grand jury in Providence refused to indict Charles Travers for his role in the *Black Duck* incident because the jurors concluded that he had "been punished enough by the Coast Guard, which shot off one of his thumbs."

AS IT MAY YET BE WRITTEN

I long for the village I knew in my youth
That dear and romantic old spot
The old-fashioned streets, where the trees overhung
The bay, where the boats at their mooring buoys swung
Old scenes that I've never forgot.

The grocery store at the foot of the road
Where bearded old men sat aloof
And talked for long hours, most gravely and slow
On licker, of "evidence, high up or low,"
Instead of their calling it "proof."

The blacksmith shop, dingy and smoky and black
Where daily the smith's hammer swung
At forging the parts for the stills in the woods
The boys kept him busy producing the goods
As I can remember when young.

'Twas sleepy and peaceful, that village by day
But when night her mantle had spread
Men hurried and scurried both hither and yon
At making and moving the hooch till the dawn
Should drive them to cover and bed.

Ah, could I but go to that village again
That village that sits by the shore
To work with the bunch as they hasten to land
The cases of happiness called contraband
As I used to do it of yore.

To walk once again down the old village street
And keep my illegalized date
When smoke rises soft from the swamp-hidden still
The rumrunner's signal is set on the hill
And the moonshiner calls to his mate.
                              —Joseph Chase Allen
                                          1923

CHAPTER XV

T HERE CAME THE DAY when all of this ended, accompanied by a holiday atmosphere, a national sigh of relief, certain regrets from the smugglers, some of whose trade sputtered on for a few years more, and generally, quick forgetfulness of an era of American history that had produced high adventure for many, money for some, and death for others.

In New York, former Governor Alfred E. Smith smiled in his office in the Empire State Building when the news was brought to him that Utah, the thirty-sixth state to do so, had officially ratified the Twenty-first Amendment to repeal the Eighteenth Amendment at 3:32½ P.M., December 5, 1933. Mr. Smith declined to pose for news photographers with a drink in his hand, saying, "I never drink in the day-time."

President Roosevelt called on all the nation's people on that date to see that "this return of individual freedom shall not be accompanied by the repugnant conditions that obtained prior to adoption of the 18th Amendment and those that have existed since its adoption." In announcing that the prohibition of alcoholic beverages in the United States had ended at 5:32½ Eastern Standard Time, the President added, "I ask especially that no state shall, by law or otherwise, authorize the return of the saloon, either in its old form or in some modern guise." Mr. Roosevelt said he wanted no return of pre-Prohibition social and political evils, which were "a living reproach to us all."

In Northport, Long Island (and undoubtedly many other places), imbibers were unable to celebrate repeal with "real stuff" on December 5. Liquor was plentiful, but none of it bore the official seal of Uncle Sam, and drinking residents postponed their celebration until the next evening, when the first legal wares were obtainable.

On December 6, H. L. Mencken observed, "It is not often that anything to the public good issues out of American politics. This time, they have been forced to be decent for once in their lives. The repeal of the 18th Amendment means vastly more than the return of the immemorial beverages of civilized man — it means, above all, a restoration of one of the common liberties of the people. It was as absurd and oppressive for fanatics and politicians to tell them what they could drink and not drink as it would have been for the same mephitic shapes to tell them what to eat or wear."

Oscar of the Waldorf drew the first legal cork (it was Vat 69) at the Norse Grill service bar in the Waldorf Astoria, and in the same hotel, the board of directors of the Association Against the Prohibition Amendment met and voted to disband at the end of the year. The Federal Alcohol Commission announced it planned to "turn the spotlight of publicity on liquor costs to cut the high retail prices reported in many localities the first day after repeal." Actually, repeal had cut the prices in half; whisky was selling for three dollars a quart and Scotch for forty-five to sixty cents a highball.

In Boston, with 200 out of an ultimate 2,000 clubs, hotels, restaurants, and package stores properly licensed to sell liquor, the city — according to an eyewitness on that first wet night — "promptly undertook a regal celebration which rapidly assumed New Year's Eve proportions. By 10 o'clock, every place which had received its license was packed to the doors and it was impossible to get within forty feet of a bar without a long wait."

On December 7, the matter already having been relegated to page 18, *The New York Times* noted that "one hundred thousand homes throughout the city uncorked legal wine and liquor; repeal reached the family stage.

"Despite the rain, hundreds waited outside wine and liquor shops of Bloomingdale's, Gimbel's, Hearns' and Macy's and Namm's in Brooklyn, which opened at 9 A.M. yesterday. The shops admitted small numbers at a time; others took a wetting."

Rum-running is the stuff of which history is made and elusive history at that; it remains one of the nation's best-kept secrets. I approached one rumrunner of consequence for an interview through a mutual friend who had known him since childhood. The response: "I don't want to remember; I want to forget."

The waterfront reporter of the New Bedford *Standard-Times* talked to a group of former rumrunners in April, 1936. Many of the stories they told him — minus the names of places, men, and boats — were gauzy in their vagueness, and that is the way they wanted it. And still want it. Yet in their recollections, there is the irrepressible spirit of the smuggler:

"The four stackers were the easiest to get away from.

When one tailed you, it was just a question of waiting for night. Then a jingle for full speed and a quick spin of the wheel to reverse your course. By the time the destroyer got her long hull turned around, we were a mile or so away. Then she came tearing up on us, searchlight glaring. When she was about 200 yards away, we shut off our engines and snapped on our two red 'out of control' lights.

"If she rammed us then, she was to blame. But her terrific speed carried her by us in a smother of propeller foam even though her engines were put full speed astern. Then we simply doused our lights and left that place and the destroyer. . . ."

"I'll never forget the time I put my boat under the Stone Bridge in the Sakonnet River. A C.G. was right on our stern and it was the only hope. The clearance under the bridge was about a foot over our deck. The pilot-house left us, but we got through and the C.G. didn't dare try it. . . ."

"Once they turned the deck hose on me after someone aboard the C.G. had fired a hunk of coal at me. When the hose struck me, I reached around and picked up an iron bolt and let it go. It went through the pilothouse window of the C.G. They didn't complain. . . ."

"Some of those nights when it blew offshore it was tough. Remember when the Madame couldn't load offshore so she and the offshore boat came up under Squibnocket and transferred 1,800 cases? And the big offshore boat rammed the Madame in the dark? Well, the Madame took her 1,800 cases and started for New Bedford. In Buzzards Bay, she began to sink and had to run back for Quicks Hole. But she didn't make it. She sank with the liquor aboard and her crew rowed ashore in the dory. . . ."

"I had a big load aboard once and two of my crew had broached a case of beer. It was thick fog and I was having a merry time of it trying to find the little creek entrance where I was to drop. At last, I got desperate and blinked my flashlight ashore in an attempt to get an answer. Will you believe it when I tell you that that flashlight beam revealed the red entrance buoy to my creek? . . ."

"One C.G. used to board me regularly and every time he'd ask me what my name was that time. He knew me and every time I'd give a different name. Once I claimed I was Carlos Henrique de Castillion Tavares, and 'no spik Inglis' ver' good.' It was lots of fun. . . ."

"Tales of danger, excitement and thrills roll off their tongues as easily as the latest weather discussion," the *Standard-Times* reporter wrote, "and none of these men would enter the game again if it were possible. They have had their fun and their money. Most of them spent every cent of their high earnings as fast as they could.

"Daredeviltry, nerve, seamanship — it was all a game with good pay for the successful. Their period of activity will go down in American history as a colorful episode outranking even that of the pirates who ravaged our coasts in times gone by."

Some of the symbols of the era faded before Prohibition ended. The cutter *Seneca* — with a show of gunfire when he tried to run for it — captured Bill McCoy and his beloved *Arethusa,* then renamed *Tomoka* and under British registry. Six years before repeal, McCoy predicted that liquor smuggling on a large scale was finished and would not return, "largely because of the high tributes exacted of the rumrunners by shyster lawyers."

I talked with McCoy on October 20, 1939, in New Bedford. Characteristically, he was in the wheelhouse of a boat and he was then making a model of *Arethusa.* "It's strange how some people just fall into adventure," he said of himself. "I took the *Arethusa* down to the West Indies and put her under the British flag. Then I brought her up off Nomansland and sold good whisky to everybody and anybody who wanted to buy and had the price."

The *Encyclopaedia Britannica,* which refers to McCoy as "a stalwart," adding that "only a few skippers of this type survived [in the liquor smuggling business], for the agents with whom they had to deal had many ways of tricking them out of their cargoes . . . ," tends to support his evaluation of himself.

But the New Bedford *Standard-Times* took issue with McCoy's claim to have sold nothing but "good whisky." In his obituary on January 1, 1949, the newspaper commented,

He won fame of a kind as skipper of the rum ship Arethusa, which in 1921 did a flourishing illicit business off Nomansland until unwelcome publicity in The Evening Standard made a change of location imperative.

Captain McCoy claimed to be coiner of the expression "the real McCoy," which he applied to the liquor he hauled from Nassau to the thirsty U.S. coastline. It was his boast that he sold the genuine article, although what might have happened to it after it left his ship was another matter.

Professional chemical analysis of two brands of whisky bought by Earle D. Wilson, Standard reporter assigned to board the Arethusa as a customer and bring home some evidence, indicated otherwise. The chemist's report was cheap rotgut whisky and rain water.

The heroes of any era fade and have their inevitable detractors.

Some rumrunners did not spend all the money they made. A fellow died in eastern Canada a couple of years ago; he had lived comfortably for a long time and it was known in the small community in which he resided that his money had come from running liquor. Among other possessions, he owned an odd-sized horse collar that almost everybody in town had borrowed at some time over a period of years, this being a town where horses were much used. Upon his death, he left a letter to his son, advising him to look in the collar. It was stuffed with thousands of dollars and had been so for a long, long time, even while it was being loaned freely.

Some money remains from the days of rumrunning, translated into businesses both related and unrelated to drinking. Some landmarks remain, too. Within three to fifteen minutes' walking distance from where I am writing, there are houses, sheds, wharves, and boatyards that figured centrally in the rum-running operation. It is so in many communities of the Northeast. And in Rhode Island, there is a house with an ingenious arrangement that allows a boat to approach the building from the water side and float in underneath it, out of sight behind closed doors.

Some people remain, too, although they are fewer each year and those whom I interviewed ranged from their early sixties to their late eighties. When I have mentioned that I was writing this book, they smile and you can fairly see the recollections coming into focus. One never knows what it is they are going to remember; one woman said: "I was three or four years old and you remember how the seats of cars used to lift up? Well, my mother and her boyfriend would put some bottles under the back seat and wrap burlap bags around them so they wouldn't rattle and then they'd put me in the back seat to have a nap. I remember a flashlight streaming into the car and my mother said to the policeman, 'Officer, I hope you don't wake my little girl.'

"Another time, her boyfriend ran the car into a tree. The police came and my mother had the bottles inside her coat and she had her arms folded to hold them up. She said to the police, 'My daughter and I are so upset that we have to go to the bathroom.' So the police let us go down into the woods and there was a barn there, and my mother put the bottles inside the barn and hid them."

What these people remember is already half-legend and I have to remember why this is: it was more than fifty years ago that I went to the docks to look at the draggers that never went fishing, listened to the laughing, booted men who did not work days and disappeared nights, heard the high whine of beautiful engines in the dark, and watched the workings of a strange and dangerous kind of history without knowing it.

And to this day, America has not really decided whether the seagoing principals of this period were heroes, villains, or simply pawns of the larger circumstance, as are we all, to varying degrees.

Recently, I mentioned to a young man of twenty-something years that I was writing a book on rumrunning. He looked perplexed and said, "I don't understand the term. Do you mean that all they smuggled was rum and no other kind of liquor?"

The thought that the term could be misunderstood never had occurred to me and that is how far we have traveled since the misty years when the *Diamantina,* the *Lassgehen,* and Frank Butler made headlines. Even the essential idiom has fallen prey to time and change. And that, of course, is the only way in which history can become history.

ACKNOWLEDGMENTS

Chapter I

Excerpts from the Reverend John Roach Stratton sermon from the New Bedford (Mass.) *Evening Standard* of July 11, 1921. Remarks by Richmond Pearson Hobson from news story by George R. Morris, Jr., New London *Evening Day* of October 6, 1927. Letter to Coast Guard commandant, dated May 14, 1931, from L. W. G., Coast Guard files, National Archives, Washington, D.C. Fannie Hurst interview, *Evening Standard,* July 14, 1921. Photos of Helen P. Gatley, *Evening Day,* January 31, 1927. Testimony of "Waxey" Gordon, *The New York Times,* December 1, 1933.

Chapter II

Documents relating to Thomas Godman and Schooners Associated Limited made available to L. J. Ekstrom, assistant U.S. Customs attaché, London, England, August 20, 1927; verified as copies of originals, August 22, 1927, by firm of Constant and Constant, attorneys-at-law, 24 St. Mary's Axe, London; forwarded to Washington, D.C., August 25, 1927, and now in National Archives. Agent "London" interview in Hamburg with William Huibers from report dated January 31, 1929, to Division of Foreign Control, Treasury Department, Washington, National Archives. Bill McCoy comments from Frederic F. Van de Water, *The Real McCoy* (Garden City, New York: Doubleday, Doran and Company, Inc., 1931). References to *Mulhouse,* Malcolm F. Willoughby, commander, USCGR (T), *Rum War at Sea* (Washington, D.C.: U.S. Government Printing Office, 1964). Information on Miroslav Schrivaneck, or Skrivanek, cable, June 9, 1929, W. Henry Robertson, American consul general, Halifax, Nova Scotia, to Secretary of State, and letter, December 17, 1927, from Owen P. McKenna, U.S. Customs agent, Boston, to H. S. Creighton, supervising agent, U.S. Customs Office, New Orleans, Louisiana. *Jenny T.* incident, letter, August 21, 1924, from Jeremiah Dillon, U.S. Customs Service, New London, to Captain Charles Root, U.S. Coast Guard, Washington, D.C.

Chapter III

Arethusa incident, New Bedford *Evening Standard,* August 9, 10, 11, 12, 1921, and conversations with my friend the late Earle D. Wilson, to whom I am indebted for these recollections; also, Bill McCoy reaction from Frederic F. Van de Water, *The Real McCoy* (Garden City, New York: Doubleday, Doran and Company, Inc., 1931). References to German submarine and one-man torpedo boat, *The New York Times,* August 3 and August 12, 1924, respectively. Mystery ship references, New York and Atlantic City, New Jersey, datelines, Associated Press, July 18, August 9, and August 12, 1921.

Chapter IV

Federal figures on Rum Row from Attorney General Stone, *The New York Times,* February 3, 1925. Nova Scotia rum vessel traffic and vessel names, memorandum from Sergeant E. B. Nickerson, Yarmouth Detachment, Royal Canadian Mounted Police, undated, to Commander, Boston Division, U.S. Coast Guard; U.S. consular cables from Halifax and Yarmouth, Nova Scotia, June 24, 1925, November 30, 1931, and other dates, and Halifax, Nova Scotia, *Morning Chronicle,* on May 21 and 23, 1925, and other dates. Informant contract, Coast Guard files, National Archives. Nova Scotia attitude toward Prohibition, letter to U.S. Coast Guard from Division Foreign Control, Halifax, Nova Scotia, August 29, 1926. Rear Admiral Frederick C. Billard's comments from address October 8, 1927, to Woman's Christian Temperance Union, Elmira, New York. *Sagatind/Diamantina* incident, report, October 17, 1924, of Eugene Blake, Jr., commanding officer, *Seneca.* I am especially indebted to the former mate of the *Diamantina* for his recollections of Rum Row. Newspapermen's tour of Rum Row, Associated Press accounts, May 7, May 16, 1925, and New York *Herald Tribune,* May 18, 1925.

Chapter V

All material from Coast Guard files, National Archives, principally from vessel operations reports. For this, and other extensive information, I am most grateful to William F. Sherman, Legislative, Judicial and Fiscal Branch, Civil Archives Division, National Archives and Records Service, Washington, D.C., who was of great assistance to me during my research there.

Chapter VI

Taboga/Homestead incident, cruise report and logbook of *Redwing,* February 5, 6, 7, 1925. *Holmewood/Texas Ranger* capture, report, October 9, 1933, by U.S. Customs agents Gordon H. Pike and William J. Finck; report, October 5, 1933, by Lieutenant Frank M. Meals, Coast Guard Intelligence; *The New York Times,* October 5, 1933. *Clackamas* material, Philadelphia *Inquirer,* February 26, 1927, and Associated Press, Philadelphia, September 27, 1927. Ensign Charles L. Duke capture of *Graypoint/Economy, The New York Times,* New York *Herald Tribune,* Associated

Press, and other contemporary accounts published July 4, 1927, and letter from E. D. Jones, commander, Coast Guard Section Base 2, July 5, to Captain Charles S. Root. Charlotte Molyneux Holloway comment, New London *Evening Day,* January 14, 1925.

Chapter VII

Material principally from Coast Guard files, National Archives. James C. Moore assault, *The New York Times,* January 19, 1925; report, January 19, 1925, from W. V. E. Jacobs, commander, New York Division, U.S. Coast Guard. Attack on Joseph Dabue, Boston *Evening Traveler,* September 22, 1924. Carl Gustafson death, memorandum, May 6, 1927, from Intelligence Officer Charles S. Root. Attack on Coast Guard ship *Argus,* Washington *Post,* January 3, 1925. Sabotage of two Coast Guard submarine chasers, Associated Press, May 9, 1925. Theft of Coast Guard vessel by rumrunners, Washington *Post,* December 22, 1925. Federal Court trial in New York City, *The New York Times,* January 7–21, 1927.

Chapter VIII

Coast Guard and U.S. Customs files, National Archives. I am indebted to the widow of the good man who owned the double-ender that finally went rum-running for sharing her thoughts with me. I am also grateful to the master boat builder, whose recollections of the Casey Boatbuilding Company, Fairhaven, Massachusetts, during this period were of invaluable help to me. *Nola* incident, Coast Guard files, National Archives; New Bedford *Evening Standard,* December 19, 20, 1931.

Chapter IX

Peter J. Sullivan report, *The New York Times,* August 24, 1924. Unidentified New Yorker's account, published New York *Herald Tribune,* May 9, 1925, copyright Universal Service. Senator Felix Hebert–Secretary Seymour Lowman–*Idle Hour* material, National Archives. I am most grateful to the former rumrunner engineer for his detailed and dramatic account of his experiences. Associated Press account of *Lassgehen* case, Boston, November 4, 1932.

Chapter X

I am indebted to the former radio operator for the interview in which he provided a unique insight into rumrunner communications and operations. Raid on Newark radio station, New York *Journal*, January 20, 1931; report, January 21, 1931, from Frank M. Meals, Coast Guard Intelligence, to Lieutenant Commander F. J. Gorman. All *Amacitia* material, Coast Guard files, National Archives, including operations reports and correspondence; also, New Bedford *Evening Standard*, November 2, 1932.

Chapter XI

John Dwight incident, New Bedford *Evening Standard*, April 7–May 13, 1923; conversations with the late Earle D. Wilson, for which I am grateful; letters from and conversations with my father, Joseph Chase Allen, which were valuable. I am grateful to Judson Hale, editor of *Yankee* magazine, for permission to use material on the *Dwight* that I wrote for that publication in April, 1965. References to *Paulding*, Malcolm F. Willoughby, commander, USCGR (T), *Rum War at Sea* (Washington, D.C.: Government Printing Office, 1964). Some information concerning *C.G.-238*, New Bedford *Evening Standard*, February 21–22, 1927.

Chapter XII

Concerning the episode of the *Ammeg/Star*, I was assisted greatly by the recollections of the late William J. Fitzgerald; other material from the New Bedford *Evening Standard*, December 3, 1931, and operations reports of *C.G.-813*. I am grateful to the "lady rumrunner" for the interview that she granted to me, and to the man who was kidnaped at eighteen, for revealing to me the remarkable details of his experience.

Chapter XIII

Principal information on the *Black Duck* incident is from the "Copy of Findings of Facts, Opinions, and Recommendations of the Board of Investigation in the Case of the Capture of Motorboat C–5677, Black Duck," Coast Guard files, National Archives. Other *Black Duck* material from correspondence in Coast Guard files and contemporary news stories from Providence *Journal,* Associated Press, New London *Evening Day,* New York *Herald Tribune,* and New Bedford *Evening Standard.*

Chapter XIV

Threatening letter to Cornell, Coast Guard files, National Archives. Story on debate in U.S. House of Representatives, by Wells Church, New York *Herald Tribune,* January 8, 1930.

Chapter XV

Along the way, there have been many who have supplied anecdotes, colorful fragments that might otherwise have been lost, and who have led me to those people with firsthand knowledge of rumrunning who were willing to be interviewed. I acknowledge my debt to all of them.

INDEX

New Bedford *Evening Standard*, xv, 29-31, 33, 34, 88, 197-198, 219, 283
New Bedford *Morning Mercury*, 82
New Bedford *Standard-Times*, 205, 238, 280-282, 283
New Jersey radio transmitters, 189, 191-192
New London, Conn., 267-268
New London *Day*, 5, 244
New Orleans *Tribune*, 274
New York, 47, 51-53, 81-82, 136, 159; bribery trial, 126-128; and *Economy*, 99-104; and *Holmewood–*"Texas Ranger," 89-96
New York *Daily News*, 61-62
New York *Herald Trbiune*, 38-41, 87, 266, 270, 274
New York *Times*, 41, 95, 128, 139, 280
Newark, N.J., 99, 191-192
Newfoundland, 30, 44
Newport, R.I., 247-248
Nichols, F. A., 163-164, 166-167, 223
Nola, 144, 145-147
Nova Scotia, 43-44, 45-46, 56-57, 96

Octon, Alexander, 125
O'Donnell, R. W., 193

Packer, Ralph, viii-ix
Pateman, Thomas, 213
Paulding, 141-142, 209-213
Paulsen, Carl C., 249-250
Pearson, Lewis R., 250-259 *passim*
Peirce and Kilburn boatyard, 166, 168
Pell, Mr. (a supercargo), 19, 20
Pequod, 54
Petrel, 215
Phalen, Alfred E., 195, 197
Picketing and trailing, 47, 55-56, 60-63
Pike, Gordon H., 90-93
Pine, James, 62
Pitman, Augustus F., 122-123
Poole, Chester, 215
Prentiss, S. N., 149
Prohibition: advocates, 3-4, 5-6, 10, 271; opponents, 9, 265, 266-269, 272, 274, 279
Prohl, Mr. (a supercargo), 15, 16, 18, 19
Providence, R.I., 165
Providence *Journal*, 115

Public opinion, 3-11, 36-37, 111, 242-244; and *Black Duck*, 262-264; editorials, 128-131, 197-198, 265-266, 273, 274; letters, 6-7, 107-109, 273; sermons, 3-4

Radio transmission, 91-92, 182-198
Raney, R. L., 115, 213-217
Rasmussen, M. W., 243
Raynor, Gilbert J., 111
Redwing, 84-87
Rees, W. E., 124
Reeves, Ira L., 99
Renear, Walter H., 201
Rhode Island, 161-164
Rice, Frank, 214
Rivenback, Jesse K., 209, 213
Roberts, J. W., 90
Roosevelt, Franklin D., 279
Roosevelt, Mrs. Kermit, 4
Root, Charles S., 115, 159, 165-166
Ross, R. M., 193-194
Rowan Park, 88-89
Rum War at Sea (Willoughby), 48, 211
Rumrunners: armed conflicts with hijackers, 238-241; deaths, 199-208, 232-233, 243-244, 247; and inshore drops, 151, 155, 219-223, 228-232, 234-238; letters, 79-80; profits and losses, 14-22, 31, 57, 94, 104, 110, 124, 148, 156-157, 216-217; strategies and tactics, 50-51, 62-73, 133-136, 148, 154, 155-156, 159, 178-181, 214, 241; women, 228-233
Rye Harbor, N.H., 77-78

SOS calls and distress signals, fake, 69-71, 88-89
Sabotage, 125-126
Sagatind, 47-51
St. Pierre and Miquelon, 44, 57, 78, 94, 97
Sandy Hook, Conn., 118
Schooners Associated Ltd., 13, 15, 20-22
Schrivaneck, Mr. (a supercargo), 16, 18, 19
Scituate, Mass., 117
Scott, Philip H., 120-122
Searles, H. R., 68, 69-71
Seattle *Daily Times*, 273
Sebago, 68, 69-70